OKINAWA

A MARINE COMPANY'S TRUE STORY

JIM BOAN

ibooks

new york
www.ibooks.net

DISTRIBUTED BY SIMON & SCHUSTER, INC.

A publication of ibooks, inc.

Distributed by Simon & Schuster, Inc.
1230 Avenue of the Americas, New York, NY 10020

ibooks, inc.
24 West 25th Street
New York, NY 10010

Previously published as *Rising Sun Sinking*
Reprinted with permission from Eakin Press

The ibooks World Wide Web Site address is:
www.ibooks.net

ISBN: 0-7434-9831-3
First ibooks, inc. printing January 2005
10 9 8 7 6 5 4 3 2 1

Printed in the U.S.A.

CONTENTS

Foreword

By

John D. Gresham

"Just what do military analysts actually produce?" Folks in my business get that question from time to time, often leading to unsure answers as we try to justify our existence. However, the reality is that we are often looking for insight into future events, namely the little kernels of wisdom and foresight that will give an edge to warriors in future combat. Our credibility comes from making good "guesses" for our customers, frequently from obscure sources or forgotten manuscripts, assisted of course by our existing base of knowledge. That knowledge, more often than not, comes from years of reading.

It goes without saying that military analysts and authors like myself are voracious readers, consuming a steady flow of email, Internet newsgroups, newspapers, and magazines with an ear and eye always attentive, keeping watch on a 24-hour television news channel. It is books, though, that provide us with the basis of our knowledge and expertise. Were you to walk into my home, you would find the walls covered with shelves and stacked with books, some older than myself. Some are valued old friends, corners and slipcovers worn by continual use and frequent visits. Each represents a piece of the knowledge base that I fall back on time and again in my work as author, analyst, and sometimes fortune teller.

So what makes a "really good book" that you might pick up in my home? It often varies, though "really good books" always have a timeless quality to them, even when newer volumes have covered or replaced the same subject or time period. Often, they form the basis for an investigation, or just represent the book that an inquiring student should start with. Sometimes, these books are just what you feel comfortable recommending to friends and family, in the hope that what you offer in advice will not bore or overwhelm the reader. And then there are the books that plant you right into the middle of the subject your are studying. Such a book is *Okinawa*.

Since 2002, following a wonderful experience helping ibooks put out a new edition of the classic book *Zero!,* I have worked to create a list of books that would been of particular interest or value to readers of military history. Such lists are quite common within the major military service schools and academies around the world, each having their own set of choices. All share a common desire to provide student readers with a wide and hefty base of military lessons to take with them into their careers. Some books however, make a lot of the lists. Robert Heinlien's science fiction classic *Starship Troopers* is on almost every American military reading list I know of from West Point to the National War College.

Starship Troopers encompasses many of the values and virtues desired for good military personnel of all levels, and is a universal favorite.

It was with this same desire to provide civilian readers of military history with a similar background that I began to make up my own reading list for the *John Gresham Military Library* at ibooks. This series is designed to give readers a list of book that will allow them to better understand military history from a "deckplates and ditches" point of view. Battles and campaigns, the real nuts and bolts of a victorious war, are rarely won in national capitals or command bunkers. Victories in battle go to the soldiers, sailors, airmen, and Marines actually in the theaters of war. Often, the "BIG" realities of a battle or campaign can be encapsulated into the story of a few men, fighting their way through to the end. Such a book is *Okinawa*.

Spring 1945 was a time of promise and dread with Allied personnel. The war in Europe was within weeks of ending, Hitler was making his final rants from a squalid bunker in Berlin, and for the battered people of the United States and England there was an end in sight of what they considered "their war." However, on the other side of the globe another conflict was still raging, this one with no end in sight and only more brutal fighting ahead. What some historians today call "The Great Pacific War" was in high gear, and only getting bloodier and more insane.

1944 and early 1945 had seen Imperial Japan lose most of its early prizes to a relentless pair of Allied advances. Across the central Pacific, the forces under Admiral Chester Nimitz had conducted a brilliant series of amphibious invasions, taking critical islands including Guam, Tinian, and Saipan in the Marianas, while bypassing Japanese strongholds such as Truk and the Marshall Islands. From the south, General Douglas MacArthur had continued his restless drive to keep his promise, "I shall return," to the people of the Philippines. In October 1944, these two drives met, and the liberation of the Philippines began on Leyte Island.

Along with losing its hold on the central Pacific and the Philippines, Imperial Japan had lost much more during this period. Supply lines for oil, rubber, iron, tin, and other critical strategic materials had been almost cut, through a relentless American submarine campaign. Almost as bad, Japan's Imperial Fleet had been decimated, and lacked the ability to put up even a token fight. The Battles of the Philippine Sea and Leyte Gulf had cost Japan over half of its battle fleet, and the rest had either been sunk by air and submarine attacks, or driven into harbor sanctuaries.

By early 1945, the prewar possessions of Japan itself were being assaulted, starting with the loss of Iwo Jima. In a bloody invasion which saw the defending Japanese force wiped out, and thousands of U.S. Navy and Marine casualties for a small, pork chop-shaped island. What had made Iwo Jima, along with all the air and sea engagements since the Battle of Leyte Gulf so vicious had been the shift by Japan to suicide tactics. Unable to produce enough aircraft, ships, submarines, and crews to credibly attack the oncoming Allied forces conventionally, Japan had begun an organized campaign of having aircraft crash their planes into American ships. Called *kamikaze* (Japanese for "Divine Wind"), the suicide planes had helped sink two small aircraft carriers and several escorts at Leyte Gulf. More Allied ships had been sunk or damaged in the months that followed, and suddenly the Great Pacific War had turned from nasty to desperate.

The Japanese, seeing that they finally had a way to get at the American Navy threw its full effort into *kamikaze* operations. In addition to the *kamikaze* planes, which had become the equivalent of anti-ship guided missiles, the Japanese quickly developed manned suicide torpedoes and explosive motorboats to ram into Allied ships. These also proved to have deadly potential, much like the Al Qaeda motorboat, which nearly sank the American guided missile destroyer USS *Cole* (DDG-67) in the fall of 2000, killing 17 sailors. By the end of winter 1945, *kamikaze* attacks were killing and maiming American sailors at a rate previously unseen even in the dark days of 1942.

The twin shocks of the Iwo Jima and *kamikaze* campaigns hit the Allied war planners hard, because there was an immense task ahead before the Great Pacific War could be won. The pending invasion of the Japanese home islands, planned to begin in the fall of 1945 and continue into 1946 was going to be the biggest amphibious operation in history. Two separate invasion operations, Operations Olympic (for Kyushu) and Coronet (into the Tokyo Plains) would have each dwarfed the 1944 D-Day invasion into Normandy. Units and personnel from Europe were already being trained and re-equipped for operations in the Pacific, including the famous "Screaming Eagles" of the 101st Airborne Division and Lieutenant General "Jimmy" Doolittle's "Mighty Eighth" Air Force were just two such formations.

There was never a question of eventual victory. The Allies had more than enough might to decimate the armed forces of Imperial Japan, and occupy the home islands in 1946. The real question for Allied planners of Olympic and Coronet was far more gruesome: how many Allied personnel and Japanese civilians would die in the process? By early 1945, the people of the United States and England were already war weary, having lost hundreds of thousands of personnel in World War II. Just how bad would an invasion of the Japanese home islands be? The answer came in April with the invasion of a group of islands just south of Kyushu, centered on the landmass of Okinawa.

Okinawa was invaded because it was capable of supporting airfields able to handle the largest bombers and transport aircraft in the Allied inventory. Fighter planes from Okinawa would be able to fly across the whole of the Japanese home islands, and there was lots of room for billeting Allied airborne units before their jumps. Along with Iwo Jima and the Allied aircraft carrier task forces, Okinawa was the last base needed before Olympic would be launched in the fall of 1945. Unfortunately, Okinawa turned out to be more than a dress rehearsal for Olympic and Coronet: it was a window into just how horrible those operations might become.

The Japanese viewed Okinawa as their own territory, and had built up a large defensive force, the 32nd Army, armed to the teeth and deeply dug in. Large numbers of *kamikaze* aircraft, boats, and manned torpedoes, and even the remnants of the Imperial Fleet would back up the ground troops. The Allied invasion force, the largest yet assembled in the Pacific, was a joint Army/Navy/Marine construct led by some of the finest field and fleet officers in America's history. The Okinawa campaign was weeks of the most vicious and desperate fighting of World War II.

Like on Iwo Jima, the American soldiers and Marines had to literally dig the Japanese out of their defensive positions. Massive battles took place on the plains of the island, including tank engagements and desperate banzai charges. Over 72,500 American soldiers and Marines were killed, wounded, or put out of action during the Okinawa campaign. Japanese losses were even worse, with the entire 32nd Army of 100,000 men either killed or captured. Both of the commanders of the American and Japanese ground forces were killed, along with many other admirals and generals on both sides. At sea, over 2,000 *kamikaze* planes ravaged the Allied naval force, hitting 162 ships, resulting in the sinking or scraping of 62 vessels. Over 9,000 sailors were killed or wounded, the worst American casualty total of *any* naval campaign of World War II, including Guadalcanal. For the Olympic and Coronet planners,

Okinawa was an ominous window into what might await the Allied force when it invaded the Japanese home islands.

Some estimates of Olympic and Coronet Allied casualties ran into the hundreds of thousands, with Japanese military and collateral civilian casualties perhaps into the *millions*. The prospect was that in less than a year of fighting on the home islands of Japan, Allied and Japanese war dead would have *doubled* from *all* the previous fighting since 1941. While these numbers remain controversial today, they represented the kinds of figures that made staff planners on both sides contemplate the unthinkable. Both Allied and Japanese forces stockpiled poison gas, and made preparations to use it without concern for Japanese civilian casualties.

There also was the emerging spectre of the atomic bomb, which was being prepared for testing by scientists of the Manhattan Program at Los Alamos, New Mexico. By the spring of 1945, there was already a growing movement among the atomic scientists themselves not to actually use the bomb. President Truman was already being faced with the terrible decision of whether to deploy nuclear weapons against Japan, and the Okinawa casualties were one of his primary justifications. Given the Olympic and Coronet casualty projections, the chance to deliver a knockout blow to Japan with atomic weapons was too tempting to pass up.

While such insights were available to Allied staff planners, where would an average citizen have gone to gain some idea of what the invasion of

Japan would have been like for our soldiers, sailors, airmen, and Marines? One of the best ways is by an intriguing book called *Okinawa* by Jim Boan. A Marine assigned to the reconnaissance company of the 6th Marine Regiment, Jim Boan saw some of the worst of the fighting on Okinawa, on point for thousands of his fellow Leathernecks. The vicious, hand-to-hand fighting of Okinawa is brought to life through his words, in all its horrors. But *Okinawa* is more than just another tale of one man walking through World War II. While focusing on his own experiences with the 6th Marines, Boan's *Okinawa* also takes the reader to other places and events in the campaign, providing important perspective to a complex story of combat in many areas.

Along with his own combat observations, Boan takes the reader to the sinking of the greatest *kamikaze* of all, the super-battleship *Yamato* as she tried to attack the American invasion fleet. Boan also takes you to the deaths of Generals Buckner and Ushijima, the opposing ground commanders of the Okinawa campaign. Thanks to his unique viewpoint during the Okinawa battle, Boan is able to bring out the nuances of the larger battle, including the pending invasion of Japan, which he would have fought in. There also is Boan's profound sense of relief when President Harry Truman makes the terrible decision to use the atomic bombs on Hiroshima and Nagasaki, perhaps saving his life and those of his fellow Marines.

Okinawa is not a book for the shy or faint of heart. This is close combat, raw and ugly as it can be. There are no marching bands or trumpets in Boan's narrative; just the kind of insight that provides readers an idea of what men at war face up close. Given what our soldiers and Marines have experienced in recent year while fighting in Afghanistan and Iraq, this is a very useful insight indeed. So here I offer you *Okinawa,* the kind of book that can make a reader see the future, with all its horrors and possibilities. And if you find yourself thinking, as President Harry S. Truman did in 1945, that the terrible consequences of using atomic weapons might be worth the cost to save millions of Allied and Japanese lives, then *Okinawa* will have done its job. I can ask no more of any book to educate and provide insight.

John D. Gresham
Fairfax, Virginia
October 2004

PREFACE

War is something our folks at home talked about; battle is something marines talked about; combat is what we experienced on Okinawa.

My objective is to present an overall view of the battle for Okinawa and a well-rounded view of the Recon marines who fought there.

There were many pleasant and humorous moments. After all, we were mostly between eighteen and twenty-two years old. We were full of bravado and prowess, but also preoccupied with thoughts of home and girls. It wasn't always Kill! Kill! Kill!, as some people would have you believe.

I wish to thank The Marine Corps Historical Center, Washington, D. C.; The 6th Marine Division Association, Inc., Wildwood, New Jersey; Individual members of the 6th Division Reconnaissance Company; and Clara, for her tolerance during the weeks, months, and years I've spent on this project.

Beached Japanese transport off the coast of Guadalcanal. Several rammed the beach with troops. On the beach near the Recon Company area was the Kyushu Maru. We could look across Iron Bottom Bay and see the island, Savo.

Excursion to Tulagi and the Florida Islands, our mail collection point. Mail call on Guadalcanal was a high point any day.

Native outrigger boat near Aola Bay, Guadalcanal. Splotches in foreground are the coral sea bottom. Reefs visible in background.

Guadalcanal shoreline from Twenty-second Marine camp area. On beach are coconuts, tree fronds and logs, and an oil barrel. In the distance, top right, is Savo Island.

OKINAWA SHIMA

Showing Principal Roads, Towns, and Villages

Scale

Miles

MAP 3

INTRODUCTION

Events Leading Up to the Battle for Okinawa

Before the Pearl Harbor attack, the Japanese were chafing under an oil embargo. They desperately needed oil to fuel their expansion into China and the southwestern Pacific. One line of explanation is that the Japanese high command figured that the United States was soft, and if they saw their navy destroyed they'd soon sue for peace, allowing the Japanese to take over the Indonesian oil fields.

At the time of the infamous attack on the U.S., the Japanese had already conquered much of the western Pacific: China, Indochina, Malaysia, and part of New Guinea. The Philippines were also in the grip of the Japanese empire, and Australia was threatened. General Douglas MacArthur was ordered to Australia in March of 1942, only three months after the Pearl Harbor disaster.

Then came a series of events that were turning points in the war with the Japanese. The naval battle of the Coral Sea, May 7–8, 1942, was not decisive, but it was a roadblock to Japanese expansion. Several other naval battles through the remainder of 1942, some of which our naval forces lost, served notice to the Japanese that their empire expansion would be challenged. Most of these battles took place around the Solomon Islands, southeast of New Guinea.

An area called "The Slot" was a waterway among the Solomons that the enemy used to ferry soldiers to Guadalcanal and other islands. The U.S. Navy seamen nicknamed this troop movement the "Tokyo Express."

Although the U.S. Navy had some success in reducing the south Pacific's Japanese fleet, the absolute turning point of the naval war had to be the Battle of Midway Island. The great loss of ships, particularly carriers, reduced the Japanese navy to a second-rate power and a defensive rather than an offensive force. The loss of ships also meant that air power would become the dominant factor in naval warfare.

It has been properly noted that U.S. codebreakers made a major contribution to the Battle of Midway. Although the Japanese code (JN-25) had been broken, American cryptographers had not yet deciphered the names the Japanese gave to individual islands. They knew that a Japanese attack was imminent, but where? Midway was suspected, but the navy admirals could not commit their task forces based on only a hunch. Someone had the idea of a ruse. An open U.S. message was sent that the water system on Midway was down. It wasn't long before the Japanese sent a message that the water system was down on (code word) island. Then our task force commanders knew for certain that Midway would be attacked.

The absolute turning point on land had to be Guadalcanal. Aerial reconnaissance indicated that the Japanese were building an airfield on the island. If completed, the Japanese air force could bomb anywhere in the south Pacific, including Australia.

On August 7, l942, ten thousand marines under the command of General Alexander Vandegrift landed in the swamps on the northeast coast of Guadalcanal, near the site where the Japanese were constructing their airfield. Taken by surprise, the Japanese soldiers and construction workers fled to the island's hills.

From the sea, Guadalcanal looked like an idyllic South Pacific island. Soon after the First Marine Division landed, they learned that Japanese weren't the only enemy they had to fight.

Steaming heat, daily rain, swamp mud, rats, bugs, scorpions, land crabs, and mosquitoes were constant, annoying companions. The place stunk. In the ocean were sharks, stinging jellyfish, and razor-sharp coral.

And if that wasn't enough, men suffered with malaria, dysentery, jungle rot (fungus), and homesickness—not to mention the Japanese who were constantly harassing by air, sea, and land.

Marines soon learned that Japanese soldiers were wily, tricky, deadly, and *banzai*-prone. They lived in the jungle like animals, surviving on rice and coconuts.

A journalist who visited Guadalcanal a few weeks after the landing remarked that the leathernecks looked like pirates. They sported rifles, pistols, knives, and loaded ammunition belts draped with hand grenades and other paraphernalia. They were grimy, their clothes dirty, and they smelled like the jungle.

But all were fighting for a common cause: They wanted to go home.

Through all of the hardships, they held the airport named Henderson Field—even completed it—despite Japanese reinforcements and air raids, often using abandoned enemy equipment and materials.

The Japanese made repeated attempts at reinforcements. Finally, during one night of the first week of February 1943, they brought in destroyers to Cape Esperance and evacuated twelve thousand troops.

By August 1943, the Japanese had given up; they had suffered their first defeat on land.

The marines moved on, up the Solomon Islands chain, but they left a legacy. Here's the way it was expressed on one Guadalcanal marine's tombstone:

> And when he gets to Heaven,
> To Saint Peter he will tell:
> One more Marine reporting, Sir—
> I've spend my time in HELL!

During this period of the Pacific war, the U.S. Joint Chiefs of Staff were forced to make a decision. General Douglas MacArthur, the supreme army commander, had argued vigorously for control of all the Pacific forces. But the navy admirals—Ernest J. King, Chester Nimitz, and William F. Halsey—pointed out that it was largely a naval war. As a result, the Pacific Theater was divided into three commands.

MacArthur would be in control of the Southwest Pacific area, including the Philippines, to which he had promised to return. Admirals Ghormely and "Bull" Halsey were to control the South Pacific. Admirals Chester Nimitz, and Raymond Spruance were assigned the Central Pacific islands.

The conquered ladder-of-islands calendar looked like this: Russell Islands, February 1943; New Georgia, June 1943; Vella Lavella, August 1943; Choiseul and Treasury Islands, October 1943; Tarawa and Bougainville, November 1943. Some islands were bombed and sidestepped: Rabaul, New Britain, and Truk.

At Tarawa, landing forces began to learn how to assault the islands, but this came at a high price. At low tide there was only three feet of water for the Higgins boats displacement; many were caught on the reefs. Marines were slaughtered as they waded ashore. Losses were 991 killed in action (KIA); 2,311 wounded (WIA).

At Kwajalein, the story was different. With prolonged shelling and proper landing equipment, only one-third as many marines were lost, although there were twice as many Japanese—4,500—on the island.

The Marianas (Guam, Saipan, and Tinian) were invaded by U.S. forces during the summer of 1944. History records the great Marianas Turkey Shoot as a Japanese invasion fleet headed for Guam, but it didn't invade.

The U.S. Navy used a new weapon to win the battle, although that weapon couldn't fire a shot. It was radar. The Japanese sent their bombers toward Guam without a fighter escort. Radar gave American pilots time to get their fighters in the air before the bombers arrived, and they swarmed on the bombers, with disastrous results for the Japanese.

In the western Pacific, MacArthur's forces moved steadily north and returned to the Philippines. In the central Pacific, Spuance's navy moved marines who swept from island to island, steadily closing in on Japan. Early in 1945, Iwo Jima was the first great battle in which Pacific marines played a part. Iwo was the site of the famed U.S. flag-raising photo by Joe Rosenthal. Now the battle for Okinawa was at hand.

Chapter 1

OPERATION ICEBERG

"Iceberg" was the code name assigned to the Okinawan operation by the United States Joint Chiefs of Staff. At that time, an invasion of Formosa (code name "Causeway") was considered instead of Okinawa, but further study proved that Okinawa was a more practical target.

Recommendations for Iceberg over Causeway were largely due to the Air Force and Army General Simon B. Buckner Jr., who said that his Tenth Field Army was large enough to take Okinawa, but not Formosa.

Reconnaissance photo missions were flown regularly over Okinawa, beginning in September 1944. Although the Japanese had cleverly camouflaged their defense positions, photos taken at different times could be compared to detect them.

At the beginning of surveillance, U.S. Intelligence estimated the Japanese garrison strength at 48,000 men, built around two infantry divisions and a tank regiment. By January 1945, this estimate was increased to 66,000, with a footnote that it could be increased to 87,000 men in four infantry divisions.

However, in February 1945 the Japanese high command withdrew

a division from Okinawa to reinforce their strength in the
Philippines. This left a fighting force of 38,000 to 39,000 on
Okinawa, but the estimated garrison quickly changed to 64,000 as
additional men were transported in. With an estimated sixty miles of
camouflaged dug and natural caves on the island, some sheltering as
many as a thousand soldiers, the enemy's strength was greatly
underestimated as to both manpower and equipment.

The Iceberg plan consisted of three phases: 1) Capture southern
Okinawa. 2) Capture northern Okinawa and Ie Shima, an island off
Okinawa's Motobu Peninsula. 3) Capture additional small islands in
the area that could be used as supply and repair bases. Due to cir-
cumstances that evolved as Iceberg developed, the order of phases
one and two was reversed.

The original schedule by the Joint Chiefs called for General
Douglas MacArthur to invade Luzon in the Philippines on December
20, 1944. The landing on Iwo Jima would be made on January 20,
1945, followed by the invasion of Okinawa on March 1, 1945. Because
of bad weather, the Iceberg operation was postponed until April 1,
1945. The delay aided logistics and helped determine the landing site
on Okinawa. Alternate plans were made to attack Okinawa from
either the east (Pacific Ocean) side, or the west (China Sea). The
delay also aided in making the decision that the Hagushi beaches of
Okinawa's west side would be more satisfactory. However, cloudy
weather had hindered good aerial reconnaissance.

It was decided that marine and army units would make a joint
amphibious landing along ten thousand yards of the Hagushi
beaches that were coded for each landing unit. The landing force
was scheduled to move inland and capture two airfields within five
days. Then the joint forces were to continue to cut the island in two
before the marines turned north and the army south. The plan
called for four divisions to land in the initial assault.

Many of us young marines in the sixth division had never seen
combat, although remnants of units that had fought on Guam and
other Pacific islands were mixed with green troops. Most were fresh
from boot camps at Parris Island, South Carolina, or San Diego,
California. Officers, too, were a mixed bag—some experienced, some
straight from officer training at Quantico, Virginia. All had been put
through rigorous combat training in the mangrove swamps and kunai
grass savannas of Guadalcanal.

In March 1945 the Sixth Division marines boarded transports, including PA 218, the USS *Nobel*, and we set sail for the staging area, Mog Mog, a small island of the Ulithi atoll in the Carolina group.

The trip itself was uneventful, but the troops were on short rations, maybe a sandwich and an apple for a meal. Griping about the food was continual. The only thing discussed more was our unknown destination. The scuttlebutt was outrageous. Some said Korea, but others said Kyushu in Japan proper.

Although our officers tried to keep us busy with work details, calisthenics, and inspections, we had a lot of time on our hands. Men read pocket books and magazines, wrote letters, played cards, rolled dice, or sunbathed.

One noncommissioned officer, Sergeant William "Wild Bill" Dawson, delighted in entertaining the new privates. They would gather around big, handsome Bill for what became known as the "Dawson Hour."

His bunk in the ship's Recon quarters was festooned with pinups of beautiful girls, including movie stars. I believe he called them "georgous babes." Some had written to him. He would read, or pretend to read, the amorous letters just to torment the younger guys. He had a picture of a girl in a bathing suit that a young blond recruit couldn't get over. "I'm going to meet her if it's the last thing I do before I go to heaven," he'd say, "and personally remove that part of the bathing suit she's stuffed into herself."

Work detail—we need volunteers. The loudspeaker would scarcely stop vibrating before a line formed. Not that we liked to scrub the deck or clean the head, but the work detail got extra chow.

Jim C. Smith of Detroit always looked out for "numero uno." He volunteered along with six others to work as a mess man in the galley. "A Marine soon learns you travel on a full stomach," he said. Then he would tell us about his meal while we gnawed on apple cores.

It was always hot in our closed quarters. We had no portholes and only one hatch door, which was always curtained after dark. No lights were permitted after taps. However, one safety light near the doorstep glowed softly—enough light for the nightly crap game. Most of us slept in our skivvies. Some of the most adventuresome would sneak topside to sleep on deck, where there was a breeze, even though this was forbidden.

As the USS *Nobel* neared Ulithi, some of us were on deck at the bow, watching flying fish race the ship.

"Look at the little bastards. They're running just like Japanese," said PFC William J. Sweeney.

"Look!" yelled John E. "Lefty" Smith of Pottstown, Pennsylvania. He was pointing toward the horizon.

There were so many ships on the ocean that the island of Mog Mog was surrounded. We stood in silent awe. In that single moment, we realized we were to become a part of something big.

"Godawmighty! What a sight!" shouted the normally quiet Private William E. Ellis. (Some of us called him "Preacher," because he was so religious). There were ships everywhere—little, big, and unbelievable. As the troop ship slipped toward anchor, it eased by the USS *Franklin*. I was standing on the main deck, starboard side, and was amazed at the height of the great aircraft carrier. Then I noticed a hole in the ship. The metal skin had been peeled back, leaving a hole big enough for a man to stand in. As the *Nobel* eased by, the hole became more obvious, and I could see the interior of the ship. When our ship came alongside, I could see that the hole went completely through the carrier, and a tingle of fear crept up my spine. I could see other ships and palm trees through the hole. *How could such a wounded ship stay afloat?* I pondered. For the first time, I realized that the war games we had played were going to become real.

When the PA system announced shore leave for exercise and recreation, Smith was first in line. Most of the troops went ashore, but I stayed aboard. I was on deck later when the Recon Company men returned.

"Ozark, you should have been with us. That was the longest goddamn bar in the world. They were serving beer halfway round the island." That was the greeting I got from a beer-drunk comrade.

Bong! Bong! Bong! General Quarters! blared the ship's PA system. Elements of the Recon Company scrambled for cover below deck. Soon the deck anti-aircraft guns began banging away, making the ship resonate like a giant bell. Then it became quiet, followed by: *Secure from General Quarters*.

Sergeant Major Cossens came along and said he had heard that the Japanese regularly harassed the gathering fleet. He also told us that Ulithi was the staging area for Task Force Fifty-three and the assembly of the greatest amphibian fleet ever to gather in the Pacific. Furthermore, the convoy would be underway when we woke the next morning, at which time there would be an announcement. Finally, we would know our destination.

I was down in the galley for breakfast when the announcement came that the Recon Company would assemble on deck at 0900. We were in line with trays for chipped beef on toast.

"Shit on a shingle again," complained Tony "Sugarlips" Bordoni, from Philadelphia.

As the sailor cooks ladled out the food, we continued to bitch. We took our trays to the stainless steel tables that were fastened to the bulkhead by metal poles.

"I hear they use these tables for the wounded during battle," commented PFC George Taylor from Tennessee.

The boatswain's whistle interrupted our conversations. *Now hear this! Belay the last announcement.*

"That figures," said Jim Smith. "The situation is normal—all screwed up."

It was a beautiful, sunny day on deck, and the *Nobel* plowed effortlessly through the rolling waves. Surrounding us was an ocean full of ships.

Whoomph! Whoomph! Whoomph! warned a destroyer as it roared by on the port side of the *Nobel*. As it passed, it belched a great rope of black smoke from its stack. The powerful propellers pushed the bow upward while the fantail was nearly awash. It looked as if it were about to spring upon its prey. Later it was announced that an enemy submarine had been sighted.

The flotilla had left Ulithi on March 25, and now we were still at sea, on our way to—somewhere. Scuttlebutt was driving most of us to distraction.

Major Walker, our commander, came down to our quarters himself to announce our destination.

"Men," he said, "we're going to Okinawa. I can't tell you much about it, but it's a fairly big island on the doorstep of Japan. You'll be called on deck later today for a description of the assault plan."

Then the major showed his humanity and restated a Marine Corps tradition.

"We will have casualties, but we take them with us or we stay."

"Right then," Sergeant Fuller Curtis would later say, "I knew we had a leader I would follow to hell and back—so would the rest of our company."

"Good luck!" concluded Major Walker, then turned and left. But the jawboning among the troops started before he reached the hatch door. "Where the hell is Okinawa? I thought we were going to Formosa. Smith, you're just loaded with misinformation."

Later, Recon assembled on deck, and we were given the scoop by our officers, who displayed a large map of Okinawa. Features of the island were pointed out, along with the shoreline of the Hagushi beaches—including Green Beach Two.

"Seriously, men," said Sergeant Harry Manion of Michigan, a veteran of previous island battles, "the fun and games are over. Now you're going to find out why you were sent over here. Get your gear and mind in order. Tomorrow may be April Fool's Day, but some of you will not be coming back. Dismissed!"

From the beach, this is what it looked like on April 1, L-Day.

What the southern tip of Okinawa looked like from the air.

Chapter 2

THE LANDING

The shrill, energetic notes of reveille cascaded over our quarters on the USS *Nobel*, in the convoy of transports on the East China Sea. Someone threw a shoe at the loudspeaker; another cursed. Three young men shooting dice under the safety light of the hatch door kept to their game. The doorway was blanketed in a blackout. When the lights came on, men began to stir. I rose on my elbow and looked around. I was in my green skivvies, as were most of the men, because it was sultry in our crowded quarters.

"There's a Jap in the doorway!" yelled a marine. He grabbed a carbine in one hand and a .45 pistol in the other and charged the hatch door. The crapshooters looked at him in amazement. Others scrambled to see what was going on.

"April Fool!" screamed the prankster. "I gotcha' that time," he yelled, slapping his legs and laughing like his lungs would burst.

"You sonofabitch," hollered Bama,who was named after his home state. "You keep pullin' your jokes and you're gonna' get your ass shot off."

I settled back and opened an issue of *Coronet* magazine. My green chow card meant that I wouldn't be called to the galley for some time. I was on the top bunk.

"Whoopee! Would you look at that!" came an excited voice from one of the bunks farthest from the doorway. A half-dozen marines rushed with youthful exuberance to see what was causing the ruckus.

"What is it?" asked Sammy Zaidain. Others were talking fast and milling about. "I can't see—what is it?" repeated the short corporal, standing on the balls of his feet.

"For God's sake," I said, "it's only Big Dick showing off again."

"Let me see!" called Dan Kvaase, jumping up and down in the crowd for a better view. "Man, you could use that as a club!"

Meanwhile, the prankster had slipped his K-bar from its sheath and sneaked over to Big Dick's bunk. He lunged at Big Dick with a blood-chilling yell, but Big Dick was too fast for him. He grabbed a pillow and wrapped it around himself protectively. "I'll make a woman out of you," the prankster threatened. "What can you do with that over here anyway?"

"For chrissake, you guys, cut it out!" I yelled.

"Cut it off, you mean," was the retort.

"It wilted," said Big Dick in a disgusted tone.

Bong! Bong! Bong! came the alert over the intercom. The piercing sound of the boatswain's whistle followed; then we heard a voice: *Now hear this! General quarters! General quarters! Marines lay below.*

"What's going on out there?" asked Private Don Wampler above the roar of anti-aircraft guns.

"The sky's full of Jap Zeros," screamed a voice from the hatch door. Fear made his voice about two octaves higher than normal. "And every ship in the harbor is shooting at them. Black puffs of smoke are everywhere up there. One plane was hit; its wing came off in a blaze of flames."

Pom! Pom! Pom! Pom! went the steady beat of the anti-aircraft guns, and the metal decks and bulkheads vibrated. We marines sat on our bunks, subdued.

Suddenly, the ship rose and lurched. The next thing I knew, I had hit the deck on all fours, bloodying my knees.

"Ozark, you lucky bastard," said Bama. "You get a Hollywood wound without touchin' land. Probably go back to Guam or Pearl."

Private William Willett rushed in screaming at the top of his voice. "I saw the goddamn plane!" he yelled. "I was on the fantail when he dove his plane right at a ship!"

The storm of kamikaze planes subsided, and soon the boatswain's whistle announced that we were secure from general quarters. That was followed shortly by the announcement we all were dreading: *Marines prepare to disembark.*

"Saddle up!" ordered Sergeant Manion.

Men of the Sixth Marine Division Reconnaissance Company slipped into the shoulder straps of our heavy packs, grabbed our weapons, and struggled up ladders to designated holding places.

Topside, I saw it was a beautiful, sunny morning. In the blue distance, I could see the hazy brown shoreline of Okinawa. As I watched, the big guns of the battlewagons opened up, banging against the Hagushi beaches with great balls of smoke—an awesome sight that filled us with fear and dread.

Nearby, the landing boats began circling in preparation for the dash to shore. Behind them were short white wakes like the spreading tails of eagles.

Sergeant Manion looked at his waterproof watch. It was 11:30. A navy officer was standing on deck above the assembled marines, barking loading orders over a megaphone. His voice was anxious, nervous. "Move out! C'mon, load up those boats. We don't have all day!" Loaded with heavy packs and rifles, we struggled to climb over the side of the ship and move down the swaying cargo nets.

In some places, men were lined up, patiently waiting their turn at the net. The officer was ranting and raving, while Major Walker patiently encouraged his troops.

A Marine yelled, his voice trailing off before he splashed into the ocean.

"Watch your hands!" yelled Major Walker. "Grab only the vertical ropes and you won't get stepped on."

The navy officer had a short fuse, and the accident set him off. He yelled a tirade at the marines. Commander Walker stepped out to where the officer could see his commanding football physique and spoke calmly.

"I understand your eagerness to unload before a Jap plane or sub plants a torpedo in our belly, but my men are in more danger than you are. So just bide your time!"

The stunned officer stood silent for a moment, then turned to his aide, saying, "There's one man who's afraid to go ashore." He didn't realize that "Cold Steel" Walker had fought his way up the islands one by one and was absolutely fearless.

At last we crowded into landing boats and joined the other circling crafts. The boats lined up and headed for shore, past big battleships, past the LSTs, and on toward Green Beach Two.

The choppy water splashed against the flat ramps of our boats. I was standing by the ramp door and was getting drenched.

"Here!" yelled the boatswain as he threw me a rubber rain outfit consisting of pants and jacket. I put them on over my green dungarees and turned my back to the huge ramp door.

As we neared the shore, it looked peaceful, quiet. Suddenly, the front of the landing craft rose high in the air with a terrible scraping sound. Men tumbled over each other. One man was hysterical, yelling over and over, "We've been hit! We've been hit! We've been hit!"

The craft reversed and pulled off the coral reef. Then it found a new path and proceeded toward shore.

Gunny Sergeant James Tabb began to sniff the air. After a few sniffs, he looked at a recruit who was squatting on the deck. "Did you shit your pants?" he asked.

The private just shrugged his shoulders and looked at his shoes.

"Well," said Tabb, "you can wash your pants as you wade ashore. You won't have time to change clothes today."

The big ramp in front of the boat rumbled down, revealing the shore.

We dispersed like a covey of quail and splashed through surf for the safety of the beach. We dove for the cover of shoreline mounds. Then we realized that no shots were being fired.

Corporal Fuller Curtis had made landings before, under fire. He couldn't believe the silence.

"The bastards are just waiting to ambush us," he sneered. "Hey Chronis," he yelled at the radio man, "any news on what's happening?"

"All along Green Beach it's just like here—little or no resistance."

"Move out!" The order was passed along the beach.

Sergeant Robert McDougal partially rose from a sand dune and waved us forward. "First squad, head for those terraces and hold up." He led us toward the objective. It was deathly quiet as we moved, just the rustle of wet clothing, feet sloshing in shoes, then grunts as we flopped to the ground.

"Dig in and pass the word. Two-men foxholes." Backpacks came off and entrenching shovels were put to work.

I was paired with "Lefty" Smith, a smooth-faced PFC who didn't look a day over seventeen. The soil was laced with sand, so the digging was easy. We had dug a trench about knee-deep when an order was passed down.

"First squad," called McDougal making a circular motion with his hand for his men to gather round him. "We're to go out about one thousand yards on reconnaissance. Headquarters wants to know what's out there. If you're fired on, return to base. Ozark, you take the point."

The squad spread out behind me, running low behind the terrace. At the end of the terrace was a narrow road, or a trail. There, crouched behind a bush, was a man. Just as I raised my rifle, he spoke.

"What's the password?"

"Hell, I don't know," I said, my voice quavering. "Where's the front line?"

"This is it!" answered the marine, and I noticed that he was manning a camouflaged 37mm gun. I moved on, leaving explanations to others.

The squad spread out behind me as I moved along the road. To either side were fields of sweet potatoes; no place for the enemy to hide. Rifle ready, I moved ahead. Each rock was an enemy's head, each growing plant an enemy weapon; each step was near an enemy mine, each man-made object booby-trapped. Up on the hillside was a cave, probably sheltering enemy soldiers. *Sneak up—It's empty*.

Ahead was a cluster of buildings. I begin to examine them with field glasses. Nothing moved. *What was that?* A rooster crowed; a goat bleated.

Bang! A shot was fired on the other side of the field. I dropped to the ground, an automatic reflex. As we waited, a message was passed. "Return to base." Later we learned that a sniper had been removed from a tree.

Lefty and I finished our foxhole, then examined the distant hillside where the evening shadows lengthened from the ancestral tombs above the rice paddies.

Two civilians wearing tattered kimonos were brought into camp. Their bodies were dirty; they had probably crawled out of a nearby cave. They cowered. They were crying, fearing death. Sergeant McDougal passed the word that we were to avoid them. Interrogators came and took them away.

I removed my helmet and sat on it in the foxhole. I took a cigarette from a pack and offered Lefty one. He refused and watched me light up.

"How did you get a name like Ozark?" he asked.

"Oh, that happened in boot camp. My home is in the Missouri Ozarks. The DI called me an Ozark hillbilly. The name stuck."

"I'm left-handed; that's why they call me Lefty."

"I figured as much."

"I'm going to be a painter."

"Paint houses?"

"No, paint pictures. You know, an artist."

"Then you'll be famous someday."

"I don't know about that. I just want to paint."

It was almost dark. The password was whispered down the line of defense. "Water lily." The Japanese were supposed to have trouble pronouncing l's. The counter word was "flower."

"I'll take the first watch," I offered. "It's going to be a long night, so try to get some sleep. I'll wake you in two hours."

After dark, an air raid began. Ship searchlights and tracer shells pierced the night like a giant Fourth of July celebration. Once a spotlight caught a plane, it was doomed, leaving a fiery path like a meteor as it plunged toward the sea.

As I watched the battle in the sky, I realized what a small part I played in such a large operation. I wondered how Okinawa had been selected and how the battle had been planned.

Chapter 3

INVASION

Lefty shook me awake at dawn.

"Ozark, wake up." His voice had an urgency about it. I stirred.

"What time is it?"

"I don't know, but it's nearly daylight . . . and I gotta go."

"Go? Go where?" I asked.

"Go pee," he said. Then, realizing who he was talking to, he amended, "I gotta piss . . . now!"

I sat up. A canteen clanked against a rifle in a nearby foxhole. I peered around in the gray dawn, but saw nothing move.

"Water lily," I whispered loudly. "Man coming out."

"Flower," came the response from the adjoining foxhole.

"Pass the word," I said.

"Now, get out there in plain sight and do what you have to do; then get back in here before you get your pecker shot off."

Not long after Lefty returned, Sergeant "Mac" McDougal was passing the word for the first squad to assemble.

"On the double!" he shouted, ignoring the fact that the Japanese liked to pick off leaders.

The griping began immediately.

"Screw you!" came a voice from a foxhole.

"I'm tired. All that shelling and bombing kept me awake all night," said a bleary-eyed private. "I didn't sleep a goddamn wink."

As the squad gathered around McDougal, a can of cold C-ration hash was passed to each.

"Eat up; we move out in fifteen minutes," he said.

"What kind of a screwball breakfast is this?" asked Jim Smith as he opened his mess kit for a spoon. "How the hell can I function without a cup of coffee?"

It seemed no time at all before Mac was back from company headquarters.

"Listen up. Here's the scoop. Leave your packs here. We're movin' out light—just rifles and cartridge belts."

"What about helmets?" asked a groggy marine.

"Of course, helmets; unless you want to get your head shot off!"

"Where we goin', Sarge?"

"I told you not to call me that. The village we saw yesterday, we're going to take it, or try to. We're supposed to secure it until one of the regiments passes through. Okay, let's move out!"

The squad assembled with the platoon, the platoon with another platoon, and soon the entire Recon Company was moving out along the narrow road toward the village. There wasn't much talking, just some under-breath grumbling, a rattling of equipment, and complaining about stinking farts.

I could see Lefty, the artist, admiring the countryside. The sun came up and took the chill out of the morning air. Great boulders rose out of the hillsides, and the fields were splashed with blotches of sago palms as thick and spiney as rosebushes. Terraces ran across the land in parallel lines. Momentarily, I forgot that this was war.

"Keep alert!" yelled Mac. "Japanese can be anywhere. Remember, some of us were shot at yesterday, so we expect resistance." I noticed that Mac was paying close attention to the lyre-shaped tombs where snipers could be hiding.

"Spread out!" came the order as we approached a hilltop above the village. "Take a five-minute break."

I saw Corporal John Krysztofik searching the village with his field glasses. Krysztofik was a short brick of a man with wide-set bow legs, a proud career marine who was both loved and feared by subordinates.

Considerable time was spent observing the village, after which there was a conference among the officers. Then noncoms were called forward for instructions.

The first platoon was instructed to move through the center of the village, with the first squad, my squad, taking the right side of the main street.

"Ozark, you and Ace take the point."

Suddenly, loud talking and banging erupted from one of the squads.

"Sonofabitch! That's not water," said Sugarlips, sputtering and spitting. "It's gas!" Other men opened their canteens and sniffed the contents. They nodded affirmatively.

"What the hell did you expect?" asked Sergeant Harry Manion from Michigan. "You filled your canteens with water from five-gallon gas cans didn't you? A little gas fumes won't hurt you, but you'll do more than belch if you drink too much."

Bitching continued as we topped the hill. As the village came into view, I could see why the officers were studying it. A canopy of leafy trees covered the entire village. With rifles held at on-guard, we walked steadily toward the village.

"We're nothing but ants," said Jim Smith to Charles Payne, the BAR (Browning Automatic Rifle) man. "We're the regiment's antenna."

"We're more like fresh meat for the Japanese," concluded Payne.

"Enemy has been seen in the village; pass the word." With this enemy sighting, we were now under high state of alert.

Japanese had been seen in a house on the right side of the street. That was my area to search.

"Ace, stay close," I said in a hoarse voice. A. C. "Ace" Brown's throat was so dry that he couldn't speak, so he just nodded his head. I edged around a stone wall into the narrow street. A hundred things had to be watched, and I had to listen, but my heart was pounding in my ears. I glanced back. Ace had me covered. I moved to the house. I clicked off my rifle's safety. I glanced into the first room through a window; nothing moved. I moved to the doorway. Nothing suspicious; no booby traps.

I motioned to Ace that I was going to dash to the second house. *Uh-oh!* Something inside moved—just a shadow. I dropped to one knee and motioned for Ace to get down. Payne moved cautiously to the side of the building with his BAR ready, I rose and walked slowly toward the house.

"Baaah," bleated a goat. What a relief! Only goats were in the house.

Slowly, cautiously, we moved from house to house. First one man moved, then the next, leapfrogging. House to house, street to street, the entire village was searched. After a while, there was less caution.

A building ahead of me had only one doorway, covered with a hanging straw mat. Slowly, I moved the mat to one side with my rifle barrel. It was dark inside. I glimpsed movement and jumped back. I felt an impulse to fire, then another to wait. Then I saw the muzzle—a bull!

The houses thinned out, and we moved through the rest of the village more quickly. Beyond was a valley with terraced rice paddies. The village was clear, so we sat beside the road on our helmets. Mission complete, with only a few shots fired. No enemy routed. We were hungry and exhausted—more from nervous tension than hard work. We ate carrots pulled from the field.

The regiment passed by on the road.

"See anything? Nice job!" They said.

"Good luck!"

They moved on.

Recon Company marched back to headquarters.

At sunset, we moved to our foxholes. We began adjusting our quarters for the night. I remembered what Sergeant Manion had told us.

"Ace," I said, "dig a small hole about a foot deep in one side of our foxhole."

"What for?"

"Two reasons. First, if you get the urge you'll have a place to go without getting your fanny shot off out there." I waved my rifle. "Second, if a grenade is thrown in here you'll have a place to shove it before it goes off."

Gunny Sergeant James Tabb had company guard duty, so he inspected the perimeter. The password is "Tally ho" and the response is "Foxtrot," pass it along. More l's.

Tabb noticed Sammy Zaidain standing nearby, watching the proceedings.

"You bunk with Ozark," he said. "Ace, come with me."

"Got room for me in there, Ozark?"

"I'll make room. Jump in."

Once the short marine was in the foxhole, I noted, "You don't have to dig a hole as deep as some of us do."

"I take a lot of kidding. Some people yell 'stand up' when I'm already standing. Some address me as 'Shorty' or 'Five-by-five.'"

"How'd you get into the marines?"

"I didn't at first."

"What happened?"

"The recruiting sergeant saw how desperate I was after the third try. I did every stretching exercise I had heard of—hanging by my heels, then my neck, but I still lacked about a half-inch being tall enough. I was standing there dejected, when he spoke to a sailor in the office.

"Bring that doormat over here. I think Sammy's feet are getting cold. Stand on that," he said.

"Why the marines? What about the army or navy?"

"That's a long story." He obviously didn't want to discuss it.

Corporal Ray Richards crept up as it was getting dark. "We have a tripwire out there connected to flares, so stay in your holes. Take two-hour watches." He moved on.

"I'll take the first watch," I said.

I sat in the foxhole and held my rifle. I noticed how blue the sky was and how close the stars appeared. As I watched, I saw a shooting star streak toward the horizon . . . toward the east, toward home. I longed for the farm in the Missouri hills, and most of all I missed my mother, who was not well. My heart ached. The thought vanished with a distant boom from a ship in the East China Sea and a closer pop from a flare. Something was out there. The eerie, shimmering light made bushes seem to move—if they were bushes.

Minutes dragged by as I listened for anything unusual among the night sounds. And when I heard that unusual sound, I wished for a flare . . . yet I didn't want a flare. It would expose me to the enemy. Minute by minute, the tension grew and fed my imagination. I held my breath in order to hear better; I looked from side to side to catch any movement, and when I saw a bush move I had to risk my life on my judgment: Was it the wind? Was it an animal? Was it the enemy? Was it the glittering light from a falling flare?

Long after Sammy had been waked for his watch, I sat cramped in the foxhole. My eyes were closed but my mind was racing. Sleep would not come. I and other marines dreaded the night and prayed for dawn; the tension would not go away.

Eventually, Corporal Richards appeared in the gray light. "Get ready to move out!"

Red-eyed men roused themselves, grumbled at the meager cold breakfast washed down with gas-flavored water, and assembled to make a reconnaissance probe deep into enemy territory.

"We're going to ride tanks today," said Manion. "Squad leaders get your men ready." In the distant dim light, a dust-fog was moving toward us. Now we could hear the roar of the tanks.

I managed to find a place on the back of a tank next to the gun turret. The metal deck sloped to the rear, but there was a gun mount and a bracket for lashing that I could hold. Private William "Detroit" Shimp sat next to me, and I held onto him. On the other side was radio man Marvin Chronis, who also held a bracket welded to the tank's metal plate.

Below us three were other marines, clinging to the tank as it roared away. Although rifles were slung over our shoulders, there was a great deal of banging, clashing, and cursing as we clung to the tank like babies on a mother possum's back. To make matters worse, the road was rough and potholed from shelling, and the tank crew was in a hurry.

"Get that damned squawk box off my hand!" yelled Sugarlips to Chronis.

"Screw you! Why don't you move your damned hand? It's all I can do to hang on," shouted Chronis above the roar of the tank.

As the tank managed a curve in the road, a cloud of dust covered the riders. There was a lot of coughing and hand-fanning at the dust.

"How are we supposed to keep our rifles clean in this mess?" I mumbled, my lips glued together with moisture from my mouth.

"My eyelids are sticking together," complained Detroit.

The tank hit a rock and we all bounced. Detroit began to slide off the tank, but Chronis and I grabbed him and held on until our fingers were numb. A hand grenade came off Detroit's cartridge belt and rolled down the back of the tank. The men watched it fall harmlessly to the road. The pin was still in it.

"Some lucky Jap will probably blow you up with it," said a sardonic Sugarlips.

"Sonofabitch," cursed Bama, wiping a mess off his sleeve. Someone had puked all over his arm and was about to repeat the process.

"It's that damned exhaust," I said. "It's poisoning all of us." The other riders saw that the tank's exhaust pipe had been extended above the tank for amphibious landing, and it was spewing foul-smelling smoke all over us.

It seemed hours before we reached the front line because of the dust, the fumes, sour puke, and clinging to the tank for dear life. Regimental marines were strung out like Christmas lights on each side of the road. They greeted us as the tanks roared by.

"Give 'em hell!"

"Bring me a Jap flag!"

"How about a Samurai sword?"

"Kill 'em all—the long, the short, and the tall," harmonized a couple of clowns.

Sounds of youthful voices faded. The tanks thrust deeper into enemy territory—one, three, seven miles. Since it was difficult to speak above the sounds of the tanks, no one tried. Eyes searched the roadside, the hills, the trees, the tombs. Where were the Japanese?

About five miles out, the tanks reached a small village. It was decimated from shell and aircraft fire. Straw sleeping mats littered the street, along with household items. Not a leaf seemed to stir as the tanks moved through.

At the north edge of town, the tanks made a sharp right turn to cross the Ishikawa Isthmus. They stopped so abruptly that Detroit was thrown off. I thought it was funny until it occurred to me that he might have been shot.

"Everybody off!" yelled Sergeant Tabb.

As we tumbled off, complaining and dusting ourselves, the reason for the holdup became apparant. A hole big as a house was in the middle of the narrow road.

"Spread out! Take cover!" yelled Tabb. "What do you think this is, a football game? Some Jap's probably sitting up there on the hill right now with you in his nambu sights."

Soon it was obvious that the tanks couldn't go farther.

"Fall in!" shouted Tabb. Squad leaders repeated the orders. "Let's move out."

The road curved along a valley. At points, it was overhung with a rocky bluff or steep hillsides. Brush and trees were ideal places for an ambush. We were tense. Each of us was acutely aware that we were deep in enemy territory. Each suspected that a firefight was imminent.

From the corner of my eye, I could see Sergeant McDougal approaching.

"Ozark, we'll soon be out of this valley. When we reach the top of the hill, I want you to be our lookout. You and Ace take the point. Here's my field glasses. Do a thorough search with them." Mac dropped back into the platoon.

At the crest of the hill, our platoon formed a flanking movement to protect one side of our company. At the sound of voices, we took a defensive position. Everyone could see women and children fleeing across a small stream and toward the distant hill. They sounded like a flock of squawking geese. I carefully searched each one with the binoculars, because enemy soldiers were known to hide among natives.

"What do you see?" asked Ace.

"Just women and children."

"Keep looking."

Soon the order came to move out. Ace and I moved down the hillside toward the stream. Except for patches of brush, the land was covered with grass. The brush outlined a deep gully. Soon I saw a trench zigzagging across the hillside. Both of us readied our rifles. We examined the trench. Nothing, not even a footprint.

"Every hair on my head is at attention," whispered Ace hoarsely as he and I jumped into the trench. I immediately began searching with the field glasses.

I was panning across the escaping women and children, when I suddenly stopped in horror. "Gawd Almighty!" I yelled. I jumped out of the trench and ran toward the stream. "Hey, cut that out!" I screamed. Ace popped up out of the trench to see a native woman wearing a kimono shoving something into the water. As he watched, I raised my rifle and fired. There was a splash in the water near the woman. She lifted her head, straightened up, and ran after the retreating natives, leaving a bundle behind.

I ran into the stream and picked up the bundle. The watching marines stood in a trance, wondering what I was doing, figuring I

would be shot at any moment. As I approached Ace, there was a
faint sound of crying from the bundle.

"What the hell..." he gasped.

"She was trying to drown her baby."

By this time the platoon had moved down the hill. Mac came up
to me. "What the hell . . ."

"She was trying to kill her baby, Sarge. I had to do something."

"What kind of people do they think we are? Hey, Doc, come up
here!" Corpsman Harold Redinger moved forward.

"What the hell . . . are we going to do with a baby?" asked Doc.

"That's your problem now," Mac answered.

Dan Kvaase, a baby-faced blond, was gaping with eyes big as silver dollars. He was probably the youngest among us. Some said he
was still carrying his own baby fat.

"Kvaase," said the sergeant, "you go with Doc."

As the sound and sight of the native women disappeared over a
distant hill, a new round of screaming broke out. This time it was
coming from the rear of the platoon—and the voices were
American!

"Hit the deck!" shouted Mac. As the men scrambled for cover,
more rifle shots were heard. More shouts, and someone called out,
"BAR man! BAR man!" That was Payne with the Browning
Automatic Rifle. He surged to the patch of brush and began to
spray it with bullets.

"There's another one in there," yelled Detroit. The BAR chattered again. Then it was quiet. Gradually, the men began to move
back up the hill to see what the commotion was about.

Detroit lay on the ground, bleeding from a long gash in his hip.
Beside him lay a bamboo pole with a bayonet lashed to it. Nearby
was the Japanese soldier who had tried to kill him. The soldier had
been shot in the heart, and he was bleeding through his clothes. On
the lip of the bushy ditch lay another soldier, still grasping a
grenade. He had been shot in the head. He was face up and his eyes
were open. In the brush, down in the ditch, was a third Japanese.
The top of his skull was nearby, with his brains still in it.

As I watched, I heard retching behind me. I felt queasy, too.

Lieutenant Robert Autry came up and observed the scene.
"Sergeant, appoint an Intelligence man to search the bodies."

"Ozark, you're the man," said Mac

I carefully went through the pockets and clothing of the men, who were still warm and bleeding. On one body I found the picture of a woman holding an infant; tears came to my eyes. There were no maps, nothing to interest Intelligence. I replaced the picture. When the search was over, my hands were covered in blood.

"We'll take a break here. Break out your rations," was the message passed along. "The tanks have broken through and will be here shortly."

I looked at the blood drying brown on my hands. I washed them in gas-tainted water from my canteen, but I couldn't eat a bite.

The tanks brought a message that the regiment had been held up by a Japanese nambu. One man was killed and several injured. But the tank probe into enemy territory was to continue.

Clinging to the backs of the tanks, we had traveled less than a mile when we heard a sound like a Mack truck grinding through the air. Just ahead, the ground exploded. Dirt, rocks, and shell fragments showered us. We jumped from the tanks and took defensive positions. The tanks pulled off the road. A small observation airplane flew low over the tanks and dropped a message: *You're heading into a trap.*

The tank men had located the enemy on a distant ridge through their high-powered field glasses. By radio, they asked for permission to fire. *Yours is a reconnaissance mission.* came the response. *You are not to fire. Repeat. Do not fire. Return to base.*

As the tanks turned, there was another rumble in the air, followed by an earth-shaking explosion. Debris and foul-smelling smoke clouded the area.

As soon as the air cleared, we dug our noses out of the dirt and headed for the tanks. We scrambled aboard; more shells followed—closer! The tanks were already moving when the last man was pulled aboard. As we hung on, the tanks nearly jumped out from under us. We raced for safety. Another shell hit near the road, splashing a wave of dirt over us.

After the tanks moved out of range of the Japanese guns, they slowed.

"Damn," said our radio man, "I didn't know tanks could go that fast."

"Well, they couldn't, but I was pushing," I replied.

At the front line, tired regimental marines were moving north.

Some had confiscated horses to carry packs, mortars, and ammunition. Again we good-naturedly taunted and encouraged each other. Recon was happy; we were going back to our command post. Already we were dreaming of hot food, warm blankets, fresh drinking water, and baths. But dark caught us within the confines of a regiment.

Sargents McDougal, Tabb, and Manion were standing by the tanks when Major Walker approached.

"Call the men together," said our commander.

Tired and dirty, we straggled up, and he told us that we were to spend the night and stand flank guard for the regiment. We started bitching.

"Men," he began, "I'm proud of you. Today you acted in the true Corps tradition. Some of you earned Purple Hearts, and I'm turning in Shimp's name for the Bronze Star."

"How is Detroit?"

"Where's the baby that Doc got?"

The questions were flying, and the major was answering.

Sarge Tabb turned to Manion: "That son-of-a-gun sure knows how to get a man's mind off his misery."

The night was dark, damp, and cold. Our dusty clothes were infested with fleas picked up from the village, as were the straw mats we slept on. We had no food, no blankets, no potable water, not even a shovel.

Seeing our plight, regimental marines shared what little they had—about three spoonfuls each of C-ration hash, and water. As the cold night wore on, we fought the biting, crawling fleas. Sleep was impossible. At about 0200, several of us gathered in a foxhole and began talking. We were stomping our feet to keep warm, smoking, and visiting quietly. Regulations be damned!

A new man, who had been sleeping fitfully, woke. "Who's there?" he yelled. Thinking we were the enemy, he lifted his rifle and fired at our noise. That roused the camp, and no one tried to sleep. It also got the new man ousted. No one in the ranks knew what happened to him, but it was rumored he left Recon by request.

Dawn found us back on the tanks and headed for our CP. Hot chow, water, blankets. Sleep never felt so good.

I woke with a start from a terrible dream.

"What happened to the baby?" I yelled.

Chapter 4

JAPANESE DEFENSE

Lieutenant General Mitsuru Ushijima realized the importance of Okinawa to the defense of Japan. One year before the Allied invasion, the Japanese had established the Thirty-second Army on Okinawa in anticipation of an attack. As the months passed, many reinforcements were added. The military, along with native *Boeitai* (national guard), began digging a network of caves, underground bunkers, gun emplacements, and trenches. These fortifications were located along the escarpments and beaches, and around airfields.

Okinawa, located only 325 miles from the southernmost empire island of Kyushu, was the largest island of the Ryuku chain. It was sixty miles long and varied in width from eighteen miles at the Motubu Peninsula to two miles at the Ishikawa Isthmus; the isthmus effectively divided the island into two parts. The northern two-thirds of the island were forested and mountainous, with peaks rising to fifteen hundred feet. The valleys were farmed, primarily growing sugar cane, sweet potatoes, and rice. The southern third of the island was rolling countryside, broken by escarpments. It was also the most populated area of the island, with two- thirds of the people, and was the location of the prefecture's capitol, Naha. Okinawa had several airports and a two-lane paved road between Shuri and Naha, a short distance. Other roads were earthen.

During early island battles, the Japanese defenders had often resorted to *banzai* attacks. On Guam, for example, marines reported that the island defenders worked themselves into a drunken frenzy before swarming toward the marine invaders, screaming *"Banzai!"* Japanese commanders soon realized that this practice was nonproductive and wasteful of manpower. Later, they selected natural defensive positions to fortify and held them literally to the last man. This Japanese tactic, called *Jikyusen*, had been used on Iwo Jima, where Mount Suribachi was literally a maze of enemy fortifications.

Although Okinawa had been fortified in this manner, General Ushijima was faced with a reversal when, in February 1945, the Japanese high command withdrew a division from Okinawa to help defend the Philippines. It was determined that Ushijima would command the Sixty-second and Twenty-fourth divisions and the Forty-fourth Mixed Brigade and defend a line formed by the cities of Naha, Shuri, and Yonabaru. Colonel Takehiko Udo, with three thousand soldiers of the Second Infantry unit, would defend the mountainous northern part of the island. The Yontan and Kadena Airfields were only lightly defended by what the Japanese called *Bimbo Boeitai* (poor detachments), or native conscripts or home guard. The Hagushi beaches were left unprotected.

During the six days of pre-invasion bombardment, warships had rained 7,000 shells, from sixteen-inch down to 40mm, on Okinawa. Just prior to the landing, the U.S. Navy bombarded the beaches with 44,825 rounds of ammunition ranging from five- to sixteen-inch shells; 33,000 rockets; and 22,500 mortar explosives; plus aerial bombardment from planes.

From his elevated command post at Shuri Castle, General Ushijima must have been elated as he watched this spectacular waste on the abandoned Hagushi beaches. At the same time, he must have recoiled at the awesome firepower of the Allied forces he faced. For as far as he could see, the ocean was dotted with ships. How he must have longed for the Japanese air force to attack.

As Ushijima watched on the clear morning of April 1, 1945, he would have seen landing ships beyond the bombarding battlewagons, destroyers, and cruisers. The LST and other transport ships disgorged their cargo of landing crafts, and the troop ships lowered their cargo nets for the marines to climb down to their boats prior to rendezvous for landing. What a sight! Some eight hundred Amtracks in as many as seven lines back carried amphibious tanks—all streamed toward the Hagushi beaches.

During the first hour of landing, Ushijima would have seen 16,000 troops storm the beaches. Following the first line of invaders came most soldiers and marines, tanks, ammunition, and supplies. By noon of L-Day, the Hagushi beaches were secured.

Chapter 5

OFFENSIVE TACTICAL PLAN

The first salvo of the Okinawa campaign came October 10, 1944. Task Force Thirty-eight under Admiral W. F. "Bull" Halsey led seventeen aircraft carriers with one thousand planes, protected by six battleships, fourteen cruisers, and fifty-eight destroyers and their support ships, on an island attack.

The carriers were surrounded by the fifty-eight "tin cans" to pick up downed pilots. The "flattop" planes were armed with bombs, twenty-one-inch torpedoes, five-inch rockets, and numerous fifty-caliber machine guns. Pilots flew 1,396 sorties over Okinawa, sinking almost everything afloat in Naha Harbor, and the capitol city itself was set ablaze.

"A typhoon of steel" was the name for that and for future air raids. Natives sought the protection of caves for their survival.

On March 18, 1945, Admiral Raymond Spruance took Task Force Fifty-eight from anchor at Ulithi Island (the Okinawa invasion assemble point) and bore down on Kyushu, the empire's southernmost island, with an intention to destroy the island's airfields. Japanese air raids had become troublesome, particularly the "human bombs" called *kamikazes*, and they threatened the Allied invasion fleet.

Kyushu's 55 airfields were defended by Admiral Matome Ugaki's Ten-Go, consisting of 193 planes, all of which were released against Task Force Fifty-eight. The Carriers *Wasp* and *Franklin* were badly damaged. And Admiral Ugaki declared a great victory, although he had lost 161 of his 193 planes.

The ordeal for the flattop *Franklin* was not over. The following morning, a Japanese bomber blasted the carrier with two 550-pound bombs. The bomber survived the *Franklin's* guns but was downed by an air attack.

On March 24, elements of Task Forces Fifty-four and Fifty-two shelled Okinawa's southeast coast in a test of strength and to isolate the Japanese garrison while minesweepers cleared the area. Meanwhile, naval radar pickets began to encircle Okinawa and the offshore islands.

Dawn of March 26 brought the first kamikaze attack by the Japanese Eighth Air Division from Formosa. The first Allied ship hit was the *Kimberly*. It was knocked out of action and the crew decimated—four dead, thirty-three wounded, and seventeen missing.

From March 27 to 29, Okinawa launched land-based planes until all had been shot down.

In preparation for the landing, U.S. Underwater Demolition Teams (UDTs) searched the waters off the Hagushi beaches. They found that 2,900 large wooden posts had been driven into the sea floor. These had to be blasted out.

During the week before L-Day, the navy delivered 27,000 rounds of ordnance but did little damage to the dug-in Japanese defenders. On L-Day, the largest battle armada ever assembled in the Pacific lay offshore to Okinawa: 1,300 ships with more than 500,000 men, 184,000 of which were in the landing force, and of which 154,000 would actually assault the Hagushi beaches.

In a diversionary move, the Second Marine Division faked a landing on the Minatoga beaches on the eastern side of Okinawa. Actually, the first casualties came as a result of this action, when kamikazes slammed into the *Hinsdale* and LST *884* during the landing feint by the Third Battalion of the Second Marines. After the fourth wave of the feinting assault was launched, the troops were recalled under cover of smoke.

The diversionary tactic served to hold the Japanese garrison in position while the actual landing was in progress on the opposite side of the island.

At 0406 on April l, Vice Admiral Richmond Kelly Turner gave the "Land the Landing Forces" order, and naval gunfire rocked the shoreline. Participating in the bombardment were ten old battleships, cratering the shore with from twelve- to sixteen-inch guns firing 1,200- to 1,800-pound shells; nine heavy and three light cruisers; twenty-three destroyers; and 177 gunboats—many of which were rocket-firing LCIs. This was followed by sorties from 138 planes from the Twentieth Air Force, the Tenth Army's tactical air force, and strafing by marine pilots who saturated the Hagushi beaches before the landing.

At 0800 navy time, armored vehicles with troops began rendezvousing for landing as ship pennant signals were hauled down from masts. Medium tanks with flotation devices on their tracks struggled toward shore, where explosives would remove their baggage and make them truly land vehicles. All types of personnel landing crafts were released from their circular gathering patterns for a 4,000-yard dash to shore.

By 0824, six waves of LVTs had landed army units south of the Bishi Gawa river.

General Simon Bolivar Buckner, son of a Civil War Confederate officer with the same name and a veteran of the U.S. Service in Alaska, was named to lead the invasion forces on Okinawa comprised of the Tenth U.S. Army and including the First, Second, and Sixth Marine Divisions.

Many of the marines had seen action in the Pacific in other commands. This was true of the Sixth under the leadership of General Lemuel Shepherd. About seventy percent of his troops were veterans of other Pacific battles. The Sixth's emblem became a silver crusader's sword and their slogan "the Striking Sixth."

Altogether General Buckner had 184,000 men, of which 154,000 would assault the Hagushi beaches, but this was only half again as many as General Ushijima's 110,000 defenders. Historically, an attack force needed three times as many troops as the defenders.

Following the LVTs with infantry, the army engineers landed and began blasting seawalls in preparation for the buildup of supplies on beaches designated Purple, Orange, White, and Brown.

While troops encountered little difficulty in landing south of

Bishi Gawa, those north of the river—along beaches designated Yellow, Blue, Red, and Green zones—had difficulty crossing coral reefs, although there was an incoming tide. Blue Beach was the roughest of all.

As a result, some troops did not land in their designated areas. However, the overall landing plan was successful, and there was surprisingly little opposition.

Marines moved inland so quickly that a gap appeared between the Second and Third Battalions of the Twenty-second Regiment, Sixth Marine Division. General Shepherd immediately released a unit of the Twenty-ninth Regiment to fill the gap. By midmorning the Twenty-second Marines had advanced to Yontan Airfield. As marines advanced rapidly, other reserve elements were released to fill the widening gaps between the assault units.

When marines approached Yontan and Kadena Airfields, units of the *Bimbo Boeitai*, or "home guard", fled. They had no stomach to fight for the oppressive Japanese. Many simply shed their uniforms and disappeared into the ranks of civilian Okinawans.

Intelligence officers could scarcely believe the reports from the front. Major General Shepherd moved his Sixth Marine Division on shore, saying: "There was glory on Iwo, but I'll take it this way."

At the end of L-Day, a beachhead eight miles long and from three to four miles inland belonged to the invaders—at a cost of 28 KIA, 27 MIA, and 104 WIA. Several of these numbers were from the Second Marine Division that had feinted at the Minatoga beaches but did not land.

Radio Tokyo announced that the landing units on Okinawa would soon be destroyed. The Second Marine Division feinted again at the Minatoga beaches, freezing the Japanese main body in a defensive position.

Chapter 6

RECON MECHANIZES PATROLS

I woke with a start, my mind still groggy—in a fog. I imagined I heard voices. The Japanese were snooping around. I grabbed my rifle but fell back into the foxhole.

"What's the matter, Ozark? You still fighting yesterday's battle?" It was Sweetpee, Ray Van Heuvelen, speaking. He had acquired the nickname when he took a urine test after eating candy.

Sweetpee laughed. I collected myself, then grinned. "Guess you could say that." I rose above the foxhole rim to see marines grouped around something on the ground. I recognized Doc Redinger among them.

"What's going on? Did someone get shot?"

"No. It's that baby girl you rescued. The whole outfit is goofing around, going 'ga-ga' and 'goo-goo' like a bunch of proud papas."

"The hell you say."

I climbed out and walked toward the crowd. I could see the baby girl sitting on a green blanket. Dan Kvaase was on his knees, teasing her. She would giggle and bounce up and down, flailing her arms. As I got closer, I could see that she was dressed in a marine's dungaree jacket with the sleeves cut off at the elbows—and nothing else. She had been scrubbed and her straight black hair combed. She was happy and laughing at all the attention. Her big brown eyes sparkled. I, too, felt loving compassion for the harmless little enemy waif.

I was sipping a cup of coffee from my canteen cup and watching the little lady perform when we were told to fall in on the double for another patrol. I didn't realize it at the time, but Recon Company was making history.

The Okinawa campaign was reported to be the only battle the Marines fought in the Pacific where armored reconnaissance probes were practical. Lack of resistance and the size of Okinawa were what made them feasible. Leading our panzer-like probes to find the Japanese were six Sherman tanks, five with 75mm guns, and one bulldozer tank to repair roads and remove obstructions. There was also the commander's radio jeep, which kept other units and the navy with their big guns aware of our progress. All that firepower supported 140 battle-ready Recon marines. We moved swiftly miles ahead of the regiments, and we must have been a tempting target many times for the Japanese.

Sergeant Harry Manion, with his knack for military history, said this about one of our trips:

"Early the next morning we moved north. Took a look at Bolo Point [beach needed for unloading ships], checked the villages of Jima, Takeskhi, and Uza. All vacated. Moved along the seawall to Nagahama, Masuya, Maeta, Kurawa, Nakadomari, and Menkaniku. Then we were called back to Nakadomari and ordered across the isthmus to assist another unit near Ishikawa on the Pacific side of Okinawa. A book author, I believe Robert Sherrod, came with us."

Our forays beyond the front lines and into the unknown attracted many visitors. Some of the others who visited Recon were Captain Phillips Carleton, Marine Historical Section; Major General Lemuel Shepherd, Division Commander; an army brigadier general from General George C. Marshall's staff; and several magazine, wire service, and newsreel reporters.

In combat, all marines were considered the same regardless of rank. Riding on a bench in a truck bed, a PFC in our outfit was sitting beside the army brigadier general. Here's the conversation as our executive officer, William Christie, recalled it:

"Hey, Sir, what's that funny patch on your collar?"

"My collar insignia identifies me as a representative of General George C. Marshall, Chief of Staff, United States Army."

"Wow, Jeez, big fugging deal."

PFC Ernest Wills tells of encountering a short, fat guy jumping and rubbernecking to see what was going on over a wall. At the time, it was pouring rain, and men along the wall were under sniper fire.

"I gave him a boot in the butt and told him to get down. Boy, was I surprised when he turned around. On his helmet were three stars." Wills didn't stay to see who he was.

But I have digressed. When we returned from our armored reconnaissance mission, I asked about the baby. One of our men, I don't recall if it was Kvaase, spoke up. "I'd like to tell you we got on the radio and called Civil Affairs and they came and took her, but that's not what happened," he said.

Here's how Corpsman Harold Redinger remembers it:

> We spent two or three days on this bluff while patrols went out. Some fellows brought a little lost Okinawan girl to me. She was probably three or four years old (about the age of my daughter in the States). She was a mass of mosquito or flea bites. I gave her a bath from my helmet, put ointment on the bites, and dressed her in a shirt one of the fellows had cut down.
>
> The next day some Okinawans came by and we gave the girl to them. A day or two later, an old Mama-San came back and gave me a block of crude sugar wrapped in an old rag. It didn't look appetizing, even after K-rations. When we left, the sugar stayed.
>
> I've often wondered if the girl lived through that mess, and if she remembered. She'd be a great-great-grandmother by now.

I also wondered about the dislocation and death of the Okinawans. How could families ever find their relatives—even if they were alive? And if they were dead from a bullet or shell burst, who would know?

I had grown up in the Ozark hills, where everyone knew each other and half of us were related—aunts, uncles, cousins, fathers, mothers, grandparents. And the marines had been a shock—a revolving door of acquaintances. I had close friends at boot camp, others at Camp LeJeune, Camp Pendleton, Guadalcanal, and finally Okinawa. They came and went—some I would never see again.

It was getting dark, and the shelling had started again. Just as I was getting into my hole, Jim Smith came by with the password. He told about capturing two soldiers on their patrol. They were discussing what to do with them, because we had no facilities for prisoners, when they were fired on by a sniper. They hit the deck and fired back. The sniper hastily retreated. When they got to their feet, the prisoners didn't. BARman Ray Miller had solved the prisoner problem.

Sergeant McDougal with a small group of Okinawan children. Note water canteens by his shoe.

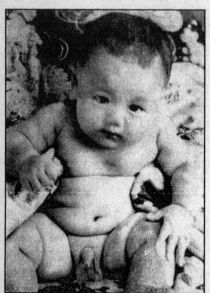

Male Okinawan babies were photographed naked to show their sex.

Japanese girl. Picture may have come from an enemy soldier's wallet.

Oriental girl. Picture found on Okinawa.

Okinawan girl.

Okinawan picture postcard.

Two marines protecting an Okinawan child as it sleeps.

Chapter 7

KAMIKAZES

Kamikazes, Chrysanthemums, *Ten-Go*, *Kikusui*—all are terms associated with Japanese suicide planes. The roots of these words go back to the late 1200s, when a Mongol fleet from China attempted to invade Japan. As the armada sailed toward Japan, it was overcome by a powerful typhoon that destroyed the fleet. The Japanese term for the storm was *kamikaze* or "divine wind."

One of the first associations of the term kamikaze with suicide planes in World War II was in Leyte Gulf of the Philippines. On October 19, 1944, at 7:40 in the morning, Vice Admiral Takijimo Ohnishi plunged his own plane into the escort carrier *Santee*.

Although Americans had encountered some historical precedence for these wartime suicide missions, nothing approached the massive action undertaken by imperial Japan. *Bushido*, warriors, were regarded with religious fervor—a pilot who died in combat for his emperor and country went directly to heaven.

This was a difficult concept for Americans to accept, although we had historical records of fighting until death at the Alamo, General Custer's last stand; and we all knew Patrick Henry's famous words, "Give me liberty or give me death," and Admiral David Glasgow Farragut's "Damn the torpedoes, full speed ahead."

The latter might be construed as an American version of the kamikaze mindset.

The Japanese high command considered the Philippine suicide attacks successful, and shortly thereafter Admiral Takajiro Ohnishi began urging flyers to sacrifice their lives. Out of this emerged their special attack units, *tokkotai*. The enemy warlords had devised a Mariana Islands defense plan that they felt was impregnable. The theory was a method of protecting all the islands north of the Marianas with naval supremacy. However, they reasoned: No navy supremacy without air support, and without naval supremacy there was no way to defend the Pacific Islands.

Therefore, a major step toward their objective was to train a strong air force. Unlike the early independent suicide missions, the new approach was highly organized. By February 13, 1945, it was reported that Admiral Soemu Toyoda, headquartered at Kanoya, Kyushu, had 11,815 planes with trained pilots.

The men were instructed to attack when the sun was low to avoid anti-aircraft fire. These pilots were dedicated and sober. They were so hardened to their fate that the last days before a flight would be spent writing letters, lounging around base playing cards, reading, and visiting. Most of their letters expressed love to their families and resignation to the glorious privilege to die for Japan.

Pilots often wore adornments. There were reports by American seamen of Japanese flight jackets decorated with dolls and religious ornaments, and the pilots also wore the popular *hachimaki* ("headbands").

At Leyte, during one of the first reports of a kamikaze attack, the plane hit the mast of one ship, lost a wing, and careened into a destroyer. Sailors reported that the pilot was wearing a white scarf.

Admiral Toyoda had his first opportunity to use the *kikusui* (a large number of kamikazes) on March 18, 1945, against Task Force Fifty-eight when its carrier planes raided Japan to reduce the Nippon air power being used against ships during the Okinawa invasion. The Japanese lost 161 planes, but considered the loss acceptable in view of the damage to the American fleet.

On March 26 Vice Admiral Mitscher's Task Force Fifty-eight planes made another preemptive strike on Kyushu. Unknown to the carrier *Franklin*, its returning planes were followed by a lone Japanese dive-bomber. The bomber was above the U.S. planes, keeping an eye on them by skipping in and out of clouds.

As the *Franklin* was busy launching a second flight group, the unseen Japanese bomber zeroed in on the carrier. The crew of the *Hancock* was nearby and saw the bomber. They called to the *Franklin*, but it was too late. Two big bombs split the hangar deck, causing fire and destruction. Bombs and rockets on loaded planes shot off with noise, fire, and smoke. Amid the chaos, sailors abandoned ship and were plucked from the ship's wake by rescuers. Some sailors were able to jump directly from the *Franklin* to other ships that pulled alongside. The *Franklin* barely managed to stay afloat, but two of her planes, launched before the attack, shot down the Japanese bomber.

The fleet commanders had devised a type of "circle the wagons" defense against enemy planes. The early-warning picket ships were first, detecting incoming planes with their radar. This was a circle of destroyers with 40mm guns firing shells with proximity fuses. The next circle was comprised of smaller ships rapid-firing 20mm shells. And finally there was the prized inner circle of flagships with the fleet commanders.

On the night of March 26–27, a few Japanese planes went scouting and harassing along Okinawa's west coast. About daylight on the 27th, seven Japanese planes streaked toward the American ships. As the approaching dots on the horizon become larger, salvos of shells were thrown at them. As one plane cleared the smoke of a shell burst, gunners could see a flame where one wing was missing. His death spiral ended in a splash. As the next circle of ships opened fire, the remaining planes dropped down for the attack. Two more planes took the deep six. The remaining planes headed for the prized inner circle. One took head-on fire and crashed into the *Nevada*.

The next one to attack, according to Vice Admiral Morton L. Deyo, was a bomber. He headed for the cruiser *Biloxi*, but he was crippled and began losing altitude. He couldn't make it. Somehow, he leveled out and dropped into the water at the ship's side. His momentum rammed him into the ship, leaving a twenty-six-foot gash. Unbelievably, the bomb didn't detonate. It was an eleven hundred-pounder. We knew, because it was found inside the ship.

The last kamikaze hesitated before making his run. That was a fatal error. He was consumed by a hailstorm of fire and disintegrated, showering parts into the sea.

Such was the story of kamikaze raids at Okinawa.

On April 2 a flight of ten kamikazes attacked a fifteen-ship convoy near Kerama Retto, an island off the Okinawan coast. Three ships were hit, leaving fifty-three dead.

Admiral Soemu Toyoda, commander in chief of the Japanese air fleet, was surprised at how quickly Task Force Fifty-eight had recovered after the March 18–19 raid on Japan. He had not expected Okinawa to be attacked so soon, and he was not ready to kill the American army at sea, which was one of the High Command's objectives.

Meanwhile, scattered air attacks from Formosa and Japan were taking their toll: a battleship, an escort carrier, two destroyers, eight transports and cargo ships, a minesweeper, and two landing craft were sunk. It was a nerve-wracking time for the U.S. Navy, but the worst was yet to come.

By April 6 Admiral Matome Ugaki, Commander of the Fifth Air Fleet, had a "floating chrysanthemum" (large number of planes) ready for "Operation *Ten-Go*" ("attack"). Although he had failed to catch the invasion fleet on the open sea with General Simon Bolivar Buckner's Tenth Army aboard, he hoped to compensate by destroying the supply ships and the materials on the beaches.

"Get the destroyers," instructed Ugaki. "Without their radar warning we will enjoy great success."

Admiral Richmond Turner had sixteen picket boats with radar around Okinawa. Numbers one and four were most vulnerable, because they faced Japan. Each destroyer had a five-man team trained in vectoring U.S. fighter planes toward "bogies" (unidentified targets).

The radar reference "Point Bolo" was a land-based radar on Zampa Misaki Cape, an area that the Sixth Marine Division, Twenty-ninth Regiment, had captured for that purpose under the direction of Lieutenant General Lemuel Shepherd.

The Japanese pilots found Task Force Fifty-eight north of Okinawa, near Amami-O Shima, and began pounding them. This chrysanthemum consisted of about one hundred bombers and fighters. They concentrated their attack on the U.S. carriers *Hancock* and *Bennington*, plus two destroyers.

An enemy bomber dove at the *Bennington*'s stern while the ship's gunners poured shells into it. The bomber exploded before it hit the aircraft carrier, but flying debris damaged the rudder.

About half of the aerial attack planes flew on to Okinawa. The first attack was midafternoon.

Following the first wave of planes came another. The second group were kamikazes headed for the Hagushi beaches and the forest of ships offshore. Hails of exploding shells and tracer bullets sought their targets. Tracer lines drew a network across the sky, which was polkadotted with black shell-bursts. The strong odor of gunpowder and smoke covered the anchored ships like a blanket. The pounding began at about 3 P.M. and lasted until dark. More than two hundred Japanese planes participated.

When the battle was over, naval commanders assessed their damage. It was enormous: six ships sunk, nine destroyers damaged, along with four destroyer escorts and five minesweepers. Eighteen other ships were damaged. More than five hundred men had lost their lives.

The Japanese lost 135 planes, but Admiral Ugaki was elated by the glowing report from returning pilots. Thirty ships had been sunk, and at least twenty more ships were burning and pouring smoke into the air. It looked like the whole anchorage was on fire. Admiral Ugaki wondered if there could be many more ships to sink after he heard the exaggerated report.

Unknown to Ugaki at the time, and perhaps underestimated by American commanders, two ammunition ships had been sunk, the *Logan Victory* and the *Hobbs Victory*. Observers said that several kamikazes had headed for the three ammunition ships, the two already named, plus the *Tulagi*. A seasoned navy veteran said he didn't attempt to go below deck, although junk from shell fragments, short rounds, and Japanese planes was falling onto the deck and splashing into the water. He expected the burning ammo ships to explode and clear the harbor, including his ship. But they didn't; they just burned down to the water.

One of the destroyers lost was the *Emmons*. It had been damaged by several kamikaze hits. Several men were below deck and couldn't see the action. When water began rising in their compartment, they knew it was time to get out. But they couldn't. Blazing fire and smoke blocked one exit. They tried another hatch door, but it had been sprung by the explosions or heat. Finally, one of the men got out through an ammunition door leading into a gun tub.

He found a fire extinguisher and was able to reduce the fire enough for his mates to escape.

The *Emmons* didn't sink. The burned-out skeleton had to be sunk by friendly fire. The cost was 64 KIA and 71 W (wounded) out of the ship's complement of 237.

The April 6 *kikusui* (major kamikaze attack) was only the first of ten that the Allied navies would suffer during the Okinawa operation.

Chapter 8

SINKING THE *YAMATO*

As the navy was the pride of Japan, the *Yamato* was the pride of the navy. In fact, *Yamato* means "Japan." It was a sailor's dream to serve on the giant battleship. Some called it the "Hotel Yamato" because it was so luxurious compared to other ships, with their cramped quarters.

The sleek lines of the ship disguised its size: 863 feet long, almost the length of three football fields, with a 128-foot beam. Her displacement was 69,100 tons. She had a complement of between 2,500 and 3,000 men. And she could cruise 7,200 miles at 16 knots. Her powerful engines not only gave her speed, but also maneuverability to evade torpedoes and bombs.

However, it was of the great ship's armament that the admirals boasted. Wrapped in steel plate one-and-a-half feet thick, with vulnerable parts even thicker, the ship had an aura of invincibility. Like the *Titanic*, she was thought to be almost unsinkable. But the Imperial admirals were acutely aware that American pilots had sunk the Yamato's sister ship, *Musashi*.

The *Yamato's* firepower was awesome. The great battlewagon had nine 18.1-inch guns, the largest in the Pacific. The guns could shoot thirty miles. The Washington Naval Treaty, to which the Japanese were a signature, stated that no guns larger than sixteen-inch would be built. A Japanese petty officer, therefore, stated that these were the largest sixteen-inch guns in the navy.

The *Yamato* bristled with secondary guns, too. There were batteries of six-inch guns, 24 five-inch anti-aircraft guns, and 150 machine guns, plus extra guns that had been added for the Okinawa expedition.

And lastly, the mammoth ship had a reputation among the ever-optimistic Japanese as a lucky ship. She had survived the battles of the Philippine Sea and Leyte Gulf with what could be considered minor scratches.

So it was that the *Yamato* left Kyushu, Japan, on April 6 under the command of Admiral Seiichi Ito. She was escorted by the light cruiser *Yahagi* and eight destroyers. Most of the Japanese commanders recognized Task Force Two, as the group was designated, as a suicide mission, a kamikaze attack by sea rather than by air. There were rumors that the fuel-guzzling *Yamato* had only enough fuel for a one-way trip to Okinawa.

Task Force Two had scarcely cleared the coast of Japan before she was sighted by two U.S. submarines—*Threadfin* and *Hackleback*. The *Threadfin* radioed Admiral Mitscher's Task Force Fifty-eight of the flotilla. The subs were advised not to attack, but to shadow. The submarine commanders must have looked wistfully at such an appealing target as the *Yamato* while they restrained their torpedoes. After all, the Pacific underwater fleet commanders had conceded that half the ocean belonged to the Japanese navy—the bottom half.

At dawn on April 7, patrol planes from the carrier *Essex* spotted the Japanese task force. They were sailing west in order to approach Okinawa away from the U.S. pickets. Their fuel-short air cover had already returned to Japan. The American air patrol shadowed the flotilla until they were about 250 miles from Okinawa.

Meanwhile, Admiral Turner signaled Rear Admiral Morton Deyo: "Hope you bring back a nice fish for breakfast."

Deyo replied: "If the pelicans haven't caught them all."

Only nine minutes after the first wave of American planes had sighted the Japanese task force, both a torpedo and bombs hit the *Yamato*. A destroyer serving as rear guard had been sunk, and the light cruiser *Yahagi* was dead in the water.

But the *Yamato* was fighting gamely. Her batteries of five- and six-inch guns were blazing away, along with her 150 machine guns. The noise must have been deafening and the smoke blinding.

After the first wave left, the *Yamato* crew thought that the worst was over, and they began to talk about how they would attack the enemy on and around Okinawa. And if the great ship should be crippled, they'd beach her and use those enormous guns to help General Ushijima's troops defend the island.

The first air wave struck at 12:30 P.M., and it was almost an hour later that the second wave attacked. Torpedo bombers speared the *Yamato* with five "fish" in the port side. She began to list. Japanese gunners lowered the great eighteen-inch rifles and fired into the ocean, hoping that the great waterspouts would down the low-flying torpedo bombers as they made their runs.

Simultaneously, the *Yamato* was dodging torpedoes and firing all guns. The huge ship must have been bobbing like a cork on the ocean. Materials crashed throughout the ship, and men fell on the bloody deck under a hailstorm of machine gun bullets from the attacking planes.

As the list worsened, it became impossible to aim the big guns above the water. In a desperate attempt to level the ship, Rear Admiral Kosaku Arriga ordered the starboard boiler and engine rooms flooded. An attempt was made to notify the men below deck to come up, but it was too late. As the great rush of water met the steam of the boilers, the men must have disintegrated.

For the American pilots it was déjà vu—the Marianas Turkey Shoot all over again. Ships without air cover could not survive. The imperial ship with polished teakwood decks was dying.

At 2 P.M. another wave of American planes attacked. A Japanese survivor said that there were so many dots in the sky that the planes looked like sesame seeds. There were all kinds of planes attacking from all directions. Hellcats and Avengers struck at will. Admiral Ito crawled from a pile of sailors and ordered the ship abandoned. He went to his cabin and locked the door.

The *Yamato* had taken nine torpedoes and was listing so far that her flag was almost in the water. The carnage on deck was beyond comprehension. Bullets and shrapnel were cutting down so many sailors, the deck was awash in blood and body parts. The smell of fresh blood and burning flesh was nauseating.

Captain Kosaku Arriga called out, "Hold on, men." It was useless. He dashed to secure the portraits of the emperor and empress
to prevent them from falling into enemy hands. Then he had himself tied to the bridge, where he calmly awaited his fate.

As American planes circled overhead like vultures, the *Yamato*
began to sink. Once underwater, she erupted with a geyser like
nothing that had been seen before. When her ammunition and boilers exploded, she sent a fireball more than a mile high, taking out
some of the planes hovering above the sinking hulk. Smoke rose
more than four miles high.

An American airman looked at his watch. It read 1423, only
twenty-three minutes after the final attack began.

The *Uikkaze* and other remaining ships of Task Force Two picked
up survivors and headed back to Japan. The attack force had been
stopped one day away from its destination.

Admiral Mitscher reported 10 planes and 12 airmen lost. The
Japanese force lost 7 ships and 4,250 men. The *Yamato* lost 3,332,
but 23 officers and 246 men survived.

As a fighting force, the Japanese navy was finished.

Chapter 9

TACTICAL PLAN TO
SEVER ISLAND

The overall plan for the Okinawan invasion was to sever the island directly across from the Hagushi beaches. Then the Tenth Army was to split—the Twenty-fourth Corps soldiers would turn south, while the Third Amphibious Corps of marines would head north.

During this initial phase, Yontan and Kadena airports would be captured and Ushijima's forces would be separated. Capture of Yontan, the larger of the two airports, would keep enemy planes from using it and provide a land-based airport for American pilots.

The Tenth Army under Lieutenant General Simon Bolivar Buckner Jr. consisted of four army divisions: the Seventh, Ninety-sixth, Seventy-seventh, and Twenty-seventh; and three marine divisions: the First, Second, and Sixth Divisions under Major General Roy Geiger. Only the Eighth Marines of the Second Division were landed, at the end.

The marines landed on ten color-coded beaches north of the river Bishi Gawa and the army on eleven color-coded beaches south of the river.

Under support as needed from the Tactical Air Force, the Third Amphibious Artillery, and naval gunfire, the landing went according to plan. Some mistakes were made when landing units missed their designated sites, and one unit failed to start on time. Lack of enemy resistance on the beaches made these errors insignificant.

By midmorning on L-Day, marines reached Yontan Airfield under sporadic enemy fire. Lieutenant General Mitsuru Ushijima had 3,473 troops left, mostly Boeitai to protect the two airfields. They were quickly dispersed, some killed or captured, some retreating to join Ushijima's forces, and some escaping north to join Colonel Takehiko Udo's northern defense unit.

The two marine divisions consisted of several battalions each— infantry, artillery, plus tanks, engineers and others. The First Division under Major General Pedro A. del Valle had the First, Fifth, and Seventh Regiments of the First Marine Division. They landed north of the Bishi Gawa next to the Seventh Army Division under Major General Archibald V. Arnold.

The Sixth Marine Division under Major General Lemuel C. Shepherd landed farthest north, on the Hagushi beaches, next to the First Marine Division. Shepherd's regiments were the Fourth and Twenty-second, with the Twenty-ninth in reserve. Both army and marine divisions held reserves, and some units were complemented by tank or artillery units.

Phase One of the three elements of the plan was scheduled for five days. Basically, the goal was to cut the island in two and secure the two airfields. With little resistance, the invasion forces exploded inland, capturing both airfields the first day.

The morning of April 2 was chilly, about fifty degrees Fahrenheit, but it was downright cold to the lightly dressed marines, who were acclimated to the tropics. They quickly lashed out toward the objective, Okinawa's east coast, with some units beginning to spread out to the north. It quickly became evident to General Shepherd that his regiments were spread too thin, some losing contact with adjoining units. He contacted Commanding General Buckner for permission to land the Twenty-ninth Regiment, which he held in reserve. Permission was granted.

At the end of the L+2, the marines were roughly one-third of the way across the island, and the army, operating over less difficult terrain, reached the east coast of the island at about 4 P.M.

The navy urgently needed Zampa Misaki, a peninsula projecting into the East China Sea, for a land-based radar station to vector aircraft toward incoming enemy planes. The first battalion of the

Twenty-ninth Marine Regiment got the assignment. They quickly captured the peninsula and pulled back to the northern end of the Hagushi beaches to prevent an enemy amphibious landing.

With the quick advance across Okinawa, many invading units were stretching or beyond their supply lines. More beach landing sites were needed to unload supplies. The Sixth Marine Recon Company was called to explore the west coast beaches north of the peninsula near Nagahama. They passed between the Twenty-ninth and Twenty-second Regiments and moved out into enemy territory. At a village along the way, they surprised and shot a few snipers, explored the beach and found it suitable for small boats, then returned by dark.

By the end of the third day, the army had pushed south through Isa and Futema, closing in on Ushijima's advance defense positions. And the marines had reached the island's east coast, near Gushikawa. All units were beyond the advanced plan's L+5. Some marines were as many as eleven or twelve days ahead of schedule.

However, resistance was increasing. The Third Battalion of the Fourth Marine Regiment, Sixth Division, entered a valley and took fire from caves on both sides. Twelve men were wounded, and it took four hours to get them out. A two-prong attack from above the caves was needed to rout the Japanese. Also during the third day, the First Battalion was halted by enemy fire. A platoon of tanks came to their rescue, killing 250 Japanese.

During the early days of the invasion, civilians became an increasing problem. After the first massive bombing by Americans on October 10, 1944, the Japanese Army began conscripting Okinawans between the ages of seventeen and forty-five mostly for laborers. The Japanese looked upon the Okinawans as inferior, and little of the Okinawan defense plans was confided to them. Intelligence interrogators were unable to get expected useful information.

During the first days of the invasion, many of these Boeitai joined other natives in caves. Of course, some Japanese soldiers used natives as hostages, so it was risky to talk large groups of women and children out of the caves without adequate protection. Several Americans were killed by what appeared to be harmless Okinawans. And the natives had been brainwashed to believe that Americans would cruelly rape women and children and then murder them. Naturally, many believed this propaganda and were prepared to kill the invaders as well as themselves.

As word spread among the civilians that Americans would not kill them, masses of destitute Okinawans surrendered and were taken to civilian compounds for safety. They clogged the narrow roadways and overwhelmed those designated to handle the crowds. Logistic commanders had anticipated the problems related to civilians, and they had unloaded quantities of rice and soybeans to provide food for them.

Stories still persisted among the army and marine ranks about natives who were marched out of caves with guns in their backs, or more likely, a Japanese soldier behind them with a live grenade that only needed a tap to light its fuse. Some women hid knives or grenades in the folds of their kimonos to kill themselves and their attackers. Old men and women would come from the caves and bow low, some exposing the backs of their necks for the expected blade or blow that would send them to their ancestors.

But Okinawans found the Americans to be compassionate. Husky, bearded marines would cuddle small children and try to get them to eat chocolate bars, eating bites themselves to prove there was no poison. All the time, the starved youngsters would be solemnly watching with wide, hollow eyes.

As the marines advanced up the island, it narrowed to two miles wide at the Ishikawa Isthmus. One marine unit was held back while the others advanced.

Learning that the marines were a week ahead of schedule, General Buckner signaled General Geiger: "full confidence that your fighting Marines will meet every requirement of this campaign with characteristic courage, spirit, and efficiency."

Meanwhile, the First Marine Division had swept across the island to the eastern shore and occupied the Katchin Peninsula. Then they turned north along the Chimu Wan shoreline. They were moving as unstoppable as the tide.

Lieutenant Colonel Hurst with his Seventh Marine Regiment dashed toward their objective, the town of Hizaonna. Unfortunately, they took a wrong road. Company K was ambushed, and Company L was sent to extract them. They had to spend the night on the beach. The next day, they reached their objective. The enemy retreated north.

On the west coast, the Sixth Recon probed up the coastal road. With the support of two tank battalions, we were ordered to check out the road across the isthmus from Nakadomari.to Ishikawa, about three miles wide and one of the narrowest points of the Ishikawa Isthmus. Near the town of Ishikawa we began receiving mortar fire. We returned under fire.

On L+4 General Shepherd moved the Twenty-ninth Regiment to Nakadomari, and by the end of the day the Twenty-second Regiment had moved up the west coast to Yakada, linking up with other units to form a line to the sea in both directions.

Supply lines had become so strained that H-Hour was delayed until 9 A.M. on April 5. But the time wasn't lost. Recon probed north along the coastal road, riding tanks and with a tank dozer in support. We moved swiftly from Nakadomari to Onna, about five miles on our way to Chuda, about fifteen miles into enemy territory. At Onna, a bridge had been blown, preventing the tanks from going farther. So we marines hiked to Chuda and back to the tanks. At Onna, we met the Twenty-ninth Regiment, freshly supplied and moving forward. During the day, only scattered pockets of the enemy had been discovered, and it had begun to rain—a harbinger of things to come.

With the First Division's Seventh Regiment in reserve and patrolling south of the Nakadomari–Ishikawa line, the Sixth Recon mopped up from this line north to the Yakada–Yaka line. Meanwhile, the Twenty-second Regiment, on line, was passed through by the Fourth and Twenty-ninth Regiments, and the Twenty-second reverted to reserve and began mopping up back to the Recon Company line.

The fresh Twenty-ninth moved rapidly up the west coast road, and the Fourth moved up along the east coast road. Enemy resistance was light. Road demolition was slight and hastily prepared. Mines were not covered or hidden, and bridges were only partially destroyed.

Leapfrogging one regiment through another, the Sixth Division troops advanced to the base of the Motobu Peninsula near Nago on L+6. Helping the marines was a platoon of Sixth Engineers to clear roadblocks and mines. They hastily repaired bridges for vehicles and tanks. Other engineers followed to further repair and build roads.

On the east coast, the Fourth Marines reached their objective north of Ora and set up a perimeter defense. The Twenty-ninth reached its objective near Nago, at the base of the Motobu Peninsula, and set up their defense. Meanwhile, the Twenty-second in reserve had been following and mopping up enemy pockets—they were either destroyed or dispersed.

The Fifteenth Artillery was hard pressed to keep up with the fast-moving infantry. They managed by substituting radio for telephone wire and using stripped-down equipment. They also leapfrogged some units but managed to keep a unit of artillery with each unit of infantry.

Down south, the army was meeting increased resistance near Ginowan and Uchitomari.

Both army and marines were swamped with great numbers of malnourished civilians who came out of their hiding places. Notably lacking were the young men and women whom the Japanese had taken with them into their deep, well-stocked caves.

Even at this early time of the invasion, some of the natives were voicing their opinion: *Nippon ga maketa*—"Japan is finished."

Hilly northern Okinawa.

Rice paddies in level area of northern Okinawa.

Waterfall on northern Okinawa's rugged terrain.

Typical Okinawan village; buildings have thatched roofs and streets are narrow.

*View of farmland in northern Okinawa.
Small figures, top right, are LSTs on the ocean.*

*Fertile valley in northern Okinawa. Rice paddies in the right center of photo.
Beyond the paddies are houses. Military vehicles can be seen by looking closely.*

Chapter 10

RACE NORTH TO NAGO

"All aboard the tanks. Pass the word."

The tanks moved along the narrow gravel road—mountains on one side and the East China Sea on the other. The scenery was beautiful, but we were too tense to enjoy it. Regimental front lines were far behind us. Now we were alone!

Corporal Fuller Curtis was acknowledged to be a seasoned veteran. No one knew how many battles he had been in, but he had been a member of the Raiders before he joined Recon. So when he spoke, we listened.

"The Japs are so close I can smell them!" he announced. Everyone tensed, but no one saw the enemy. The tanks moved on, deeper into enemy territory.

"They'll let us pass through," said Curtis, "and we'll catch hell on the way back."

As the tanks moved around a curve, two Japanese appeared—one on a bicycle and the other on foot. A rifleman on a tank cut down the one running up a hill. The lead tank's machine gunner knocked the rider off his bicycle, and it moved aimlessly into a ditch.

"We sure helped those guys join their ancestors," said Ernest Rasar, from eastern Tennessee.

"Look at the length of those shadows," I said. "We'll never make it back to the front line before dark." As if on cue, the tanks turned around and started back. They had gone much farther than planned.

As the tanks pulled to a stop at the front line, one of the guards said, "We didn't think you'd make it. An observer plane pilot said the Japs were watching you all the way. We don't know why they didn't take you out. They could have done it any time."

"Damn," said Sweetpee. "Another hill to climb, another cold camp, cold food, cold weather. When are we going to return to headquarters?"

"Maybe tomorrow," said Sergeant McDougal.

The night was cold and clear, and we lay on the ground. I looked at the countless stars in the sky. Occasionally, I would see a distant flash, like lightning, followed by a boom. But the war seemed remote.

"If we're attacked, don't wake me," I said. "I'm too tired to care."

Up at dawn, we were miserably tired. We grumbled and bitched about conditions. We drank hot black coffee, then boarded trucks for an area that needed mopping up behind the main line. We spread out over a hillside. Ace Brown was as jumpy as a cat.

"Why can't we dig in and wait for the little bastards to come to us, instead of us having to ferret them out of their advantageous positions?" he grumbled.

As we reached the hilltop, civilians were seen approaching. We were very alert, because Japanese soldiers were known to shield themselves with civilians. As the women and children passed, there was a group sigh of relief.

"Oh, no you don't!" yelled the rear guard. I looked back to see a marine wrestling with a Japanese soldier, who was holding onto him with one hand and banging the firing pin of a grenade on his helmet with the other. The marine broke free, and before he could fire his rifle, Bama had cut loose with the BAR, slicing the enemy soldier in two and scattering guts all over the area.

"You lucky sonofabitch," said Bama to the fortunate marine. "Anyone else would have been blown to kingdom come." The marine was too stunned to reply.

After we swept the area, we boarded trucks to the front line, then tanks. Our objective was the town of Nago.

Our tanks moved through the town, which was larger than most villages we had seen, without resistance. The tanks stopped, and we dismounted to search the shops and buildings.

This was a comedy. Marines came from clothing shops wearing high white straw hats, kimonos, and other clothing. They looked like circus clowns. And the entire area burst forth with music, recordings of sing-song string instruments from record players. Amid all this street activity, one marine was trying to start a motor-cycle he had found.

Sarge McDougal and I were searching a store-front building when we came across a large lepidoptera collection in several glass-top cases. Each butterfly was carefully impaled on a pin, and there must have been hundreds of them.

"It's a crying shame," said William Gadbois, who came up behind us. He was a scout in the Third Platoon.

"What?" I asked with concern.

"It's a crying shame that our old captain from the 'Canal could-n't have seen this collection before he shipped out."

This is what Gadbois told us:

> I don't remember our commanding officer's name when I joined Recon, but he was a captain.
>
> I soon found out we were doing all the dirty work, you know, policing up, digging latrines, all that crap for the Headquarters Battalion.
>
> One day we actually went to the boondocks and did a little scouting. Walt Curtis and I were laying in the grass when we heard this threshing in the brush. Although Guadalcanal had been secured, we knew a few Japanese were still around. They had been seen steal-ing clothes and even in the chow line. We figured it was a Jap, and he was coming toward us.
>
> Suddenly we see this white thing waving above the brush and figure he wants to surrender. We ready our weapons.
>
> Out steps our captain with a butterfly net. He innocently asks if we'd seen a large butterfly.
>
> "Holy shit! We're dead in combat," I thought. "He's definitely not in the right outfit." He was transferred.
>
> When Major Walker became C.O., all that crap stopped. We real-ly started training.

"Back on the tanks! Back on the tanks!" barked Sergeants Tabb and Manion.

Soon the tanks could go no farther. The narrow shoreline road has been mined and the bridges blown up.

"Watch for mines. Pass it on. Walk in single file." The order didn't have to be repeated.

"Look at that, Ozark!" said Ace. I looked at where he was pointing and saw an exposed mine fuse. Looking around, I saw more mines. Fresh dirt and yellow powder were on the ground. An acrid smell was in the air. A light observer plane flew low over the road and dropped a message.

You are being observed from the hilltop, the message read.

"Chronis!" yelled the Major. "Bring me that radio." The column stopped, but no one dared fall out.

"What was that?" asked Ace. Before I could answer, a roaring *whizzzz* filled the air, and the road ahead exploded.

"Gawd Almighty, they're shelling us!" cried Sugarlips Bardoni. "Everyone get down," yelled Corporal Bill Dawson.

"That's from the ocean," explained Sergeant Manion. "Those are our ships shelling this area. That's what the major wanted the radio for. If those Japs don't head for the hills, they'll be blasted to eternity."

A cheer went up from the Recon marines.

"Guess the major got our tit out of that ringer," said Sugarlips.

The probe had reached the point of danger. That's what Recon was all about. We retreated to the tanks and headed for the regimental front line. We were safe within our invaded territory before the tanks stopped for the night.

We had a warm meal of ten-in-one rations and were told we could sleep in some vacated native houses.

We found straw mats to sleep on.

"Someone must have raided the army commissary for a meal like that," said a belching marine in the dark to no one in particular.

"Something bit me," I said.

"I feel something crawling inside my pant leg," added Sweetpee.

"Hell, this mat is full of fleas," I shouted, slapping my thigh. We were too tired to look for another place to sleep. As I lay there, I could hear men scratching, slapping, and cursing all around. I quietly pulled my rifle butt to me, opened the plate, and took out a vial of gun oil. I dripped some in my hand and rubbed my hands together, then smeared the oil on my legs, arms, then my whole body. I slept like a baby.

Morning brought hot coffee and a good breakfast of regimental food.

"I'm beginning to feel like a human again, if only I could take a bath and get rid of some of this crud," I said to Mac. The sergeant didn't say a word, just pointed to a pond below the rice terraces.

I led the way, running, jumping, and shedding clothes as I went. We were more like schoolboys than fighting men as we splashed, swam, and dunked each other. Private Jim Smith was one of the first out of the water. He dressed, and soon I joined him on the pond bank where the men had left their clothes.

Before long, Corporal Krysztofik went exploring along the pond bank.

"Hey, guys, look what I found!" he yelled. I could see some iron contraption by his feet.

"What is it?" I asked.

"A double machine gun."

"It's a twin stinger out of an airplane," explained Sergeant Manion.

"What's the matter with Preacher?" I asked. As the swimmers looked back, Preacher was hopping from one leg to the other and jumping all over the bank. His trousers were about half down, and suddenly he splashed into the lake head first, clothes and all.

Preacher came up yelling bloody murder, mad as a wet hen. If he hadn't been religious, he would have burned even our ears.

"What son-of-a-gun tied my trouser legs in knots?" he screamed.

Jim started laughing and slapping his legs. I joined in the hilarity. Then the whole group teased Preacher as they realized what had happened.

But the laughing stopped when Krysztofik ordered Smith to carry the stinger, which appeared to be operational. Tempers flared. Threats were made. And a fight would have erupted if it hadn't been for some others stepping between them. Since Krysztofik was a corporal, Private Smith could not refuse the command.

While we were boarding trucks to return to our headquarters area, it began to rain. It continued to rain, not heavily, but steadily. By the time we reached our bivouac area, the ground was muddy.

We ran from the trucks to find any cover we could for our foxholes. We scrounged old sliding doors from destroyed houses, along with straw mats, boards, poles—anything that would support our ponchos for a roof or go under our feet in the foxholes.

I was bunking with Jim Wheeler, who said he'd take the first watch. I lay back and watched Jim dig a small hole in one corner of the foxhole. Then he adjusted himself so that he could see all around between the makeshift roof and the top of the foxhole. Last, he plunged his K-bar into the earthen wall at shoulder height.

"What'd you do that for?" I asked.

"'Always be prepared' is my motto."

A drop of rain seeped through the roof and hit me on the nose. I moved my head, and the next drop hit me in the eye. I could hear the rain pitter-pattering on the GI shelter half-roof. It was falling heavier. More drips began falling through the roof. I was annoyed and found sleep difficult.

It seemed I had been asleep no time at all when Jim woke me for my watch. But my clothes were wet, so I must have been sleeping. On my watch, I was sitting hunched over, listening to the rain, when I heard a sound I thought was the wind. I cocked my head and heard it faintly again. I jabbed Jim in the ribs.

"Jim, wake up!" He jerked alert, and in one motion pulled the K-bar from the soil. As he drew back his arm to strike, I froze. Jim hesitated as he blinked the sleep from his eyes.

"Jim!" I grabbed the knife-wielding arm.

"Is it my watch already?"

"Listen!"

"I don't hear anything."

"Hold your breath."

"What is it?"

"Sounds like someone crying."

"You nuts; they already took the baby.

"Listen!"

The sound of soft sobbing drifted in and out of the rainy night.

"That's coming from one of our foxholes," said Jim.

"That's what I thought," I whispered. "You think he's losing it?" Wheeler didn't answer.

"You don't think . . ." I began.

"It happens," he replied, "men go crazy."

He returned the knife to its original spot and dropped down to sleep. I listened to the wind and the rain. My ears strained to hear the pitiful, muffled sound. I tried to imagine the outcome, then I tried to forget what I imagined.

The night in the foxhole was a disaster. The next morning, everything was wet. It was chilly and still pouring rain. Jim and I decided to dash for a nearby native house, taking only our weapons. As we rushed in, we were greeted by Sweetpee, Mac, Chronis, Preacher, and others. There was a small fireplace in one corner, and the group was trying to get a fire started. The wood was wet, and the place was filled with a strong smoke that burned our eyes.

"What was that?" asked Mac. There was a Japanese voice in an adjoining room. Wheeler and I, still holding our rifles, edged toward the choking sound. At first we didn't see anything through the smoke, then we saw an object move on the floor. It was an old Okinawan lady, and she was trying to talk. With hand gestures, she finally made it known that she didn't want her house burned.

The old lady sat hunched over on a straw mat. Her stringy hair had streaks of gray and her face was a maze of wrinkles. She had no teeth, and her cheeks were sunken. Her arms and legs were bony and her muscles sagged. Her back was deformed, and she showed pain when she moved. Her eyes were listless.

"That poor old soul," said the sympathetic Preacher. He offered her a cracker with jam on it. She licked off the jam. Wheeler and I lowered our weapons and went into the other room.

"Where's Preacher?" Sergeant Manion asked after getting the fire started.

"He's with the old granny," someone said. About that time, he returned to the group.

"I gave her a cigarette," said Preacher, "she broke it, saving half and putting the other half in her opium pipe. I lit it, and she smoked. She was trying to tell me something."

"Food's ready!" called Sugarlips. Small tin cans of food had been placed around the fire to warm. After eating, we began to strip to our skivvies. We rigged our wet clothes by the fire to dry.

Nights were not safe. Japanese and Boeitai came out of caves and attacked. So despite the rain, that night it was back to the soggy shelters for another foxhole vigil. During my midnight watch, I noticed that the clouds were breaking up and at times stars could be seen. There was no enemy attack. Morning brought a clear sky—and the sun!

As I crawled out of my muddy hole, Preacher was returning from the house where the old lady lay.

"How is old granny?"

"Still alive. I offered her some cooked rice, and she ate it. Then she just closed her eyes. She looked cold so I found an old comforter in a pile of stuff. When I covered her, she threshed about and threw the cover off."

"We just got word we'll be cleaning out caves today," I said.

"That's dangerous business, Ozark."

"Tell that to Sweetpee. He's happy as a lark at mating time; thinks he'll find souvenirs to trade with the sailors."

"If he finds a flag or anything, it'll probably be booby-trapped."

The squad was passing a beautiful blue pond, and I was thinking how wonderful it would be to bathe, when word came that a cave had been located. The squad halted while Mac observed.

"Ozark, you and Ace, front and center." summoned Mac. "One of you get on each side of the cave, and I'll try to talk them out."

"Deh-ta-koy! Deh-ta-koy!" There was no response.

"Deh-ta-koy!" shouted Mac at the mouth of the cave. Silence.

"Guess we'll have to use our grenades," said Mac. At that moment, an old man with a gray beard and dressed in black clothes with a high black hat appeared like an apparition. He bowed to Sergeant McDougal.

"Deh-ta-koy!" said Mac, motioning for the man to step out. The old man was apprehensive and stumbled as he came forward. Mac asked him if there were others. But he didn't seem to understand. After a few minutes the old man believed he wouldn't be shot, so he returned to the cave and spoke in an Okinawan dialect.

An old woman came out, then another. Younger women and children followed. Many had flea-bitten sores. One woman's eyes were swollen completely shut. Ten, twenty, fifty, and more drifted out of the tiny opening, blinking in the sunlight.

"Boy, would I like to screw that one," I said as a beautiful dark-haired Oriental girl emerged with the others.

"Hey, keep your mind on your business!" yelled Mac. "You don't know if she has a gun or a grenade in that kimono."

We moved the civilians away from the cave.

Sergeant Manion and some others volunteered to search the cave. No one else was in the cave, but Sweetpee found a small silk

Japanese flag. He bragged that it was worth at least a bottle of bourbon, maybe a case, back at headquarters.

Meanwhile, Major Walker had been on the radio, and headquarters was sending a truck to take the civilians to the retention compound. We were kept away from the civilians.

Sweetpee came up showing off his enemy flag.

"I wonder if I'll ever see her again," I said.

"I don't know about that, but I'll bet you have a wet dream tonight." He waved his flag and left.

Community cave on northern Okinawa. American air raids forced the natives to dig in. Civilian clothing, which was often infected with fleas, in foreground.

Japanese mined the road near Nago, northern Okinawa. See wrecked Jeep. We were forced to abandon trucks and walk.

Marines at Sunday church service, Nago, Okinawa.

Round-up time on Okinawa. Al Zimmerman guards civilians taken from a cave.

Blown bridge on coastal highway, northern Okinawa.

Okinawan child peers from her underground home.

Chapter 11

BATTLE FOR MOTOBU

If the back of your right hand were northern Okinawa, your thumb would be Motobu Peninsula, with the thumb joint being 1,500-foot-high Mount Yae Take, stronghold of Colonel Takehido Udo.

Udo was overbearing and self-centered. The natives he oppressed greatly disliked him. Even his soldiers disapproved of his lifestyle, which included three native women attendants. It was evident that his personal feelings came before the country's war efforts.

The defender of northern Okinawa had 2,500 men from mixed units, about sixty of which were survivors of the Toyama Maru that had been sunk by the U.S. submarine *Sturgeon*. Udo had tried to sneak the bedraggled men past natives, but they noticed the gaunt, oil-blackened troops and knew that the war wasn't going well for the Japanese.

Although it was evident that Okinawan Commander Ushijima didn't expect Udo's relatively small force to defend nearly sixty percent of the island, it was imperative that he delay the marines as long as possible. This he did.

Mount Yae Take was surrounded by steep hills and sharp valleys, and the enemy knew the territory well, using every natural advantage for his defense. Heavy guns were mounted on tracks in caves where they could fire a few rounds, then retreat to safety from artillery and naval gunfire. Mortars were located to lob shells over protective terrain onto the enemy. Heavy Hotchkiss and light nambu machine guns were positioned to protect fire lanes that marines were certain to use. Riflemen were dug in or positioned in concrete pillboxes, and snipers were positioned to harass advancing marines.

Following a stalled probing action, the Sixth Marine Reconnaissance Company was allowed to move up the East China Sea coastal road to Bise on the tip of the peninsula, where they set up a defense to prevent an enemy landing by water.

When the Sixth Marine regiments began advancing, a bloody battle ensued that raged for several days. As men began moving up the steep hills, they soon found themselves in a fire lane, subject to lethal machine-gun fire. They had to retreat, often pinned down by sniper fire. When artillery or naval gunfire was directed to the enemy location, and the marines were again able to advance, they would find no evidence of the machine-gun nest. Nothing. Both men and guns had simply vanished.

In addition to the steep hills, the ground was covered with scrub brush, vines, and short pine trees, making it easy for the enemy to hide and difficult for the marines to proceed. Also, one of the marine regiments had been overtrained, and the fatigued men could not maneuver up the mountain.

Earlier, marines had captured civilians who had lived in Hawaii. They said the Japanese had more than a thousand men on the mountain, south of the Manna-Toguchi road. They said that Colonel Udo had a 150-man artillery unit under Captain Hiruyama. They were in possession of both 75mm and 150mm guns, and they had two six-inch naval guns with a ten-mile range. The marines knew from aerial reconnaissance that Colonel Udo could see from shore to shore across Motobu and all the way to Ie Shima, four miles off the point of the peninsula. With this information, General Shepherd decided that more than a regiment would be needed to take Mount Yae Take.

Colonel Victor Bleasdale's Twenty-ninth Marine Regiment was ordered to try clearing the Toguchi–Itomi road across the peninsula east of the mountain and in the process join the First and third Battalions. They immediately came under 20mm canon fire. When the Twenty-second Battalion attempted to enter the fray, they came under fire. At this point, marines were on both sides of Mount Yae Take, and when the Fourth Marine Regiment moved up two battalions, the Japanese mountain stronghold was caught in a noose from both the north and south sides, with reserves to the west and the ocean and Recon Company to the east. General Shepherd then began to pull on the rope.

To soften up Mount Yae Take, an intense artillery, naval, and aerial bombardment began before the marines moved in. But it would take more than that. The marines had to battle from ridge to ridge under intense fire, often halting to call in support from the USS *Tennessee*, located offshore in the East China Sea. Even so, the Japanese used predetermined lanes of fire very successfully, often letting advance units pass before opening fire. Officer casualties were very high.

With continued pressure from all sides, it was evident to Colonel Udo that he could not hold out much longer. He began to make plans to abandon his mountaintop underground headquarters. On April 13 (April 12 in the States) marines guarding the coastal areas could hear loudspeakers on nearby ships. One announcement they heard was that President Roosevelt had died. This dismayed many troops, and they discussed the relatively unknown vice president, Harry Truman, wondering how he could replace a four-term man like Roosevelt. Colonel Udo heard that the President had died, and he had his own reaction. It was recorded in a note found later.

Meanwhile, marines were pressing the attack, and as was often the case in the race north, supply lines were stretched until they broke. This time it was at the base of the mountain. As marines scrambled up the hilly ridges, motorized supplies were stalled at base dumps along the roads. Ammunition, water, and food were piling up.

At this point, every available man, including headquarters personnel, began carrying materials up the mountain—some sweating and cursing as they struggled with loads of five-gallon water cans tainted with gasoline; some with bandoleers of ammo; some with cases of rations. Even native horses, which we were previously forbidden to use, were loaded with desperately needed supplies.

In many ways, the return trip was just as critical, as the weary men evacuated the wounded.

As the noose was tightened, Colonel Udo directed his remaining troops to form guerrilla units and continue fighting. The mountain stronghold was abandoned, and Udo moved his headquarters by way of Itomi and reestablished them in the mountainous forest of northern Okinawa.

When the marines found Udo's abandoned headquarters, there was a note for the Allied forces. It suggested that Roosevelt's death might have resulted from his knowledge of defeat on Okinawa.

Marines quickly reorganized and began mop-up operations. As they swept across the mountainous terrain, they found quantities of food, clothing, and arms abandoned by the fleeing Japanese. There were also numerous corpses.

But the departing enemy was not through with the marines yet. Many mines and roadblocks hampered engineering efforts to construct roads and bridges. The guerrilla units delayed progress both day and night, inhibiting movement of troops and supplies. An order was issued that no vehicle was to venture out alone at night.

Mop-up troops found extreme difficulty in their efforts, because undergrowth on the mountainsides came down to the very edges of trails and roads.

Large numbers of civilians, including many who had fled from Naha and the populous areas to the south, hampered marine efforts to clean out warring units that often dressed as civilians or used civilians as shields. Native boeitai and civilians with Japanese affiliations, even children, used deadly means to kill or disrupt marines.

When a civilian processing center was established at Taira, northeast of Nago, much of the local population was taken out of the equation. Other detention centers were established at Chimu and farther south on the Katchin Peninsula.

On April 20 the Motobu Peninsula was declared secured. The Japanese had lost more than 2,100 killed. Marines had 207 KIAs, 757 wounded, and six missing in action.

As Udo had planned, his pockets of guerrillas continued to harass and disrupt marines. They targeted communication lines, hospitals, heavy equipment, and water facilities. At times, they would ambush repair parties as well.

At one point, a party of about two hundred Japanese troops, thought to be a part of Udo's forces finding their way south through the forested mountains, were detected. Marines were force-marched to the area, where a battle ensued. Nearly all of the Japanese were killed. Some among the dead were found to be disguised, wearing kimonos.

As a part of the northern Okinawa mop-up operation, three nearby islands were invaded: Yagachi Shima on April 21, Sesoko Shima on April 22, and Kouri Shima on April 23. These were leper colony islands and no resistance was found on them.

When the northern end of Okinawa was declared secured, marines were limited to mop-up action and guard duty. They began acting like off-duty marines. They improved their bivouac areas, cleaned weapons, played cards, sunbathed when weather permitted, and raided local villages for building materials or anything they could use—even old alarm clocks, which could be rigged to announce nighttime perimeter prowlers. Many spent their spare time searching for souvenirs, particularly Japanese flags, swords, or other weapons. As roads were opened, marines visited area supply dumps for fresh food, canned fruit, and delectable 10-in-l rations. Beer and alcohol were in great demand.

Unknown to the infantry marines at this time, a conference was being held at the Tenth Army Headquarters that would greatly affect them. Their feelings that the battle for Okinawa would soon be over and that they would be celebrating Christmas at home would be nothing more than shattered dreams.

Chapter 12

ENEMY ISOLATES RECON

The morning of April 12 was fresh and sunny, a beautiful spring day on northern Okinawa. Recon broke camp, mounted six-bys, and moved up to the front line. We were bitching and cracking jokes until we saw what we were up against.

"Jesus Christ!" yelled Preacher. The silence that followed was deathly. Only the clanking of equipment was heard as we dismounted from the trucks. We quietly walked by the line of corpses, all buddy marines who had not survived the night.

"Fall in over here," shouted Sergeant Manion. "Spears, you take the point." Spears was a lanky Texan.

"Whatinhell we gettin' into?" I whispered. All the men appeared to have heavy thoughts.

"Look sharp and stay alert," said Manion. "Pass the word." Manion was aware that regimental marines on the line we were passing through were watching.

The company had walked less than a mile, traveling on both sides of a mined road, when Spears held up his hand. The platoon stopped, and Manion came forward. "What's the problem?"

Ellis, a sharp-eyed scout, was holding his M-1 at port position. In answer to the question, he pointed his rifle to a hedge about two hundred yards down a hillside.

At that moment, I saw a Japanese army cap bobbing above a distant hedgerow. I had fired "expert rifleman" at Parris Island, and I was sure of my marksmanship at this distance. I dropped to one knee, aimed, and fired. The cap disappeared.

Cautiously, the patrol approached the target, expecting to be fired on with each step we took. Sweetpee was the first to reach the hedge. "It's just a boy!"

I moved to the hedge and peered over. The boy was lying on his back, whimpering, blood spurting from his chest.

What came from Spears' throat was spine-chilling. It wasn't a scream; it was a wail, like from a wild animal.

I have never discussed my feelings of guilt with anyone since that day, nor has a day passed without pain. I'm telling this for the first time in my life, although it happened more than a half century ago. You cannot imagine the blame you feel as you look upon the face of a young boy who is dying because of your actions. I turned away in grief, not able to stop the misery.

When I was a few steps away, I heard a rifle fire. I could tell by the sound that it was an M-1. Two or three of my buddies, who had witnessed my shooting, had M-1s. One of them had finished the humanitarian job I didn't have to guts to do. I'm sorry!

As we regrouped and moved ahead, we were aware that the sea coast was near on our left and that Mount Yae Take crowded us on the right. At times, we could feel the eyes of the enemy upon us, yet we moved mechanically, like a machine, toward our objective. Why were the Japanese letting us pass? Were they curious as to what this group of marines was up to?

Recon was to take the coastline of Motobu Peninsula at Bise and hold it to prevent enemy reinforcement from the sea, or an escape to Motobu from an island, Ie Shima, four miles offshore. Bise looked as if it had been a pleasant seacoast town at one time, before the bombing and coastal shelling. Recon found little opposition.

At Bise, Corporal Walter Curtis and Private William Gadbois caught a Japanese naval officer carrying a briefcase. It looked stuffed, so Walt grabbed it, but the Japanese officer wouldn't let go. They got into a tug of war, and the Japanese pulled his sword. There was a fight of sword against bayonet. Curtis won. The briefcase contained maps and a lot of papers, good information for Intelligence.

Four of our men (Corporal Ray Richards, BARman Ray Miller, and Privates "King" Burkhart and Jim Smith) were exploring outside Bise and saw an Okinawan wading toward a small offshore island. They followed him and surprised two men wearing kimonos. During a search, the marines found that the men were wearing uniforms under their robes.

The men were discussing what to do with the prisoners when a sniper opened fire. Everyone hit the ground, including the prisoners. The marines fired at the sniper, who hastily retreated. They got up, but the prisoners didn't. The BAR had been firing at the prisoners.

The three men separated themselves from Miller. Then they saw an object snagged on a reef several feet from the beach. They discovered that it was a dead sailor who had washed ashore. They buried him and took his dog tags back to headquarters.

While we were deployed along the coastline, a radio message informed us that the Japanese had cut us off from the regiment. We could ask the navy to rescue us, but this wasn't considered. We formed a tight perimeter defense and dug in for the night.

James McConnel, from Boston, was assigned to bunk with James "Pappy" Payne, from Charleston, South Carolina. Sergeant Manion warned them to be quiet.

"No talking," said Manion. "You two guys speak a foreign language anyway, and you might be mistaken for Japanese."

"Pappy," said McConnel, "you take the first watch and I'll take the next. Here's my watch; it has large illuminated numerals. Remember, just nudge me in two hours; don't say anything."

It was a quiet night. Recon was too far away from flares and gunfire to be disturbed. Before long, McConnel was asleep—and snoring. The noise frightened Pappy. He imagined it would attract nighttime infiltrators. The weather had deteriorated. Clouds rested on the ground and a misty rain was falling. Pappy punched McConnel, and the snoring stopped.

Pappy heard a noise, but he dismissed it as a leaf blowing in the breeze. McConnel began snoring again. Pappy punched him.

"Is it time for my watch already, Pappy?"

"Yeah, you were not only snoring, but snorting. If you watch, maybe I can sleep."

The next morning, a Recon patrol flushed a native from some bushes, according to Lieutenant Paul Curtis. The guy ran out with his hands up, shouting: "Don't shoot! Don't shoot! American! American!"

His English had a New York accent, but the patrol didn't believe him. However, they didn't shoot. The man pulled out his wallet and showed Curtis his driver's license and a picture of himself leaning on a taxi under the 42nd Street sign in Manhattan. He had come home to Okinawa just in time for the Japanese occupation. Like the man said when he was discovered in a woman's clothes closet, everybody has to be somewhere.

Since we were separated from other units, the Japanese decided to test us. We had a strong perimeter defense, expecting an attack. Corporal Krysztofik had his squad on the beach road, and that's where a large Japanese unit hit. We were ready for them.

Boy, were they surprised at our firepower: machine guns, BARs, M-1s, grenades, 75mm tank guns, and even a few planes dropping bombs.

Although Recon was on our own, cut off from other troops, there was no further enemy harassment. Most had retreated to their mountain stronghold, pursued by Sixth Marine Division regiments.

Supplied by parachute drops, we found ourselves with little to do beyond perimeter patrols and guard duty. We cleaned our weapons, washed clothes, built shelters from the rain, played cards, sunbathed when weather permitted, bathed and swam in a nearby lake, prepared meals from air-dropped 10-in-1 food cartons, and visited.

From one drop, Sergeant McDougal recovered a gallon can of pears and shared them with us, a half-pear per person. To a man, we said that was the tastiest food we had eaten during the Okinawan campaign.

After a multi-plane supply drop one sunny day, I commented to Sweetpee that fighting this kind of war wasn't so bad. We were talking about Bise and what a beautiful picture it would make. I told him I'd always been interested in cameras and had taken a course in news photography at the University of Missouri School of Journalism. I don't know if he told anyone, but I wasn't surprised when I was selected to be among those issued 35mm cameras. It was rumored that a big event was about to take place, and the navy wanted it recorded.

Before anything occurred in our view of the sea, one of our squads was sent on a rescue mission to Mount Yae Take. They arrived to see several dead marines. Dan Kvaase recalled recovering the body of Lieutenant Chavez. Dan was on the front of the stretcher going down a path that was steep and muddy.

"I was aware of his foot tapping me on the rear all the way down the mountain."

Another Recon patrol was sent to recover the body of a pilot who had been shot down on the mountain. Zack Brandes said he had never realized that a dead body could be so heavy. Bodies were taken to the Grave Registration Unit.

Corporal Sammy Zaidain, a radio man, was on a body recover detail. One of the casualties was a teenager. A battle-hardened marine sergeant was standing there crying like a baby, reported Sammy. The boy had been like a son to him. That brought the realization that marines were getting killed, yet I had no fear that it would happen to me. In fact, most marines had supreme confidence that it would be someone else who would be killed.

Although Recon had probed quickly into enemy territory and moved swiftly onto the Motobu Peninsula, one unit was always dogging our heels, urging us to get out of their way. Major Walker was leading Recon as fast as he and General Shepherd felt was prudent, but Colonel Victor Bleasdale, Commander of the Twenty-ninth Regiment, said Recon was holding up his progress.

Recon reluctantly stepped aside to let him pass. Some of us had been on a night patrol and were resting in a ditch when they went through.

"What outfit are you?" asked one of their men.

"Recon."

"You ought to join the infantry. That's where the real action is."

Colonel Bleasdale pressed onward into a narrow valley on Mount Yae Take. The Twenty-ninth was ambushed and lost many men. Japanese Colonel Takehido Udo had planned his defenses well. The tired, overtrained Twenty-ninth Regiment was easy prey.

General Shepherd arrived and questioned Colonel Bleasdale concerning his regiment and their whereabouts. Not satisfied with the colonel's answers, General Shepherd replaced him with Colonel William J. Whaling on April 15.

In less than a month, our part of the battle for Okinawa appeared to be almost over.

"Hey, Sweetpee, rub a little more of that rifle oil on my back," I said. But before Sweetpee could move, someone yelled, "Mail call!"

The corporal reading names on letters and packages was standing on the entrance to a womb-shaped tomb. The mail had been air-dropped.

"Burien! Cochran! Goulden! Bordoni!" The corporal held the letter to his nose and sniffed. "James! Keel!"

The reader looked at the envelope. "Where in God's name is this place in West Virginia?"

"Morley! Hansen! Bordoni!" The corporal looked at Sugarlips who was smiling broadly. "You got a whole sorority writing you? Phillips!"

"Which one?"

"Lyle W.! Zig, Zig . . . that's spelled Z–g–a–i–n–e–r!"

Names were called until all the mail had been distributed; then magazines and packages were distributed.

"Spears!" The corporal sniffed the package. "Smells like something gone bad," he said.

"My Mother's tamales. Oh, please," said Spears, looking toward the sky, "let them be good." He opened the package gingerly, with anticipation. "Wrapped in green corn husks!" he exclaimed, then threw the package to the ground in disgust. "Rotten," he said. "The whole lot is spoiled."

One man was sitting away from the others, his head down. I suspected a problem. "Bad news?"

When he lifted his head, I could see the tears.

"From home?" I asked.

"No," he sniffed.

"Dear John letter, then?"

He nodded. I left to read my letter from Mom. As I read, I thought of home and how I longed to see her again.

During the next two days, an old red rooster and a half-grown chicken were killed and boiled in helmets. A pig was dressed and roasted over an open-pit fire. The cooks' culinary efforts didn't add to their reputations, because salt and seasonings were scarce. And the two men who owned the borrowed helmets were furious because the straps had been burned off.

Recon cheered when regimental men appeared. That meant that we were no longer isolated. Within the hour, a party was sent back to the supply dump for food, water, and ammo.

Some of the men returned with more than had been requisitioned. Now we were short-handed.

"If we only had one of those Okie ponies," said Ace.

"Well, we don't. And fat chance we'll find one," I said, looking around. "Unless . . . How about you, George? You feel like a horse?" George saw what I was looking at. An ox cart was backed up against a nearby tree. We filled it with our supplies and took off down the trail, one pulling and the others pushing.

We arrived in camp after dark. Sergeant Tabb met us and took us to the commander's tent. "You boys get the supplies?"

"Yessir."

"The cameras, too?"

"There's a box that could be cameras."

"Bring it."

The major turned away.

Next morning, Sergeant McDougal noticed that some of the supplies were gone.

"What happened to the food, Smith?"

"Damned if I know."

Mac saw that the cart was moved to headquarters and the supplies distributed. In a few days, "Smith & Payne's General Store" was opened, with all kinds of goodies for sale. With tables and dishes scrounged from the abandoned native houses, we were beginning to live like home-folks.

I found a clock and rigged it to telephone wire on the perimeter. If the wire was disturbed, the alarm would sound.

"That reminds me of Grandfather's Irish limerick," I told Sheridan Yost, the bugler. It went like this: "Now Briny O'Lynn he had no watch for to wear. He got him a turnip. He scraped it bare. He put a cricket right under the skin. I swear she's a-ticking, said Briny O'Lynn."

"Ozark, they want you up at the headquarters tent." It was Mac. "You and three other photographers are to make a record of the big show tomorrow."

United States Pacific Fleet

PHOTOGRAPHER'S IDENTIFICATION CARD

No. 2830   Void after 31 DEC. 1945

This is to certify that

JAMES O. BOAN
PFC   USMC 389573

is an official photographer of the United States Navy. He
is assigned to making official photographs of naval subjects,
in accordance with existing security instructions. Commanding officers of ships and stations are requested to cooperate
with and assist the bearer in obtaining official pictures.

Commander in Chief
United States Pacific Fleet

By Direction T.B.Williams

Unit D-2

Color Hair L.BRO
Eyes GREY
Weight 155
Birth 9-1-2

Motobu mountains under attack on the northern end of Okinawa.

Ellis and the .45 he used during the attack on our C.P. during a raid the previous night. In the background, another corpse is under observation.

Our C.P. on Motobu. We were cut off for a time and had to be supplied by air drops. In the distant haze is Ie Shima.

Company command post on Motobu Peninsula. Heat and moisture damaged film, giving a mottled look to the photo.

This camouflaged Japanese landing craft was found on Motobu Peninsula.

Little lost girl who joined us one morning for breakfast. Her parents were glad to get her back later in the day.

Note observers in foreground. "What does the distance hold?" We were always guessing. Short sago palms (foreground) were everywhere.

Chapter 13

CAPTURE OF IE SHIMA

The Sixth Division's race north had been so quick that the Okinawan battle planners had to reassess their Phase I and II operations.

First, naval requirements were reduced to providing supplies and supporting gunfire.

Second, Admiral Turner could use ships and supplies that had been designated for Okinawan amphibious operations for an early attempt to capture the island of Ie Shima with its long airfield runways.

Ie Shima was a rectangular island, relatively flat, measuring five by two and a half miles. It was located about four miles off the northeast coast of Okinawa's Motobu Peninsula where the Sixth Recon was located at Bise during Ie's invasion.

Toward the eastern end of Ie Shima was Iegusugu Yama, a 600-foot-high mountain. Otherwise, the airfield with three-mile-long runways was unobstructed. The village of Ie was at the mountain's foot.

Major General A. D. Bruce's Seventy-seventh Army Infantry Division was selected for the assault. Working with Rear Admiral L. F. Reifsnider, General Bruce completed invasion plans in two days, and W-Day was set for April 16 at 0800.

During the two weeks before the invasion, the Seventy-seventh boarded ships and moved to a safe area three hundred miles southeast of Okinawa. It turned out not to be so safe when Japanese kamikazes found them on April 2. Although all eight Japanese planes were terminated, the invasion fleet took hits on two transports, the APD *Dickerson* and the APA *Henrico*. American losses were heavy among both officers and enlisted men: 22 KIA, 76 WIA, and 10 MIA.

The *Henrico* was too damaged to continue, so command was transferred to the transport *Sarasota*. Commander of the 305th Regiment, who was KIA, was replaced by Colonel Joseph B. Coolidge, and men from other outfits were transferred to complement the Seventy-seventh.

Aerial reconnaissance in January had indicated that two Japanese infantry battalions, plus airfield service troops, were on Ie Shima. More recent close aerial photos, however, showed no defense on Mount Iegusugu Yama. Battle strategists were positive, though, that the mountain and the city of Ie were heavily fortified.

As mid-April approached, observers were mystified, because gun placements previously seen now disappeared. Mines and trenches, on the other hand, began appearing, along with obstructions on the runways, but only five people had been seen by observation planes making daily flights over the island in the two weeks prior to landing.

General Bruce was not convinced that the island was unfortified and the invasion proved how right he was. The mountain, Iegusugu Yama, was a maze of fortifications, honeycombed with tunnels, caves, and hidden firing positions. Nearly seven thousand people inhabited Ie Shima, and they were full of fight.

The island garrison was a detachment of Colonel Udo's defense of northern Okinawa. Unlike Udo, Major Masashi Igawa, who commanded the Ie Shima troops, was liked and respected. Not only did his soldiers fight bravely, but nowhere else in the Okinawa campaign did civilians, fighting with spears and guns, battle the Americans with such ferocity.

Altogether, Major Igowa had more than two thousand Ie Shima defenders: 930 men in his own battalion, plus 350 members of a special infantry battalion. In addition, about 1,500 men and women of the island joined his troops.

The army's first move was to occupy the nearby island Minna

Shima, 6,500 yards from Ie Shima, where they set up two howitzer battalions to shell Ie Shima.

Major J.L. Jones' Underwater Demolition Team (UDT) checked the landing beaches of Ie Shima and found no mines or obstructions. They also determined that the landing beaches were lightly defended.

Sailing under dense smoke, the invasion fleet approached Ie Shima on the morning of April 16. Unfortunately, the Japanese Third Chrysanthe-mum was underway. The navy's defense picket line took a beating, but only seven planes broke through, and they were downed by Admiral Reifsnider's invasion fleet.

On Okinawa, the observing Sixth Marine Recon Company at Bise had a panoramic view of NGF (naval gun fire) from two battleships, seven destroyers, seventeen mortar boats, and ten gunboats as they blasted Ie Shima. That wasn't all. Both fighters and bombers zoomed over Bise in protective maneuvers for the sixteen attacking fighter planes of the invasion fleet.

By nightfall of the first day, Colonel Aubrey D. Smith's 306th Infantry had moved more than a mile inland with little opposition. The 305th Infantry under Lieutenant Colonel J.B. Coolidge wasn't as fortunate. Stiff opposition from caves and tombs contested every yard of land. Even after dark, infiltrators hassled his troops. It was during the 305th's attack on April 18 that a sniper shot and killed renowned war correspondent Ernie Pyle.

Although progress was made on the lowland, the enemy on strongly fortified Mount Iegusugu Yama laid down layer upon layer of defensive fire. The city of Ie was also well defended from positions on Bloody Ridge, particularly Government House. These strongholds were not secured until April 20, with a final bayonet and grenade charge. Because of inland mines, artillery and tanks could provide only limited support in many areas, including the City of Ie. Infantry had to dig out the defenders one position at a time.

After capturing Ie, the full force of the invaders was directed to Iegusugu Yama. Following a concentrated artillery shelling, Colonel Smith's regiment broke through a minefield, gaining access to the mountain's base. Then it was strongpoint-by-strongpoint fighting with grenades and flamethrowers to rout the enemy.

By noon on April 20, the 306th was halted well up the mountain for further bombardment with heavy weapons. The final assault on the sheer mountainside was by trained mountain infantry, who braved grenades rolling down the slopes as well as satchel charges tossed at them.

After six days, on April 21, Ie Shima was declared secure. A count of enemy losses indicated 4,706 dead and 149 prisoners. The American Seventy-seventh Infantry lost 239 KIA, 879 WIA, and 17 MIA.

*Main highway along coast of northern Okinawa. Recon Company made a beyond-
the-front-line patrol along the road and through this pass.*

Tunnel on the main coastal road in northern Okinawa.

Typical manmade cave on Okinawa.
Note carbine near entrance marking a fallen comrade.

Ie (pronounced Ee-uh) Shima ("island") was bombarded by air and naval guns before it was invaded. We watched from Motobu Peninsula, Okinawa. A few days later, Ernie Pyle, famous war correspondent, was killed there.

Ie Shima as seen from Okinawa. This is the island where Ernie Pyle was killed.

Cave entrances were often camouflaged with sago palm fronds. The island was hollow with caves.

Some of Recon Company's men advancing on northern Okinawa.

Chapter 14

PLANES, RAINS, AND KOURI

"Jeez!" yelled Murphy. He was dancing like a sailor trying to regain his sea legs. Some of his buddies "hit the deck" in a reflex action, as they would to incoming artillery. But this wasn't "incoming mail." It was outgoing—our own.

A plane roared by just feet off the ground along the level seacoast. As it pulled up, the air crackled and roared.

"Welcome to the invasion of Ie Shima," said the veteran, Curtis. He was smiling at the fright he saw on the younger faces.

Located at Bise on the tip of Okinawa's Motobu Peninsula, Recon had a front-row seat for the operation. We watched as ships emerged from their protective smoke. We could see puffs of smoke as the big naval rifles fired. Artillery from a nearby island and bombs from the circling planes raised a cloud of dust over Ie Shima, a scant four miles away.

Sound waves could be seen rippling across the water, allowing only a few seconds for us to clasp our hands over our ears. Giant phosphorus shells sent their silvery tentacles high into the sky.

"It's just like a movie," said Private John Hart of New Rochelle, New York. "See how small the ships look—the planes, too."

In a short time, dust and debris filled the air over Ie Shima. Gradually, the entire area was obscured by a man-made cloud of destruction.

"Did you get some good pictures, Ozark?" asked Lieutenant Autry. I was busy trying to fit a piece of broken amber-colored bottle glass over the camera lens.

"I shot a few before dust covered the island. Now I'm trying to get a picture of that dirt cloud."

As the battle progressed and we became accustomed to the action, we began to go about other duties.

The plane was so near that the roar of its engine and its appearance were almost simultaneous.

"Hit the deck!" someone yelled. As the plane roared closer, it became obvious that it was in trouble. A wisp of smoke trailed the bomber. It appeared like a wounded bird looking for a place to land, gliding along with its tail down.

"Oh my God!" yelled Sergeant McDougal. "There's a loose bomb hung up under the wing." As we gawked, unaware of our peril, he shouted again. "Stay down! For God's sake, keep down!"

As he was warning us, the bomb slipped loose and came fishtailing into the marine compound. The explosion was horrendous. Dirt and debris showered over the camp, knocking down the commander's tent and anything else standing.

"Corpsman! Hey, corpsman! There's a man hurt over here!"

Doc Redinger hurried off in the direction of the call. He saw a mangled arm lying on the ground before he reached the wounded man. Blood was spurting from an artery in the flesh-torn shoulder. Doc reached for gauze to pack the wound and stop the bleeding.

"Get another medic over here!" Doc shouted at Private Joyce, who was standing immobilized with his mouth open. "And tell Chronis to get on the radio and tell headquarters what happened here."

There was another explosion on distant Mount Yae Take. The plane had crashed.

Major Walker shuffled up to a wounded Recon man as he was being evacuated in a Jeep. "Hang in there, son," he encouraged. Then he turned to Manion.

"Sergeant, get a search party up there and see if that pilot is still alive. If he isn't, bring back his body—or at least his dog tags."

It was a hot day for late April, and the men were sweating profusely during the forced march, even before the mountain climb. Using a compass heading, the search party made its way up the mountain, fighting vines and underbrush.

One of the smaller men was mumbling as he brought up the rear.

"What did you say, Shorty?"

"The sweat running down the crack of my butt is hot enough to boil an egg."

The men chuckled and began bitching. Their leader knew then that they would make it to the plane. What they saw when they got there was a tangled mess of wreckage, and as much as they wanted to rush in and search for life, they knew better. The party was halted and divided into pairs to search the area for signs of the enemy, particularly snipers. Meanwhile, others inched forward looking for mines or booby traps. Finding none, the crumpled body of the dead pilot was removed.

If they thought it was hot going up the mountain, coming down with a corpse was worse, according to Zack Brandise. Their dungarees were drenched with salty sweat and their canteens were empty when they returned. The next few days, the rescue party was excused from duty to rest.

Now that the battle for Ie Shima was over and Motobu Peninsula was declared secure, the marines had little to do except for short patrols and perimeter guard duty. However, there was plenty of scuttlebutt.

Smith came running into camp one day from his guard post on the beach.

"President Roosevelt is dead," he shouted. "I heard it over the PA on one of the boats." As it turned out, he had it right for once. Another time, it was reported that the war in Europe was over.

At this time, nature set about doing what the Japanese could not. A miserable rain began to fall. Mud was everywhere—on clothes, weapons, and particularly shoes. Walking was difficult, sleep next to impossible. When the rain stopped and the skies cleared, men relaxed.

Sweetpee had fallen asleep at an outpost. In the dawn light, he felt a shadow come over him, and he woke to see a man standing on the rim of his foxhole peering down.

"I was scared stiff," he said. "I couldn't even reach for my weapon. I just knew I was a goner. Then I saw that cone-shaped native hat, and the man had a pole across his shoulders. At first, I thought it was a spear. Then I saw a bucket on each end of the pole. It was a doggone farmer heading out to his rice paddy. Neither of us said anything. Then he just vanished in the morning mist."

"We're seeing a lot of natives around here," said Sergeant McDougal, "and the major is concerned. Some of Udo's Japanese are dressing in kimonos with the natives. The soldiers are using them for shields. The major wants us to clean out the caves and send the natives to the detention centers."

A cave had been reported near a burial vault about a mile from the Recon camp. Manion took his squad to remove the occupants.

"Deh-ta-koy, deh-ta-koy!" shouted the Sergeant at the dark hole in the ground. He had men posted around the mouth of the cave, and at a side entrance they had found.

"Deh-ta-koy," he shouted again. Nothing happened.

"We'll have to throw in a phosphorus grenade," he said, preparing to start the fuse. Just then, an old man came out of the cave, walking slowly and bowing with each step. He was given a cigarette. After a while, he was convinced to bring out the others. Soon old men and women came out, followed by mothers with children. When no more came out, there was a call for a flashlight so that the cave could be searched.

The cave smelled damp and musty as we entered. My light played around the floor. It was a mess—straw mats, piles of clothing, cooking utensils. As our eyes became adjusted, we saw rifles stacked along the cave wall. I was inspecting them while PFC Walker searched the rubble. There was movement under some bedding, and a girl stood up, holding a pillow over her breasts. Walker lowered his light; she was naked.

When the girl noticed his light on her body, she lowered the pillow. Walker lifted his beam to her breasts. She lifted the pillow. He lowered the beam of light. She lowered the pillow.

He lifted.

She lifted.

He lowered.

She lowered.

He lifted.

She lifted.

"Walker, what the hell is going on over there?" I asked. "Get your ass over here and help me with these weapons."

As we were gathering up rifles, swords, and grenades, gunfire broke out at the side entrance to the cave.

"Let's get the hell out of here!" I yelled. I ran toward the main entrance with an armload of rifles. Walker passed me.

Outside, Lieutenant Newton asked what all the shooting was about. One of the side entrance guards pointed to three dead Japanese soldiers, crumpled where they had fallen.

"What about the girl?" asked Walker. At that moment, she walked out of the cave fully dressed in a kimono and joined the other civilians.

For the remainder of the long day, Recon men searched and sealed caves, mopped up, and patrolled the area. Exhausted and hungry, sundown found us digging in a perimeter defense. It included a brushy hilltop and a small valley. A dirt road ran along the trickling stream in the valley.

It was a beautiful spring evening. Those on guard saw a full moon shine brightly with a soft light until after midnight. At about 0200 the guards heard sounds of a firefight in the valley. Major Walker and his crew had erected a tent near the center of the perimeter, behind a light machine gun. Somehow the enemy had penetrated unnoticed.

Corporal William Ellis was sleeping in the road behind the gun and near the tent entrance. Sergeant Iola Evans and Major Walker were in the tent.

"God woke me!" said Ellis, a religious person. He looked up to see a Japanese soldier, silhouetted against the sky, staring at him. In one motion, he rolled over and drew his .45 pistol, just as a spear plunged into the ground where he had been. The blast from the pistol woke Evans, who began shooting. Five enemy were killed before they could throw a grenade. By this time, Ellis had reached the machine gun and began firing. The raiding party fell back and moved up the hillside.

Ace Brown and I were manning a machine gun on the ridge. We had strung telephone wire in front of our position, to which we had attached tin cans filled with rocks. When firing broke out, Ace was on watch. He nudged me awake. We listened. When the firing ceased, it became very quiet. We tensed.

A flare popped open above the hillside and the light danced, making moving shadows in the brushes. Motionless, we strained to see a human form. As the flare fizzled, darkness closed in.

We felt vulnerable.

Then rocks began rattling in the cans. Ace opened up with the machine gun—and he didn't stop firing until the bullet belt was empty. As he fired he was saying Hail Marys.

Later I said, "I don't know which was faster—the bullets or the Hail Marys."

After the remaining enemy withdrew, moans and cries of anguish came from the brush. Obviously, a wounded enemy soldier was out there in no-man's land. Another flare popped, followed by rifle fire, but the moans continued. Someone threw a grenade, but the soldier was concealed. More cries. No one could rest, much less sleep.

In daylight, the area was combed and four more enemy dead were found.

By afternoon, Recon boarded trucks to move across the peninsula. We dismounted and dug in near a village.

"Where are we?" asked Sweetpee.

"Right here," I said, pointing to the ground. "Hell, I don't know. They only tell us what they want us to know. I think it's Nakooshi or Nakasoni. I haven't seen a map since landing on Okinawa," I continued. "A lot of good that map-reading course in Camp LeJeune has done me."

We dug in. At about midnight, the stinger, the twin .30 airplane machine gun we had found, began firing bursts, alerting everyone. By the time the camp was awake, a flare had been tripped near a rice paddy in the valley. All hell broke loose—guns were firing and grenades were being thrown.

"What's going on?" yelled Sweetpee to me. He put on his helmet and peeked over the edge of the foxhole at the valley. Orange tracer bullets were drawing crisscross lines through the air.

"Who's firing that damned stinger?" asked Lieutenant Autry.

"I don't know," I said, "I think someone in Krysztofik's squad."

"He must have froze on it. Either he'll burn it up or shoot all his ammo if someone doesn't get him off it."

He used all his ammo. All he shot was a bull that had strayed into the rice paddy and tripped the flare. It was badly wounded and was still bawling the next morning when Recon left on its mission. Major Walker sent a message to the stinger crew. That was the last of the twin machine gun, but the gunner was known thereafter as a guy who could "shoot the bull."

"Look down there!" I said. Lined up at the water's edge were several amphibian tractors.

"Wonder what they're doing here," mused Sweetpee.

Lieutenant Autry called his men together.

"Here's the scoop. See that island over there? That's Kouri Shima. We're going to board these amtracks and invade that island."

The silence of trepidation smothered any bitching.

"That place is less than half the size of Ie Shima," noted Sugarlips Bardoni, "and we sure in hell ain't no army."

Recon boarded the amtracks, and we crunched our way over the coral into the open sea. The boats approached Kouri in a double line. While still too far out to see most objects on the island, the amtracks opened up with their 75mm guns. Boats shuddered and men trembled.

"Damned if I don't believe my ears are bleeding," complained Chronis. He had been sensitive about his ears since fungus was found to be growing out of them on Guadalcanal. He put his finger in his ear and pulled it away. No blood.

I looked at Sweetpee. He was working his jaws and pounding his ears. "I can't hear myself! I've gone deaf!" he yelled.

The guns fired again.

When the amtracks rammed the beach, we were more than glad to be ashore. It was the landing on Okinawa all over again; no enemy resistance.

"What's that?" I asked Sweetpee.

"Looks like a civilian." A man was walking nonchalantly down the narrow road toward us.

"Halt!" I said, stepping out in front of the man menacingly.

Sweetpee searched him but found nothing of interest. The squad moved down the road.

"Ozark, see that cave over there? Check it out," said McDougal.

I crept through waist-high grass until I figured I could see into the dark hole. Slowly, I rose to my feet.

Bang! A shot was fired, and I dropped like a rock. It was a reflex action. I determined that the sound had come from my own group. I rose slowly and returned to my squad. I was furious that no one had warned me before the shot. Then I learned that it was Murphy who had fired into the cave. I was chewing him out with a descriptive piece of mind, when someone shouted, "There goes a Jap!" A figure dressed in a dark kimono was running toward a cliff. I headed him off. The man grabbed me by the ankles, bowing and begging. He seemed to think I had saved him from some terrible fate.

As the patrol moved along, the man willingly went with us. Occasionally, he would stop and pick red berries growing on the roadside. When the man handed me a berry, I noticed that his hand was deformed.

"They taste something like strawberries," said Sugarlips, who was picking his own berries.

Back at the beach, Doc Redinger was trying to save a boy with deep gashes in his legs. The boy was lying beside a dead horse, probably killed by the 75mm shelling.

"He's bleeding faster than I can feed plasma into his veins," said Doc. Then the boy died.

Lieutenant Autry was talking to a visitor from another outfit after the expedition returned to Motobu.

"You know," said Autry, "we didn't find a single soldier on Kouri."

"Well, you really didn't expect to did you?"

"What do you mean?"

"You hadn't heard that Kouri is home for a leper colony?"

"We didn't know."

When I overheard the conversation, I had a sudden attack of the heaves, trying to throw up the red berry I had eaten.

During the next two days, Sweetpee and I shared a foxhole.

"I've never understood why they call these pits foxholes," said Sweetpee. Actually, they're more like mole holes. Why don't they call them moleholes?"

I didn't answer. I was concentrating on the letter I was writing home. Mail call a few minutes earlier had produced two letters from Mother.

Chapter 15

KAMIKAZES, KAKAZU, AND THE ARMY

While the marines on northern Okinawa mopped up enemy pockets, guarded heavy equipment, made patrols, and improved creature comforts, primarily food and shelter, the army in the south faced an increasingly stubborn enemy.

Many marines were writing letters, sunbathing, receiving mail regularly from home, and dreaming of liberty stateside. War wasn't so bad, after all. They had won *their* battle of Okinawa. Northern Okinawa was declared secure.

Between April 6 and 15, the Army Twenty-fourth Corps advanced less than a mile in some areas. Between April 18 and 30, they advanced another mile in central Okinawa. They had bumped against the outer perimeter of Japanese outposts along the hills of an area known as Kakazu Ridge.

Enemy resistance in front of the Seventh and 96th Divisions was so fierce that their advance stalled. It took four battalions of artillery, three air strikes, and the fourteen-inch guns of the battleship *New York* to clear a path to the village of Kakazu.

The next day, it became evident that the American Twenty-fourth Corps was facing the Japanese Thirty-second Army's main zone of defense.

Aerial reconnaissance could not show what a formidable defense was built into this large stone hogback. Positioned to form a natural defense, Kakazu Ridge was honeycombed with caves and tunnels. It was an enemy hornet's nest that Colonel Munetatsu Hara had been building for months. He was confident and ready for planes, guns, tanks, or men—anything the Americans wanted to throw at him.

Major General John Hodge called General Buckner for more artillery battalions. General Buckner called the marines. He ordered the Third Amphibious Corps to release the Marine 155mm Artillery, the Eighth and Ninth Gun Battalions, and the First, Third, and Sixth Howitzer Battalions to join army field artillery units.

Meanwhile, the Japanese planned a counterattack for April 8, but it was canceled when aerial scouts saw a large U.S. convoy off western Okinawa. A previous counterattack scheduled for April 6, in conjunction with the first kamikaze attack, had been canceled for the same reason. What the Japanese didn't know was that the Second Marine Division was held in reserve to feint a landing on the eastern coast of Okinawa. This threat froze the Japanese in their positions. But the staff officers were pressing for a counterattack anyway, and they would soon persuade General Ushijima to agree.

During this period, the Thirty-second Army Infantry reached the boundary of the Ninety-sixth Division near Ouki, placing the Seventh Division in range of the enemy's first line of defense. Now the U.S. Army's progress would be measured in feet per day instead of yards. They had clashed with Ushijima's renowned Naha–Suri–Yonabaru stronghold.

In a classical assault on April 9, Colonel Edwin T. May sent two of his three battalions forward with one in reserve. This meant two companies, with one in reserve, would strike the main Kakazu line, and two more companies would strike West Kakazu. For surprise, he had requested no softening up by artillery.

Colonel Edwin T. May's attack was repelled by the embedded enemy soldiers. He pulled back and called for artillery to bombard Kakazu. This didn't stop the enterprising Japanese, who popped out of holes on the reverse slope and showered the Americans with gunfire, grenades, mortars, and satchel charges of explosives designed to disable tanks.

Fire from preregistered enemy pillboxes, artillery, and mortars was devastating. Soldiers were cut down, and by dusk on April 9, the 383rd Infantry Regiment was down to 45 percent of effective strength, but they had finally crested Kakazu Ridge. All day, the Japanese fired hidden weapons from below and behind Kakazu, raining mortar shells and bullets on the troops, shutting off reinforcements and supplies. At dark, cut off and low on ammunition, the survivors retreated. The American loss was 23 KIA, 183 WIA, and 47 MIA.

Although the attack on Kakazu had failed, the army was ready to try again the following morning. Using a massive frontal attack supported by artillery and tanks, the infantry charged. Tanks became bogged down in the mud. Attempts to move down the finger-like ridges of Kakazu met withering fire. A wedge drive also failed. Fresh troops tried an end run from Kakazu west and met a wall of fire. Again they were driven back. However, some elements using armored bulldozers closed a few Japanese artillery caves. Heavy rain prevented planes from joining in the attack, but the downpour covered the army's retreat or casualties could have been worse.

On April 12 the army tried again to dislodge the Japanese and was confronted with a mortar barrage unlike anything they had seen before. Shells showered down on them at the rate of one per second. That was enough.

The army called a halt to assess the battlefield situation. They had lost 2,890 men killed, wounded, or missing.

General Hodge and his advisors concluded that a heavier bombardment of every position was needed. Not enough ammo was ashore, so ships began shelling Kakazu. The earlier loss of the two ammunition ships, *Hobbs* Victory and *Logan* Victory, to kamikazes would delay the battle.

The Japanese, sensing the delay, decided to counterattack on the night of April 12–13.

Exaggerated news of the kamikaze attack on April 6 buoyed the spirits of General Ushijima's commanders. When they heard another Floating Chrysanthemum was scheduled for April 12, General Isamu Cho urged the staff to stage a counterattack in conjunction with it. Colonel Hiromichi Yahara, tactical planner in charge of the staff, was adamantly against the idea, emphasizing that it would fail because infiltrators would get lost in the dark and be cut down. He reminded them that orders from Imperial Headquarters were for delaying tactics. However, Ushijima was finally persuaded to counterattack.

The plan was for small groups to infiltrate the American lines during a nighttime bombardment. These groups were to penetrate rear areas where soldiers would be reluctant to fire among their own men. The Japanese were to gather and hide in known caves and other places during the day. After the bombardment, the infiltrators were to launch their attack and decimate rear echelons.

The kamikaze attack came at about 1300 hours and lasted until dark, destroying a dozen American ships, including two battleships and three destroyers. The navy lost 124 KIA, 364 WIA, and 130 MIA. The Japanese lost 147 planes.

Three flares were to start the Japanese attack. First, a red flare would signal the start of the artillery bombardment of 5,000 rounds, the heaviest Japanese barrage of the campaign. A second red would announce that the all-out counterattack was ready to begin. The third flare, a dragon, was to start the attack.

Soon after midnight the Japanese laid down a mortar barrage on Americans and began their counterattack. The American lines held under the light of navy star shells. At 0300 the Japanese threw an artillery barrage of 1,000 rounds against the 96th Division line and attacked in battalion strength. But American artillery, mortars, and naval gunfire prevailed. At dawn the Japanese survivors retreated.

Coordinated with the early morning attack, the Japanese Twenty-second Regiment hit the Seventh Infantry with small groups of infiltrators. Flares caught the Japanese, who were eliminated by mortars, grenades, and small arms fire.

On April 13 another kamikaze attack damaged the carrier *Enterprise* and battleship *Missouri*. The destroyer *Kidd* was badly damaged, with 38 KIA and 55 WIA.

Meanwhile, supplies continued to come ashore at Hagushi Beaches. During the first fifteen days of battle, more than a half-million tons were delivered.

The Japanese counterattack failure of April 12–13 convinced Major General John Hodge that he could break Ushijima's Naha–Suri–Yonabaru line of defense.

At dawn on April 19, the army and marines released a fierce bombardment for twenty minutes. In front of the Seventh and Ninth Divisions, 354 pieces of artillery roared into action. In addition, they were supported by a barrage from 21 ships of various sizes, including battlewagons. In the air supporting the bombardment were 650 navy and marine planes.

Off the eastern Okinawan coast, the Second Marine Division feinted a landing, but Ushijima held his ground; he was not deceived. Then the bombardment ceased for ten minutes, while troops along the front line showed themselves, hoping to lure the Japanese from their concealment. They stayed underground. The army probed but found no soft spots in the enemy line.

On April 20 General Hodge tried again. Fighting raged back and forth across Ushijima's strong front until April 25.

Many acts of heroism were performed during this time. For example, PFC Paul Cook killed ten Japanese before he was killed. In hand-to-hand fighting, he broke his M-1 over an enemy soldier's head, took an *Arisaka* rifle from a Japanese and bayoneted him with it, then shot a third Japanese.

Resistance by the Japanese continued until the 28th, when Machinato Airfield was captured. Meanwhile, Captain Tadashi Kojo had taken over command at Suri Castle.

April 29 was Emperor Hirohito's birthday, and at Japan's Okinawa headquarters a fierce debate was raging about what action to take next. The result dramatically affected the careers of Lieutenant General Cho and Colonel Yahara.

Chapter 16

RECON GUARDS SEABEES

I was setting the table with china plates and silverware scrounged from the vacant Okinawan houses. What appeared to be a white sheet made a tablecloth. The table was constructed from sliding doors taken from village houses.

"Man, you guys live like kings," commented one of the men from Mississippi who had walked up.

"I admit we've made the most of what the enemy and the quartermaster's supply dump provides, both marine and army."

"You bastards stole half this stuff."

"No, it was requisitioned by Sugarlips and Smith."

"I hear you lost a man. What happened to him, Ozark?"

"Damned if I know. It was after dark and he was warming coffee over this open fire when everything exploded. Smoke, sparks, dust, and coffee flew everywhere. When Doc Redinger got there, he was lying on the ground with his guts hanging out. Shrapnel had sliced his belly open neat as a knife. He wasn't bleeding a lot, and didn't seemed to be in a lot of pain. They put him on a stretcher and hauled him off. He just lay there and waved goodbye."

"You think it was a Jap grenade?"

"Could have been. Or maybe the fire was built on a land mine."

A man from another unit walked around the table examining items and looking at things on the shelves. This was known as the "General Store." I kept an eye on him.

"Guess your squad will be leaving today?" he said.

"Yes, and I guess you're looking to see what you can make off with when we leave," I accused.

"I understand the guys left here will inherit all the loot," he said, "not that we don't hate to see you go."

"Yeah, but they have to cook a farewell meal for us first. They've promised hamburgers, fried potatoes, canned veggies, and fresh fruit, coffee, and milk . . ."

"Bull! If you get any milk it'll be that vanilla-flavored powdered stuff we had on the 'Canal."

"That's probably better than you had growing up. Where was it, Turnip Green, Mississippi?" I kidded him, just to make him mad. He had a short fuse and would get red-faced when it was lit. Color was seeping into his cheeks now.

"I hope you get run over by one of those Seabee trucks you'll be guarding," he said as he walked away.

After the promised banquet, the first squad under McDougal boarded trucks and headed south, toward the Seabees' camp. They had requested guards because guerrilla elements were sabotaging their bulldozers and heavy equipment at night.

It had started raining again by the time the trucks reached the Seabees.

"Dismount and put your packs over there on the ground," yelled Mac. "We'll cover them with a tarp until you come back in the morning. Then bring your rifles, cartridge belts, and helmets and get back on the trucks."

"Look at that, Ozark!" said Sweetpee. "They've got electric lights and a mess hall." But Recon didn't have time to look around before the trucks pulled out.

The road-building equipment we were to guard was pulled into a a flat area with large trees and brush nearby. Without shovels, we couldn't dig in. There was an abandoned building nearby. It could have been a schoolhouse. It was pouring rain as we moved in.

Dark came early, and we began rotating two-hour watches. I drew the ten to midnight watch. I stood by a glassless window and looked out into the blackness. I could see nothing, but I could hear rain hitting the leaves of the bushes, some so close to the window that I could touch them. I wished for a flare, or for moonlight, and neither was available.

Halfway through my watch, I heard a scratching on the gravel road. I stiffened and held my breath to hear better. Nothing, so I let my breath out. Just then a twig broke almost under my window. I froze, with every nerve in my body alert. My skin crawled. I slowly raised my rifle until it pointed out the window. I waited. I wished that the bushes weren't so close.

Although I couldn't see, I knew where the men were sleeping on the floor, and I remembered someone was manning the machine gun on the front steps. Suddenly, I thought what might happen if a grenade were tossed through that open window. Out on the road there was a muffled cough. The machine gun opened fire. Men woke and began firing through the open windows. The noise was deafening. The smell of gunpowder filled the room.

The firing stopped, but my ears were ringing. In the quiet, my hearing returned. As I listened I could hear noise in the bushes. Someone was moving around. Inside the building, I heard a click. Then another click. I identified it as someone snapping his fingers to let me know that he also heard the sounds outside. *Rustle—snap! Crack—snap! Crunch—snap!* But the sounds were moving away. The enemy was retreating.

A terrible screaming noise came from the direction of the Seabee equipment. I dropped to the floor, expecting an explosion to follow. Nothing happened. Then I grinned as I realized what it was. The machine gun had shot a hole in one of the huge rubber tires on an earthmover.

I felt someone snuggle against me, shaking like a leaf. It was our corpsman.

"Are you cold?"

"Hell, no—I'm scared," Doc replied.

Come dawn, the sky was clear and we sleepless marines hunted down four dead and two wounded Japanese. There were some stinging-mad Seabees—until they saw the dead Japanese.

Trucks returned us to the Seabee camp. We marveled at the mess hall and ate cereal and hot rolls and drank hot coffee while the grinning cooks watched.

"I don't know if it's the fatherly attitude or the food," said Pappy, "but marines always get along well with Seabees."

After breakfast, we grabbed our gear from the pile and spent the rest of the day sleeping in Seabee bunks.

"We're going to a different place for guard duty tonight," Mac told our squad. The heavy equipment was parked in a graveled area near a low hill. With no shelter, the men crawled under the equipment to try sleeping and to stand their two-hour watches. I was glad for the moonlight. At least I could see if anything moved in the dim light. I was remembering a moonlight sojourn with my girl on the banks of the Hinkson Creek, when I heard a faint buzz. Instantly, I thought of the poisonous snakes we had been warned about before the landing. Then it occurred to me that the sound was above and on the other side of a little hill.

The next time I heard the droning sound, I recognized it as an airplane. The plane came closer but showed no lights. It had to be an enemy bomber from the sound of its engines. The "bomber's moon" was setting and there were stars in the sky.

The engines accelerated into a whining roar. I knew that it was diving. Two earth-shaking *whoomps* followed. Sparks flew high above the little hill. I ducked as shrapnel and debris fell around me. The plane left as quickly as it had approached.

When daylight came, I led an inspection crew to assess the damage. None of the equipment had been hit, but half the little hill was gone. Fortunately, it was the half opposite us. Total damage to the Seabees was two severed telephone wires.

Back at the Seabees' camp, we guards were introduced to our first hot-water showers since landing on Okinawa. What a thrill!

"Boy, these Seabees know how to live," said Sweetpee, as he soaped down.

"I can't get over the food," said Mac. "You know they have their own bakery?"

"Mail call!" yelled Sergeant Tabb.

We were feeling good after hot food, hot showers, and mail from home. Then our two platoons began arguing who had the toughest guard duty. The sergeants joined the discussion.

"Tell you what," said Mac, "why don't we trade assignments for tonight, and we'll find out who has the toughest job."

That night, I was on duty again when I heard the bomber returning. I heard the bombs exploding in the direction of our previous watch by the small hill. As I listened, I recalled a bomber that had harassed us on Guadalcanal. We had named it "Washing Machine Charlie."

The other platoon wasn't as lucky as ours, because PFC John Hutchinson was hit in the shoulder with a flying fragment. Medics took him away for x-rays to find the shrapnel.

"Another lucky bastard with a Hollywood wound," said a resentful marine.

As we left the mess hall, we heard big booms to the south over the East China Sea. They were followed by the rhythmic pounding of the anti-aircraft ack-ack guns. As we watched, the sky filled with so many puffs of exploding shells that it was polkadotted.

"Look at that!" Chronis was pointing to a dot that was moving through the smoke puffs. As we watched, the dot became red and it separated. Then it left a long plume of spiraling smoke as it plunged to the sea. In the bold daylight raid, other planes disappeared from the sky.

Not long after the aerial battle, it began to rain again—a slow drizzle with a chilly breeze.

"Damn this weather. Ain't it ever gonna warm up?" complained a born Southerner with tropical blood in his veins. He was shivering. "I can't say that I'm religious, but I'll be answering my mail in the chaplain's quarters where it's warm."

I had the good fortune to be offered a Seabee's bunk to sleep in. The goodhearted man woke me with a steaming hot cup of coffee.

"Thank you," I said. "I haven't had coffee in bed since I left the States." Next, we got another surprise in the mess hall.

"Boned chicken for dinner," said Sweetpee. "I must be dreaming."

Mac came in and joined us. "Have you heard the news? Germany surrendered. The war in Europe is over."

After a moment of silence for the impact of the news to sink in, someone yelled, "Yahoo!" Then there was applause and laughter.

"That's the good news," said Mac. The men stopped laughing.

"What's the bad news?" asked Sweetpee.

Mac stood. "The army's bogged down in the south; we're going to replace them." Mac left.

"Oh, shit!" I said. Others shared my sentiment.

Back on guard duty, Chronis was close to Lieutenant Autry, as was the custom of a radioman.

"What are they saying about President Truman's speech last night?" I asked.

"He did a good job," said the radioman, "but it wasn't like Roosevelt's fireside chats."

"Did he mention Okinawa?"

"I don't remember, but he gave the Japanese hell."

Although the rain had stopped and the sky had cleared, the ground was sloppy mud. The guards had found the driest spots available to place their ponchos for beds. A few had found straw mats or old doors for a foundation to their beds. As a lot, we were miserable, sleepy and grouchy. Some were grousing when a firefight broke out with a Japanese patrol. None of the marines were hurt, but we could hear a wounded enemy groaning. No one could sleep.

I believe it was Curtis who found the wounded Japanese at dawn. He had been shot in the hip. A heated discussion followed as to how we could get the wounded man back to the detention compound for medical care. The argument was settled when the someone took Mac's carbine and said he would do it.

The two of them started down the road. Soon after they were out of sight, a shot was heard, followed by another with a different report.

As the men looked in the direction of the sound, the marine came walking back.

"The prisoner escaped," he smiled.

"You shot the bastard," accused Mac.

"Well, he was trying to get away, so I plugged him with the carbine. You know, that little gun isn't worth dog crap. It didn't even knock him down. I had to use my .45."

Mac turned away, shaking his head.

We boarded trucks for the trip back to the Seabee camp, relishing the thought of dry bunks, but as soon as we arrived we were told to get our gear and reboard for the trip to the front near a stream called the Asato Gawa.

Unknown to us Recon Marines, our ordeal had just begun.

Chapter 17

JAPANESE COUNTERATTACK

Indecision about the merits of a second front and the loss of ammunition ships caused a delay in the land drive to conquer Okinawa. The Japanese commanders felt the pressure ease. This gave them confidence for a counterattack.

During the early weeks following the landing, enemy commanders were wary about the intentions of the Americans. They had feinted a landing as if to open a second front at the Minatoga Beaches. The Japanese felt it could be done successfully, although it would sever their Thirty-second Army, leading to a quick defeat.

Upon orders from the Imperial Command, the Okinawan defense was to be a delaying action. Ushijima was to inflict as much damage as possible and, at the same time, give the home island a longer period during which to build its defense.

By the last half of April, it was apparent to both sides that the line of defense north of Shuri could not hold without reinforcement. General Ushijima's commanders decided to risk an American second front, which they did not think would materialize, and they began moving troops north on a line from Gaja on the east coast to Maeda on the Urasoe-Mura Escarpment.

The Japanese would not completely withdraw from the south. Naval forces under Rear Admiral Minoru Ota were left to defend the Oroku Peninsula and miscellaneous units of engineers; service and supply units were left on the Chinen Peninsula. The defensive shifts had been made by the last week in April, but the Americans were still gaining ground.

At this time, a movement began among the Japanese commanders urging a counterattack. A meeting was called by Commander in Chief Ushijima, and his advisors entered a heated discussion. A coalition of field officers led by General Isamu Cho argued vehemently for the counterattack. Arguing just as rigidly against the attack was Colonel Hiromichi Yahara, senior staff officer and operations chief, who pointedly reminded them of their orders from Japan, to wage a defensive battle. He reinforced his argument with a warning that fighting a stronger enemy would only lead to an early defeat. He pointed out that the Americans now held the most advantageous position and could inflict heavy casualties.

Despite Yahara's warnings, General Cho, backed by the unit commanders, convinced Ushijima to counterattack. The plan was ambitious. The attack would be all along the front, plus amphibious incursions from each coast. The day was set, May 4 at 0500. The Japanese Twenty-fourth Division was to lash out north with three regiments on the line. They would be followed by other units of infantry, artillery, engineers, and even Admiral Ota's navy personnel. It was an all-or-nothing gamble, with all units except the Sixty-second Division attacking; and the Sixty-second was to be committed later to destroy the First Marine Division.

At sea, the attack plan was to use boats, barges, and even canoes to land men behind the First Marine Division at Oytamma on the west coast. About seven hundred men were committed to this phase of the attack. A similar plan for the east coast would land about five hundred men behind the Seventh Army Division near Tsuwa. Once ashore, both regiments were to infiltrate the enemy's troops and destroy equipment and supplies with grenades and satchel charges. They were to target command posts. If successful, they were to press on toward the middle of Okinawa and merge, assisting the Twenty-fourth Division's forward thrust.

The plan was well prepared, including the Fifth and Sixth Floating Chrysanthemums, with planes attacking from both Japan and Korea. The fifth kamikaze attack began May 3 at dusk, first to destroy planes on Yontan and Kadena airfields. Later waves of planes were to attack Task Force Fifty-one. The first attack by the bombers from Korea was mostly unsuccessful, because anti-aircraft fire forced the planes to drop their bombs from such high altitudes that they were inaccurate. The kamikazes from Kyushu were more damaging, plunging through curtains of bullets and shrapnel toward their targets. The U.S. Navy gunners downed thirty-six planes but lost two ships, and three other ships were damaged.

American field commanders were aware that the Japanese could counterattack but believed it more likely that they would hold their fortified positions until annihilated. The American officers also realized that the Japanese were bringing reinforcements north to the battle lines, but the counterattack plans were cleverly concealed. This was partly due to the fact that the enemy had continually counterattacked to recover lost ground.

The Sixth Chrysanthemum was a more serious raid than the Fifth. A flight of sixty Japanese bombers came at around midnight. Again ,American gunners kept the bombers high above their most effective altitude, but anti-aircraft radar was less effective because of metal foil scraps that the planes dropped to obsure the number and location of planes.

At daylight, the kamikazes attacked again, from 0600 to 1000, with heavy damage to the guarding picket ships. However, only one plane reached the Hagushi anchorage. This aerial attack was timed to complement the Japanese Thirty-second Army's land counterattack.

On the evening of May 4, kamikazes again attacked Task Force Fifty-one. One suicide plane made a destructive direct hit on the flight deck of the U.S.S. *Sangamon*. The Japanese lost 95 planes, but U.S. Navy casualties were 91 KIA, 280 WIA, and 283 MIA.

When the full force of the Japanese counterattack was realized on May 4, Americans opened up with devastating naval gunfire from two battleships, five cruisers, and eight destroyers. Joining the bombardment were ground artillery and air support. The Japanese Thirty-second Army advance was smashed, along with its supporting artillery.

Shortly after 0100, navy armored amphibian tractors guarding the Machinato Airfield shoreline heard unidentified voices on the beach and from small boats in the water. They opened fire. Several minutes later, elements of the First Marines heard enemy barges in the water near Kuwan. The barges were far short of their designated landing Oyama; having had trouble navigating the reefs, they had become lost in the dark.

Some of the Japanese landed quietly, but they began yelling during their attack, awakening the marines who had previously sighted in machine guns and mortars in case of such an attack.

In the flickering light of flares, the First Battalion opened up on the barges, some carrying one hundred or more Japanese. Soon the air was alive with tracer bullets and blobs of light from burning barges. Riflemen picked off enemy soldiers, whose heads were bobbing like coconuts in the water.

The Japanese who managed to infiltrate were soon sealed off and eliminated. In the early morning light, at least seventy-five enemy dead were counted in and around the marine positions.

On the opposite coast, the Japanese infiltrators met a similar fate when they were caught at sea in a crossfire between armoured amphibian ships patrolling the coast and the Seventh Army Infantry Division. A few Japanese escaped, but they left behind more than four hundred dead.

With American positions now protected from the flanks, marine and army commanders could concentrate on frontal attacks. At 0430 the Japanese opened a vicious artillery attack ahead of the 24th Division's counterattack. Nearly half of the sixteen thousand rounds fired during the day were fired in the first half-hour of the attack. Thousands of mortar shells and grenades were also launched on the American forces.

As the Japanese attacked on May 4, they met gunfire from fourteen-inch rifles on the *New York* and *Colorado* battleships, 16 battalions of artillery, and 12 battalions of 155mm guns and howitzers. At daybreak, 134 planes joined the battle with bombing runs.

Because the Japanese were attacking under a smoke screen, the observers at Shuri could not see the battle, but early reports were extremely favorable. On the east coast, the battle was over by noon, and the Army Seventh Division began mopping up.

In the center of the Japanese attack, progress was limited as tanks were turned back. The remainder of the day was spent by enemy infantry attempting to wrest control of the Urasoe-Mura Escarpment. They fought gallantly, often hand-to-hand, but without success, actually losing some positions to the Americans.

To the west, the marines found a soft spot in the Japanese defense and moved within sight of the north bank of the Asa Kawa.

On the eve of May 4, an aura of gloom settled on the Japanese commanders at Shuri headquarters. It was evident to almost everyone that the counterattack had failed. Despite the facts, the 32nd Regiment was ordered to try again at night.

On May 5 at 0200, following artillery shelling, they plunged into the Army Seventy-seventh's front line. They were repelled by artillery. Undaunted, they tried again at dawn with tanks. Six were stopped, but during the melee some Japanese broke through and recaptured Tonabaru village. They were able to hold their position for three days before the Seventh Division recaptured the strongpoint.

General Ushijima commended those who had escaped the death trap, but all knew that their major efforts had failed. Although the U.S. Army had lost 714 dead and the marines 649 dead, the Japanese had lost 6,227 members of their best infantry. They never fully recovered.

On the evening of May 5, at Shuri headquarters, Colonel Yahara was summoned to General Ushijima's underground office. In Yahara's own report, he said he walked stiffly into Ushijima's quarters. When Ushijima saw him waiting, he greeted him warmly and invited him in where he was sitting on the floor, Japanese style.

Speaking softly, Ushijima recounted the events of the futile counterattack, while General Cho could hear from an adjoining room. Ushijima promised Yahara that the fight would continue to the last man on the final inch of Okinawan soil. Then the remorseful Commander in Chief threw himself on Yahara's mercy, admitting that the counterattack was wrong and wasteful. He tearfully promised he would follow Yahara's advice from now on.

Yahara was outraged and frustrated. Now that it was too late, Ushijima was willing to listen to him.

Later, the talkative General Cho got in the last word to Yahara. "Are you going to tell me when it's time to commit hari-kiri?" he asked Yahara. "Is it now?"

Chapter 18

MARINES JOIN SHURI BATTLELINE

While the Sixth Marine Division, including the Recon Company, was mopping up guerrilla units and conducting guard duty in northern Okinawa, the army divisions fighting in the south were making grudging progress against the Japanese forward wall of defense. As Kakazu Ridge was bypassed, a series of ridges on the Urasoe-Mura Escarpment were fiercely defended. Places like Skyline and Tombstone Ridges and Rocky Crags caused heavy army casualties. By April 23 the Japanese had pulled back from their defense along Kakazu, Nishibara, Tanabaru, and Skyline to a secondary defense of Naha, Shuri, and Yonabaru. On April 24 patrols were sent out to determine the location of the new line of defense, and General Hodge soon learned that enemy resistance had stiffened.

The army pressed onward through the village of Nakama and reached Machinato Airfield, but Item Pocket and Kochi Ridge held out. The sheer rock cliffs of the Maeda Escarpment and heavy rain slowed progress to a crawl.

Meanwhile the Army Seventy-seventh Infantry Division, fresh from the invasion of Ie Shima, boarded ships for their return trip to Okinawa. The short campaign had left them in fair shape, and they recovered quickly on hot navy meals, warm showers, and comfortable beds.

During this period, General Buckner told General Geiger of the Third Amphibious Corps to alert one marine division to be ready to replace the Twenty-seventh Army Division at the front. The Twenty-seventh would then move back to northern Okinawa for garrison duty, and the Sixth Marine Division would move from their area near Chibana to join the front on the East China Sea coast.

While discussing the troop rearrangements on April 28 at General Buckner's headquarters, Major General Andrew Bruce of the Army Seventy-seventh Division suggested that a second front be opened behind the Japanese defense line near Ormoc with an amphibious landing from the Pacific side of Okinawa.

When General Buckner resisted, his supply officer came to his defense, saying that they did not have enough food and ammo for the operation. He was right. Kamikazes had sunk two ammo ships previously, and during the fourth Chrysanthemum another ammo ship, the Canadian *Victory*, would be sunk.

At this time, Marine General Lemuel Shepherd suggested that the Second Marine Division, held in reserve aboard ships and used previously to feint landings on Okinawa, had ample ammo and rations for the expected thirty-day mission.

General Buckner rejected the idea. Later in the meeting, General Shepherd again advanced the idea that the Second Marines had more than enough supplies for the second front. No action was taken.

Several planning officers agreed that a second front would have been most effective at this time. Later it was learned that the Japanese were reinforcing their defense line with two major units and were concerned that an attack from the sea would split the Thirty-second Japanese Army.

After rejecting the idea of a second front on Minatoga beaches, General Buckner had to face Admirals Turner and Spruance, whose fleet was continuing to take a pounding from the air.

During April 27, 28, and 29, Japanese Admiral Soamu Toyoda continued to believe that he could separate the Tenth Army from their supply ships with his (Kikusuis) aerial attacks. With the ships destroyed and supplies cut off, the Americans would soon surrender, he theorized.

During the Fourth Crysanthemum, the Japanese lost 150 planes, but the U.S. Navy lost twelve ships including the ammo ship and a hospital ship.

Buckner's response to the admirals, who were prodding him to hurry, was that it's better to move cautiously and save lives. Admiral Spruance countered that more time didn't save lives, but just spread out the death rate. After the shelling was over, troops still had to go in and take the enemy.

Both sides may have had their reasons. Some speculated that General Buckner wanted the army to get the credit for taking Okinawa. But it was known that the army preferred to soften up the enemy with artillery before sending infantry forward. The navy, on the other hand, preferred that their marines move quickly against the enemy before their ships were sunk. And the navy was hurting, reportedly losing an average of three ships every two days.

As a result of the planning and shifting of units, the Marine First Division, under General Pedro del Vallee, replaced the hard-luck Twenty-seventh Army Division, known as an undisciplined, screwup outfit.

Regardless of how they performed on the line, someone in the Twenty-seventh had garrison duty foresight. Before one unit of the First Marines knew that they were to move south, a strange jeep with two men was seen in the area nailing a sign onto a building. The sign read, "Reserved for Chaplain, 27th Army."

On May 3 the Japanese launched their Fifth Chrysanthemum at about 0600 with planes from Formosa. In a two-hour battle, kamikazes plowed through a thick curtain of anti-aircraft explosives and flying fragments to raid Hagushi beaches. They sank three picket ships. At Hagushi they sank and damaged more ships. The Japanese lost thirty-six planes.

After midnight, Japanese bombers attacked the Tenth Army's rear echelons, sparking a spectacular night display with searchlights and tracer bullets crisscrossing the sky. Anti-aircraft fire kept the bombers at such heights that their bombs fell erratically, but an evacuation hospital was hit, with thirteen killed and thirty-six wounded.

An hour later, marines stationed in amtracks along the seawall heard voices and discovered barges moving from Naha north toward the Hagushi beaches. The barges headed for shore far short of their destination, bumping into B Company of the First Marines.

Meanwhile, the amtracks moved out to sea, then came toward the barges, catching them in a crossfire with the marines. It was estimated that five hundred Japanese died.

The kamikazes continued their attack on May 4, both in early morning and late evening, times preferred because of the sun's position. Ten ships were 'hit and some sank, including the mine-layer *Shea*. It was hit with a *baka* bomb. The baka is a piloted suicide bomb, not well made, and named to mean foolish or difficult to guide to a target. At dusk, the carrier *Sangamon* was hit.

The navy's loss of personnel was heavy: 654 casualties, of which 94 were KIA. The Japanese lost 95 planes.

During this period of heavy kamikaze attacks and an aborted landing from the sea, First Division marines were pressing hard against the Shuri bastion, making small but steady gains. The Japanese had reformed a line of defense from Awacha through a ridge north of Dakeshi to Uchima and Jichaku. Powerful elements of the Thirty-second Japanese Army were still holed up in caves and spoiling for a fight with the First Marine Division.

On May 5 the marines bumped hard against Ushijima's main line of defense. Lieutenant Colonel J. C. Murray Jr. faced an L-shaped deep ravine along his entire front. The north–south road across it was closed with a deep crater. To make matters worse, enemy anti-tank guns were preregistered to disable anything on the road.

Troops met strong opposition at the village of Miyagusuku. They called in the First's Tank Battalion with flamethrowers. They dowsed the town with three hundred gallons of napalm and reduced it to ashes.

The Seventy-seventh Army Division failed to advance on the west flank when faced with withering fire and showered with grenades and knee mortar shells. They called for a smoke screen and retreated. Day after day, assault forces probed and dug in, sometimes retreating, but tentatively moving forward.

On their right was Naha, the Sixth Marine Division's assignment, and between the two divisions was a series of fortified, interlocking ridges awash in rain and mud.

Wet, despondent marines slogged through mud so thick it sucked the shoes off their feet, smelly socks and underwear molded to their wet bodies, and constant rubbing of wet clothes caused the softened skin to peel and bleed.

Marines weren't the only ones suffering. The Japanese losses had been heavy, but their main units were intact and on the Shuri line. Their commanders were confident, and the desire among them was growing for a counterattack.

General Shepherd selected the Twenty-second Regiment of his Sixth Division to spearhead a drive across the Asa Kawa. The river was rising, and rain was still falling. The only good news that day, May 8, was that Germany had surrendered, VE Day. A typical marine reaction was, "What else is new?"

When the troops tried to cross the Asa Kawa on May 9, they found that the water was still rising, the river had a mud bottom that wouldn't support a truck or tank, and the bridges were all out. What to do? Call the engineers.

After dark, the engineers built a footbridge across the river. As soon as they had finished, two Japanese laden with explosives hurled themselves at the far end of the bridge, blowing it and themselves to smithereens.

That didn't stop the engineers. They took boats down the river to the sea and returned to the seawall, which they blew open. Backed by reinforcements, they returned to the river on the opposite bank and provided cover for the infantry to cross. At 10 P.M. they began building a Bailey bridge across the river. Tanks began to cross and attack the enemy immediately. Hand it to the Sixth Division Engineers.

Farther east, the Army Seventy-seventh was locked in combat at the Awacha Pocket. Then they developed a tactic of concentrating all their offensive efforts on a small area until they broke through and could provide flank fire for other units. They continued to use this successful device over and over.

Although kamikazes were unsuccessful in their primary mission to split U.S. sea and land forces, the Japanese air raids continued. The Sixth Chrysanthemum came at 0630 May 11, attacking the Americans' new base on Ie Shima as well as the Hagushi anchorages. Altogether, ninety-three Japanese planes were downed, but they sank or damaged four ships.

Also by May 11, the Tenth Army had four divisions abreast, striking south. From east to west, they were General Hodge's Twenty-fourth Corps consisting of the Ninety-sixth and Seventy-seventh Divisions; and General Geiger's Third Corps, composed of the First and Sixth Marine Divisions.

The Ninty-sixth faced Conical Hill; the Seventy-seventh, Shuri Castle; the First Marines, Dakeshi and Wanna ridges and their valleys; the Sixth Marines, Sugar Loaf Hill and Naha.

Fighting was fierce on all fronts as the Tenth Army faced off against the best defense the Japanese could muster. Here's just one account of the fierceness of Japanese resistance on Sugar Loaf Hill.

Sugar Loaf, the strongest of the Japanese defenses, consisted of three hills on an oblong ridge about fifty feet high. It was protected on the left rear by Half Moon Hill and on the right by Horseshoe Hill, both bristling with mortars. Gunners from Shuri Heights could also fire on Sugar Loaf.

When the Sixth Division's Third Battalion, twenty-two marines under Lieutenant Colonel Woodhouse, reached Sugar Loaf Hill, he had only forty exhausted men left from two companies, F and G, and they were running out of supplies. Again and again, he sent his marines against the hill, each time facing murderous fire from automatic weapons, knee mortars, grenade launchers, and artillery. Woodhouse requested more troops, but was told to keep up the attack. He sent F Company up for the second time under an artillery smoke screen. They were stopped at the base of the hill. Woodhouse sent twenty-six more men to them with supplies.

It was getting dark when Major Henry A. Courtney Jr., Battalion Executive Officer, called his remaining men together.

"We have to reach the top of the hill tonight, or we'll get picked off one by one in the morning," he explained. Then he called for volunteers. The silence was stifling, but the men knew he spoke the truth.

As Rusty Golar looked from eye to eye, some men looked back, some looked down, some fumbled with their weapons.

"I hate to sound like a guy in a dime novel," he began, " but what the hell did we come here for?" That broke the restraints; all volunteered.

Throwing grenades, the brave fighters charged the hill. The barrage of fire that they faced can only be imagined. And as they approached the top of the hill, a barrage of grenades came rolling down toward them.

Finally, they reached the hilltop and dug in for a night of constant shelling and counterattacks. Only twenty-five survived. Major Courtney was killed instantly by a mortar burst. He received the Medal of Honor posthumously.

As marines pressed against the Shuri line, the Japanese exploited a weakness that they had discovered. When darkness approached, marines would stop fighting and dig in for the night. During this period of twilight, the Japanese could infiltrate groups to wreak havoc among the Americans, who were preoccupied with preparations for the night.

The marines were learning from Japanese tactics, too. The Japanese would fire on approaching enemy from concealed caves on hillsides, then retreat through tunnels to the reverse side of the hill and lob mortar shells and artillery fire on approaching marines from their protected positions. Leathernecks learned that if they could cross the ridge and lay down fire from both sides of the hill, they could trap the Japanese in their caves. Armed with flamethrowers, grenades, and satchel charges, the marines would then seal the caves.

As the U.S. Tenth Army battered the Japanese Thirty-second Army, advances were slow and uneven. Combat varied from hand-to-hand to long-range shelling from ships and artillery. So much ammunition and so many supplies were used on the Shuri stronghold that extra supplies had to be delivered from the ships to the Hagushi dumps.

The hard land fighting for Okinawa was now in earnest.

Chapter 19

RECON CROSSES THE ASA KAWA

Frazzled and tired, the guard detail dismounted from the trucks and headed for a Seabee shower and bunks. Sergeant Tabb stopped them.

"Grab your gear and get back on the trucks; we're heading South," he yelled. "Full packs, everyone. We're moving out."

"My eyes feel like sand was in them," complained Herb Walker.

"How the hell we gonna sleep on a truck?" asked Wampler.

Grumbling, the Recon guards shouldered their heavy packs and scrambled to the long bench seats on each side of the truck bed. Someone's rifle clunked against the helmet of John Winn.

"You sonofabitch!" he yelled, but when he turned to see who was to blame he couldn't identify the culprit.

"Settle down," I said. "It was an accident."

As the trucks roared along, the men jostled but kept quiet. They marveled at changes that had occurred since they landed here earlier.

"Hey, look at the dogfaces!" screamed Sweetpee above the roar of the trucks.

"Bow-wow!"

"Woof, woof!"

"Owoohoo!" howled another, followed by the baying of a fox-hound.

Hollow-eyed army infantry were heading north, straggling on both sides of the road. They looked beat.

"What's it like down there? Couldn't you guys lick those little yellow-bellies?

"You'll find out," a soldier shouted.

"Keep it down," calmed Mac, "can't you see everybody's armed?"

"Eat our dust!" shouted a marine.

"That's enough!" said Mac in an angry voice, as he stood.

The trucks moved between the lines of soldiers and the men were quiet.

"Look at the equipment piled up on that beach!"

"See what they've done to Kadena? They've Americanized it." Buildings were up and planes were everywhere, some parked, others moving. Jeeps and trucks roared by in a steady stream.

"Gawd Almighty, you'd think we're in downtown Chicago," said a gawking marine.

"Wow! They've even got a USO."

"For the pilots, not us bastards."

The comments turned somber as the trucks passed a cemetery with rows and rows of perfectly spaced white crosses. There was foreboding in the air.

The guards perked up when the trucks stopped and they joined other members of the Recon Company.

There were a lot of hellos and handshakes. And more than one newcomer wanted to know what it was like on the front. We were assigned an area and began to dig in when we were summoned for an urgent work party.

Grimy with dust, weary, and sleepy, Mac's platoon moved in a group to company headquarters.

"Board those trucks!" said a sergeant. "We have to unload a Bailey Bridge down by the Asa Kawa."

"Hold on while I get my helmet and rifle," I said, turning to retrieve them.

"No! It's urgent. We need you men on the trucks now."

The engines started and the trucks began to move. Men jumped on, or were pulled on.

"I feel naked," said Jim Smith, running his fingers through his mop of red hair.

In a few minutes, we reached the Sixth Engineering Battalion.

Dusk was settling in. An eager sergeant directed us to the bridge sections. We began to load them on the truck. Some parts were very heavy, taking ten or fifteen men to load them.

"Take it to the river and unload it," said the sergeant. Then he turned to other trucks that were being loaded with bridge parts.

I counted a dozen men on our truck, not including myself.

"Wish I'd stayed behind," I told Sweetpee. "Thirteen is a helluva unlucky number."

Along the way, we are amazed at the battlefield destruction. Tanks and trucks had been knocked out by enemy explosives. Some were still barely out of the road. Trucks creept along in the twilight. Shell holes scarred the roadway and nearby rice paddies with saucer-shaped pocks. Among them sprawled dead Japanese. The truck pulled out at a wide space to let returning jeeps pass. They were loaded with marine casualties.

"Whatinhell are we getting into?" moaned a marine.

"Damn, I wish I had a helmet," said Murphy.

The trucks stopped near the river, and we got off to unload the bridge sections.

"Hey, look on the ground," said Sweetpee. "There are guns and helmets all over."

Each man scrambled for a weapon and a helmet left by a fallen comrade, but most weapons were broken and damaged beyond firing.

"Some outfit caught hell here, didn't they?" Sweetpee whispered to me.

The air screeched. "Take cover! Take cover!" I couldn't see who was giving orders, but I recognized Mac's voice.

Men scattered like rats, running in all directions. The screaming shell went over our heads and hit the beach where the river emptied into the sea. Against the skyline, a geyser of water was rising. Men stood to see.

"Incoming mail!" someone shouted. The terrifying screeches came steadily now, one after another. And the explosions were getting closer. They were in the rice paddy, moving toward the road and the trucks.

"Look!" said Sweetpee, "someone's been hit." Two men ran by with a stretcher. "Oh, Lordee, more have been wounded." There were screams of pain.

"Corpsman! Corpsman!" The appeal came first from one direction, then another.

After the shelling ceased, we moved back to unload the truck.

"How many were hit, Sergeant?"

"I heard about a dozen, but none from our group."

One of the trucks was turned over in the roadside ditch. We strained to right it, then a bulldozer was brought in to set it on its wheels. The heavy bridge span was reloaded.

It was dark when we finished reloading the truck, but it was still about five hundred yards down the shellholed road to the Asa Kawa bank. The road was possibly mined, too.

"Several of you men lead the truck," the sergeant directed. "Walk slow, and move your feet around for shell holes, mines or debris. These trucks have to get through."

The trucks crept forward to the riverbank. Flares were shooting up everywhere, blinking on and off like fireflies. The hills across the river belonged to the Japanese.

"I'm tired enough to drop," said Sweetpee.

"Keep unloading," came the sergeant's voice. He was helping with the work.

One hour. Two hours. Three hours later, the trucks were unloaded and began backing out.

"Wow!" screamed Ski, as an enemy shell rumbled overhead. More followed. A shell exploded in the rice field. The next one slammed in the soft soil of the paddy but failed to detonate. Mud and water splattered on me as I dove into the roadside ditch. Someone jumped in on top of me. I reached for my K-bar before I realized it was back at camp. I hoped it wasn't a Jap. Then I realized the man had a death grip on my leg. He was squeezing it so hard it hurt, and the guy was shaking like a leaf. I could feel his heart beating like a trip hammer.

"Move out! Move out! Pass the word," shouted the sergeant.

Sweetpee and I were together as we ran for the trucks. Each time a shell roared by or a flare burst overhead, we threw ourselves onto the road. The shelling was farther away, back toward camp.

"Thank God I can breathe again," said Sweetpee, puffing. Behind us we could hear someone sick, retching. "Man, I didn't realize how tired I am until now," I said. "If it wasn't for those confounded shells, I'd sit down right here."

The trucks found a place to turn around, loaded up with bushed marines, and headed back to camp. We didn't attempt to dig fox-holes; we just lay on the ground and slept.

I woke to see men stirring.

"We got the day off," chortled Sweetpee. "C'mon, let's go take a bath." We bathed by dipping water from a well with our helmets and pouring the water over each other. We settled down to writing letters home. Other men were doing similar activities, as well as washing clothes and cleaning equipment.

At dusk, condition red was flashed, indicating that enemy planes had been spotted on radar.

Lefty Smith came running up to where we were watching the air battle.

"Hey, look at those two Jap planes," he exclaimed. Two kamikaze pilots had turned their planes into a dive toward anchored ships. Tracer bullets swarmed toward them like bees to honey. As the planes closed on their targets, more anti-aircraft fire opened up. The sky was literally full of fireworks. Flack was so thick that at times the planes couldn't be seen. Suddenly, one plane flared in a fireball and was gone. The other roared on, clipping the ship it had targeted, but the ship remained afloat.

I sat on the ground. "As soon as I recover, I'm gonna finish my foxhole and turn in," I said. "I don't know how much more of this I can handle. If a Jap comes along and wishes to share my foxhole, he's welcome. I'm too tired to care."

Zing! A shell fragment ripped through Chronis' shelter while he was on the radio, missing his head by inches. The earth began to quake from artillery fire. "Thank goodness we're firing back," said Chronis as he looked at daylight through the ripped shelter.

I looked at the hole and heard someone say. "An enemy shell got two men in Engineering. Killed one, and the other isn't expected to live."

A marine came in as I was reporting. "Shelling and bombing is so impersonal," he said. You feel so helpless to defend yourself—don't you agree, Ozark?"

"Yeah, long-distance killing has never interested me. Talk about cruel, inhuman fighting. You drop a bomb on a target you don't even see. Maybe you see a distant explosion, but not the women and children you kill and maim. Blasting a ship is a little better, because you expect to kill the enemy."

"I prefer personal fighting," the marine continued. "If you shoot a Jap, you see him fall. If you stick him, you can look him in the eye and see pain and the wild fear of death. You hear the death gurgles and gasps, and you know you're exacting 'pay back' time for the death of your buddies. *Semper Fi*, I say, to the friends I've lost."

"Don't you think that's a little extreme, to watch them die like that?" I asked.

"Many marines have been killed by supposedly dying or dead Japanese. My motto is, 'If they don't stink, stick 'em!'" He pulled out his K-bar and made a stabbing motion.

"Someone once said war is controlled chaos," I mused. "Chaos leads to extinction, but controlled chaos offers a safety line. A defeated enemy can retreat into peace, although it may be tumultuous. I think it's chaos with you, live or die."

"If I had my way, I'd prefer being one of the coastal watchers," said Preacher, who had arrived unnoticed.

"Why's that?" asked Chronis.

"They call them Ferdinands," he explained, "you know, like the cartoon bull: Smell the flowers, but don't fight."

"Move out!" It was Mac calling.

"Assemble over here!" yelled Manion. "Lieutenant Autry wants to talk to you."

As soon as the Recon men gathered, Autry told us that we had a new assignment, to guard the seawall against an attack from the sea. "Get your gear and be ready to load into the trucks in ten minutes," he ordered.

Evidence of a terrible battle lay all around as the trucks approached their destination. Articles of clothing, both marine and Japanese, were scattered about, as well as broken firearms, cartridge shells, ammo, and K-ration boxes. There was a line of zigzagging muddy trenches. The trucks crept along to avoid mines, coral chunks, and holes caused by artillery explosions.

The air began to rumble and whistle as enemy artillery zeroed in on the trucks. Men flushed from them to seek shelter without a word from the officers. The ground shook as we cowered from flying shrapnel.

When the shelling stopped, Recon counted their losses: one truck, several dead or wounded, including a Japanese Naval Officer.

"Where'd he come from?" I wondered. The man died with a grenade in his hand.

"He must have been hiding here somewhere, probably waiting to blow up the last truck passing," I said. The Japanese was lying face down, so I turned him over with my foot.

"He's still bleeding," I observed. Then I added, "We better search him for Intelligence." Both Ace Brown and I knelt and began searching. I found a small silk Japanese flag with a beautiful red rising sun in its center. Ace saw something glitter. It was the handle of a small dagger.

"Look, Ozark! An instant hara-kiri knife."

Hearing rifle fire, we abandoned the search.

"Where's it coming from?"

"That tall building above the seawall."

"What's he shooting at?"

"Us!"

Mac and a few others had come up to see the dead naval officer. Some of our outfit slipped away to a nearby cave to hunt souvenirs. A few found Japanese rifles and flags, and one found a sword. PFC Norman Slattery wasn't so lucky. He was gut shot. The next day we got the report: Slattery was dead.

Chapter Twenty

SHURI–NAHA–YONABARU LINE CRACKED

It took four days of relentless marine charges to hold Sugar Loaf Hill, but on May 17 General Shepherd sent the Twenty-ninth Regiment along a shallow groove in the terrain between Sugar Loaf and Half Moon Hills, choking off Sugar Loaf and causing it to fall.

The Fourth Marines replaced the spent Twenty-ninth, and during the next four days Sugar Loaf was secured. It cost 2,662 marines killed and half again as many battle-fatigued.

Over on the East China Sea coast, other elements of the Striking Sixth Marine Division were poised to take the capitol city of Naha, but Japanese artillery from Shuri Heights stopped them. Naha would have to wait.

Meanwhile, the First Marine Division took Wana Draw after fierce hand-to-hand fighting that followed tank incursions.

Marines tried some innovations to rout the dug-in Japanese. In one instance, two platoons lugged fifty-five-gallon drums of napalm to a hilltop with the intention of splitting them open and rolling them down the steep reverse slope upon the Japanese, then setting the fuel afire with white phosphorus grenades. The drums were so heavy and difficult to handle that only three were brought to the hilltop. The plan then went as hoped until an enemy trench caught the barrels before they reached their objective. The idea had limited success. Finally, the reverse slopes of Wana were bathed in fire by flamethrowers, roasting and suffocating Japanese soldiers in caves and pillboxes.

Hill by hill, the Allied juggernaut was crushing the opposition, but the enemy wasn't capitulating yet. Many skirmishes seesawed in fierce eyeball-to-eyeball fighting. Often, the enterprising Japanese were both above the marines on the hilltop as well as below them in caves. Using their knowledge of the terrain and the inclement weather, the enemy often won. At times it appeared that the invasion forces would have to settle for a stalemate.

Here's the way the battle progressed from May 10.

Fresh American army troops moved on line to make progress where exhausted Seventh Division Infantry had stalled. The Japanese continued to fall back near Conical Hill and to reinforce their depleted numbers with less effective Boeitai, navy, supply, and service personnel.

However, the Japanese had a lot of fight left in them from their fortified defensive positions. For example, they pinned down an advancing marine battalion so effectively that they couldn't remove their dead without a smoke screen.

Defense in the Awacha Draw was eventually overpowered by flamethrowing tanks that washed the steep terrain with a wall of fire, followed by a shelling barrage from supporting tanks, and finally by troops following tanks to eliminate the enemy flushed from caves and fortifications.

At last, the Awacha Pocket was cleared on May 11. The next strong point the invaders faced was Dakeshi Ridge. As marines approached, the Japanese mounted a fierce counterattack. This gave way to another line of defense in depth on Wana Ridge. But before the First Marines could attack, they had to be resupplied by air. Not only was ammunition low, but they needed food, water, and medical items.

Meanwhile, the Japanese were preparing to make a stand at Wana Draw, and Dakeshi Ridge was still under contention, with Japanese holding the reverse slope, the location of the Sixty-fourth Brigade's command post under the command of Tadashi Kojo.

Knowing that the U.S. Navy usually took a break at 1700 hours,

Kojo left his cave with a few men on this mid-May evening to assess his situation. His Japanese training led him to assume that his commander, Colonel Masaru Yoshida, knew if he needed replacements and would assign personnel as needed. Kojo also relied on his training and experience as an officer to show confidence to his few remaining troops. There was none of the sharing of information that occurs between officers in command of American troops. Kojo merely reported his situation to Colonel Yoshida.

Kojo recalled that he had been ordered to pull back a few hundred yards on May 10, but he knew his forces were inflicting great injury on the Americans. He didn't know how frustrating it was for them to be stalled.

The Japanese attrition was beyond comprehension. The Twenty-second Regiment had begun battle with 3,300 men; now they had 300. And they were exhausted. They moved in a daze. Kojo didn't have enough men to supply ammunition and fire his guns. Yet he must have felt that divine intervention had saved him. He and his medical officer were contemplating killing themselves when American tanks approached their headquarters, but it began to rain so profusely that the tanks turned back.

The end came on May 16, when part of their line of defense caved in. The Americans poured through, slaughtering the remaining Japanese, who were so bushed that they became aware of what was happening only moments before they died from bullets or hand grenade fragments.

Kojo was also surprised, but he escaped through phosphorus smoke to a cave that had two entrances, one a hatch reached by a ladder. A few men were still with him; the others were dead.

Some wounded men were already in the cave. They were crying out and moaning in pain. Kojo advised them to be quiet when he heard enemy voices outside.

One of Kojo's officers could take no more. He turned to Kojo and said, "I'm going to die here." At that moment, Kojo weakened and agreed to join him. Meanwhile, the Americans above were shouting for them to come out. Kojo knew that a grenade or explosive charge dropped from above would kill or wound them.

"*Shiawase*," he said, meaning that he was content or fulfilled. "I have fought honorably, and this is the end." He placed the barrel of his pistol to his head and pressed his finger against the trigger. At that moment, a satchel charge hurled through the hatch exploded, ripping the pistol from Kojo's hand and knocking him unconscious.

When he regained his senses, Kojo thought no more about suicide. He checked around and found that the other officer and a private were all who lived through the explosion. He asked them to leave with him after dark, but the officer refused, saying he wanted to die there.

Some time after the American voices could no longer be heard, Kojo and the private approached the entrance to the cave. It had been sealed. They clawed at the dirt with their hands. A long time later, they crawled out of their living tomb like moles. Running from shell hole to shell hole, they made their way down the hill, until a American sentry saw them and began firing. He missed as they dove into a shell hole. Later they crawled out, and, dodging the American soldiers, made their way to Colonel Yoshida's command post.

Yoshida knew that Kojo's position had been overrun, and he was surprised and delighted to see him.

Yoshida expressed regrets that he had placed Kojo in such a vulnerable position, saying he had had no choice. Yoshida then congratulated Kojo for a brave defense. Physically exhausted and mentally thrilled at the compliment, Kojo fought desperately to hold back his tears.

Captain Tadashi Kojo had pulled his forces from Kochi back to Shuri for reinforcement as the Seventy-seventh Army Division slammed into Shuri with its fortified headquarters, Shuri Castle.

The Seventh U.S. Army Division crushed Yonabaru, and the Sixth Marine Division was poised to jump on Naha.

The American battle commanders were now aware of the value of reverse-slope defense to the Japanese, so they trained the navy's big guns on these areas, pounding them mercilessly around the clock.

Dick and Oboe Hills were taken. Conical Hill, highpoint on Razorback Ridge, took more time. The rough ground meant that armored bulldozers had to prepare roads before tanks could be brought in.

On May 14, an attempt to break through the Wana–Naha line of defense was unsuccessful. Eighteen tanks were lost. Naval gunfire, artillery, and rockets pounded the area, but the enemy held.

On the west coast, the Sixth Marine Division was attacking the north bank on the Asato Gawa under fire from across the river. The Japanese were trying to hold their positions at all costs, as Lieutenant Colonel Woodhouse learned at Sugar Loaf. The pressure was buckling Ushijima's battleline, but it was evident to U.S field commanders that their troops were in for a prolonged tank-infantry assault.

It was now mid-May, and the navy declared the amphibious phase of the Okinawan operation complete. Command was shifted to General Buckner for the land phase of the battle.

Chapter 21

RECON GUARDS
THE RIGHT FLANK

The strain of combat was taking its toll. Herb Walker had left for the hospital that morning. He was suffering combat fatigue. Corporal Bill Dawson had also turned himself in a few days before. We waved to his squad as he left in a jeep. We'd miss the "Dawson Hour" and his love letters.

There was plenty of nervous trepidation in the air. Enemy shells were falling all around.

We walked across rubble that once was a village and boarded trucks. I was lucky to get a seat, but my heavy wet pack was hanging over the side of the truck bed. Shelling had left destruction everywhere. We went up a hillside where some Twenty-second marines were blasting tombs that Japanese had been using as pillboxes. We passed a dead Japanese major. His blood hadn't congealed yet.

"What happened?" we asked as we slowly passed by.

"He attempted to throw a grenade, but we got him first."

"Fire in the hole!" someone yelled. An explosion rocked the truck. The truck moved on in a hail of falling debris.

We passed a pandana thicket. It had been scorched by

flamethrowers. Ahead were freshly dug foxholes. The ground was littered with empty ammo boxes, K-ration boxes, and .30-caliber bullet casings. We crept down a steep, narrow cliff road to a flat area near the seawall where we took positions in zigzag trenches dug by others. An enemy shell screeched through the air and exploded nearby. That was our welcome as seawall guards. We expected more shells. None came. We waited. The silence was excruciating

Fuller Curtis and I took a pair of fieldglasses up a tomb-decked hill for a view of Naha. An outcropping of flat limestone rocks covered the crest, surrounded by brush. There was evidence that it had been occupied by the enemy as an observation post.

"Look over there!" shouted Curtis, pointing as he grabbed the binoculars. We watched as pimples of dust rose from the explosions on a distant hill. First only a few, then many. The whole hilltop began to seethe and boil in flying dirt and smoke. It sounded like a whole pack of mortars had been set off. *Whomp! Whomp! Whomp!* As we watched the distant shelling, beyond the skeletal remains of Naha, the sound of exploding mortars and artillery shells continued to bang our ears. First only a few explosions, then many. Soon the entire hill was obscured by a cloud of dust, smoke, and debris.

The shelling stopped, and gradually the cloud drifted away from the exposed and denuded hill.

"Man, they really blasted that hill," said Sweetpee Van Heuvelen. He, Don Wampler, and Bob Phillips had joined us.

"This is the second battle we've watched from a distance," I said. Remember Ie Shima?"

"Yeah, that's where Ernie Pyle bought the farm," added Sweetpee.

We noticed that the hill really was shaped something like a loaf of bread.

"That hill is as bare as a baby's butt," said Wampler.

"There it goes again," said Curtis, still watching through binoculars.

As we watched, the earth boiled and bubbled on the hill. Soon there was a continuous, thunderous roar. Then the shelling stopped, and we could hear the firecracker popping of small arms fire.

About fifteen minutes later, there was another round of shelling. All of us except Curtis were watching from behind stones and bushes. He was standing fearlessly, watching through the glasses, when there was an unusually large explosion on the hill.

"What was that—logs?" I asked. I had seen something fly through the air.

"No, Japanese!" said Curtis.

There was a roar in the sky above us, and we crouched lower. It was one of our planes.

"Is he going to crash?" asked Wampler.

As we watched, the plane dropped a bomb on a high-rise building in Naha. It was a skeleton of a building with arched windows. More planes followed dropping bombs and firing rockets. Some ricocheted out the open windows without exploding. The strong girders continued to stand, with chunks of concrete hanging from the steel frame.

Finally, a lone plane flew over, and we could see leaflets fluttering down.

"Wonder what that is?" said Wampler.

"You can bet it ain't toilet paper," said Curtis. Then he said, "Show's over." We moved down the hillside path toward the seawall, marveling at what we had seen.

Soon it was chow time. We took our food to a large rock in the sea, just beyond the wall, to avoid the large green blowflies that swarmed over dead bodies. Some dead Japanese were so full of maggots that they appeared to be alive.

Harry Sortal, Jim Wheeler, and I watched the sun grow larger, then melt and run into the sea.

Enemy shelling started again. During a lull, we heard the dreaded call: "Corpsman! Corpsman!"

"Damn," said Doc Redinger under his breath. He was examining the shredded left arm of Lefty Smith, the artist.

"How bad is it?" someone asked.

"He'll never paint again," replied Doc.

Another call. "Hey, Doc, over here."

Lieutenant Newton had been hit. A shell fragment had struck his back below the base of the neck. Sergeant Manion burned his hands removing the fragment from a gash nearly ten inches long. It cauterized the flesh, preventing serious bleeding. Both Smith and Newton were evacuated.

Since we were at the seawall to prevent the enemy from landing by boat, we were very interested to hear that enemy small boats had been active. The navy had probably sunk them. We had noticed great beams of searchlights playing across the water during the night.

Naha, just south of us, was taking a tremendous naval shelling and aerial bombing. Our stomachs were still in knots.

We were in trouble. Enemy shells had cut our supply and communication lines on the hilltop road.

I bravely crossed the seawall and threw my dirty dungarees into the incoming tide to wash them. Later I had to wade into the surf to retrieve them. I spread them on a rock to dry.

Shelling had increased, so we stayed in our holes except for necessity trips.

I was worried about one of my buddies. He seemed to be digging his way back to the States. He was offended when I questioned him.

"In boot camp they told us a defensive position is never finished." He kept on shoveling.

It was now dark, and an enemy gun opened on us from across the bay. We dove into our holes, which caused minor injuries.

"Halt!" yelled Vernon "Lucky" Murphy, a radio man from Virginia. "What's the password?" The challenged man continued to walk. Lucky noted that he was wearing marine dungarees, but he wasn't responding. "Halt, or I'll shoot!"

The Japanese soldier turned, and in one motion cracked the firing pin of a grenade against his helmet and threw it hard at Murph. It hit him in the head and knocked him down. Miraculously, it didn't explode.

Sergeant Manion was in a nearby foxhole and heard the commotion. He grabbed his carbine and turned just as the enemy soldier approached. He fired, but the Japanese ran into the brush and disappeared.

After dark it became quiet, and the man on watch in Manion's foxhole heard moaning in the brush. The guard woke Manion.

"Hear that?" Manion heard.

"I can't stand that; we've got to do something. He's driving me crazy."

"Alert the others I'm coming out."

"Man coming out," said the sentry. "Pass the word."

Manion called for a flare. In the glimmering light, he dashed out of the foxhole; three rapid shots were fired and he was back in the foxhole, long before the flare had burned out. The moaning had stopped.

Murphy returned from the hospital with a beautiful shiner. The eye was discolored for several days. He had to tolerate numerous jokes.

Enemy shelling started early, and the men of Recon kept to the trenches again.

I noticed that my buddy was deep in a hole, wearing a helmet and still digging. He had sandbagged the sides of his hole and was attempting to cover it with sandbags. He hadn't come out for water or to eat.

I was on my way to give Buckheit, Winn, and Walker the password for that night, when *Wham!* The earth shook. The three were under a low outcropping near a tomb. It was small and crudely built over a natural cavity. *Wham!* The exploding shell was less than one hundred feet from me. Winn yelled for us to get into the tomb. He squeezed in, but there was only room for one. Still he kept insisting that the rest of us join him. He didn't realize there was no room for us. After the shelling, he was embarrassed, but we didn't let him forget it.

As night fell, the enemy hit us with a fusillade of mortar and artillery shells. A thick, pungent cloud of smoke and dust enveloped us. Flares looked red in the cloud, but gave little light.

Asa Kawa River rice paddies. Shell holes are where Japanese were trying to blow the bridge erected by marines. Some of us were called to help with the pontoon bridge before we had time to collect our gear, including helmets. When the shelling started, we hit the deck. One marine, I never knew who, squeezed my leg so tight I thought he'd stop the circulation. Several died before we completed the bridge.

Submarine pen and ship off coast of Okinawa.

*Battlewagon in the distance off Okinawan shore. Big boomers would
cause the earth to shake.*

Marine shanty town under the brow of a pointed hill.

(Above) Torrential rains made MUD! Casualties could not be transported, the dead could not be buried, and the living could not be fed. (Left) "Roast 'em out" was sometimes the only way to protect your rear when the Japanese hid in cave bunkers.

Muddy walk through the rice fields.

Chapter 22

THE JAPANESE RETREAT

A new enemy took over the battlefield in early May. Sprinkles and intermittent rain quickly became deluges. Torrential rains for the next two weeks averaged an inch every day, but it didn't fall by averages.

Trucks sank to their axles where they stood; tanks nearly buried themselves. Infantry stalled. Taking a step meant the risk of losing your shoe or stripping off the sole. Rifles were slung barrel down and cleaned frequently to prevent a misfire or explosion if mud clogged the muzzle. Dungarees became camouflaged with mud. Sleep became impossible.

As rain fell amid star shells and flares, marines did what they did best—improvised. Boards, poles, and doors from vacant buildings were at a premium for building shelters. They were covered with ponchos, tent halves, or anything that would turn water.

Matches were useless and cigarette lighters valued. The only dry place for cigarettes and letters from home was in the helmet liner, tucked above the straps. Pencils and pens swelled and split apart. Wet feet shriveled, blistered, and bled through muddy socks inside shoes. Pocket books and paper turned to pulp. Body rashes developed and spread. K-ration crackers turned into inedible mush.

As foxholes filled and streams gushed, we soaked marines cursed the rain, wondering why we had to tolerate such misery while the Japanese rested warm and dry in their caves.

Regardless of the weather, the Americans had to cut off the Shuri stronghold. To do this we had to control the blocking Ozata hills to protect our rear and flank.

This was accomplished by the Army 184th Infantry in a surprise move. Starting at 0200 from Gaja Ridge, they moved silently and quickly through Yonabaru Village and by dawn had taken up positions on top of the first hill.

The surprise was so complete that Japanese were shot as they came out of their caves at daylight. Apparently, they had thought that Americans would not attack without tanks. Having seized the advantage, the Seventh Division exploited it by taking other strategic hills.

Along the eastern Shuri front, the Fourth Marines forged ahead to the Asato Gawa, despite the sluggish progress in heavy mud. Patrols crossed the river and probed some two hundred yards into Naha, meeting light opposition.

The marines made plans to cross the river in force next day, although the water was high.

Where the army units rubbed against the Shuri line in the middle, progress stalled. Much-needed artillery and motorized equipment was mired in deep mud—some pieces swallowed by the bottomless morass. Lakes formed around gun placements. The infantry, handicapped by relentless rain and little support, wavered. The feared stalemate was at hand.

Added difficulty came as the distance between supply lines and troops widened. Heavy storm clouds prevented air drops. Exhausted men were pressed into service as human bearers of ammo, food, and water.

Nature had stopped the Americans when the Japanese could not.

On the East China Sea coast, the Sixth Recon Company probed across the Asato Gawa in a night patrol and determined that the area along the south bank was not heavily fortified, so General Shepherd decided to make a daylight infantry crossing without tank support when low tide was in the river.

Japanese in fortified tombs on the hills facing the river stopped the advance with mortars and machine guns.

Meanwhile, pouring rain runoff had raised the Asato into a raging torrent. While engineers struggled to build a bridge, men stood in chest-deep water, passing supplies hand-to-hand across the stream.

Japanese commanders, foreseeing the disastrous results if the Seventh Infantry advanced through the Naha–Yonabaru Valley, decided to put every available man to the area's defense.

When the army attempted to advance, they immediately felt the stiffened resistance that ended in an enemy counterattack on the clear night of May 24.

This effort was augmented by kamikazes, who either damaged or sunk nine American ships. The navy casualty list included 38 KIA, 183 WIA, and 60 MIA. The Japanese lost 150 planes.

As a part of their aerial attack, the Japanese made a bomber raid on Yontan and Kadena airfields. Eleven of the bombers were shot down by airfield anti-aircraft, and some abandoned their mission, but one broke through the curtain of fire. It was a twin-engine bomber carrying about fourteen Japanese air raiders.

The plane came screaming and careening down a runway, flipped over, and plowed into a fuel dump.

"There was instant daylight," as one observer described it. When the plane stopped skidding, a half-dozen men dashed out with guns blazing, grenades and satchel explosives at the ready. The other Japanese in the plane were dead.

Men stationed around the airfield panicked. Gunfire, explosives, fires, yelling—it was pandemonium. Planes were blown up. Both enemy and friendlies were shot. It was daylight before the last Japanese was killed.

When airfield defenders assessed their losses, they found that eight American aircraft had been destroyed and twenty-four damaged. Two fuel dumps were burned. Two marines had been killed in the hailstorm of bullets and eighteen were wounded.

The failure of the attack did not lessen the resolve of the Japanese to hold the Shuri line. Any attempt on our part to advance encountered fierce, even fanatical action.

Conical Hill, a part of the Japanese line of defense, was to the Seventy-seventh and Ninty-sixth Army Divisions what Sugar Loaf Hill was to the Sixth Marine Division.

Evidence of the fierce fighting in May was the number of marines and corpsmen who earned Medals of Honor—nine of the thirteen awarded during the entire campaign. Major Henry Courtney Jr. was one of the nine.

The army, too, had hero medal winners during the terrible Shuri fighting. One was so unusual that it deserves mention.

Pacifist Desmond Doss, a Seventh-Day Adventist who honored his country's call, served his fellow soldiers as a medic. This was his way of fighting without harming another human—just the opposite.

During the battle on Maeda Escarpment, at the front door of Ushijima's line, PFC Doss rescued many wounded GIs under fire without regard for his own safety. He would attend their wounds, drag them to a ledge, then lower them to safety in a sling he had rigged.

He was so fearless and lucky that some soldiers believed he was invincible and tried to stay near him. For his bravery beyond the call of duty, Doss was awarded the Medal of Honor.

But the story doesn't end there. On May 11, while the Seventy-seventh was fighting to take Chocolate Drop–Wart Hill–Flattop Hill, Doss's luck ran out. An enemy mortar shell wounded both his legs. He dressed his own wounds and waited a long time to be rescued. On the way to the aid station, another mortar attack drove off the stretcher bearers.

Lying on the stretcher, he heard a call for help. He crawled to the suffering soldier and treated his wound, then crawled back to his stretcher, where he was hit again, fracturing his arm. He managed to crawl to the aid station on his own for treatment and recovery.

Back at the Asato Gawa, Sixth Division Engineers were fighting high water, heavy weather, and enemy shelling in their attempt to span the river with a Bailey Bridge. The break in the storm on May 24 allowed the bridge to be completed and tanks to cross, but they were quickly mired in the mud. Then the rains began again.

Once across the Asato, the marines found themselves divided by a north–south canal, about twenty yards wide, connecting the Asato with the Kokuba Gawa. The Fourth Marines were on the east side of the canal and the Sixth Recon on the west.

The Japanese tried to mount a strong counterattack on the Fourth Marines during the night, but the enemy activity was noticed early by the marines, who called in artillery, dispersing Japanese troops.

Rain fell in torrents. One unit of the Army Ninty-sixth was asked to report on its progress. They replied that troops on the forward slopes were sliding down, and those on the reverse slopes were sliding back.

The First and Fifth Marines made progress toward Machisi, driving a wedge between Naha and Shuri and threatening an encirclement of Shuri.

Terrible weather continued to reduce visibility, but on May 26 marines noticed unusual activity south of Shuri. No scout planes had been up because of the weather, but one was now sent up from the battlewagon *New York*. The pilot reported as many as four thousand troops and vehicles choking the roads south of Shuri.

In fact, General Ushijima foresaw the threat to his headquarters at Shuri before May 22 and had called a staff meeting on that day to decide where they should move. Some wanted the Chinen Peninsula, jutting into the Pacific. It offered great natural defense but lacked roads for movement of equipment and supplies. The Kiyamu Peninsula on the southern tip of Okinawa had natural defensive terrain in the Yayu-Yuza Escarpment, and it was accessible by roads. Furthermore, it was an area with numerous large caves and tunnels sufficient to accommodate Ushijima's remaining Thirty-second Army. Some of the caves already held arms and stored supplies. Kiyamu was chosen.

First, Ushijima had to move his entire force to its new position. To do this, he reinforced his flanks. But he was too late on the west, where marines had rushed into Naha, encountering suicidal resistance. The Japanese counterattacked on the east flank, but the army held.

Under cover of rain and low clouds, nature helped as the Japanese retreated. Within minutes after the retreat was detected, about fifty corsairs from U.S. ships began strafing with guns and rockets in what was reported to be a "field day." Ground artillery within range joined the attack.

Aerial reconnaissance reported that the mud roads were littered with wrecked equipment, and they estimated more than five hundred enemy dead. But the attack wasn't over. During the night, artillery and NGF from the big ships continued to pound the roads. Marine General del Valle congratulated all units for their quick response when the "Japanese were caught with their kimonos down."

However, the Shuri defense was not yet broken. The army infantry lacked artillery support because of the mud, and all attempts to break the deadlock met with a wall of mortar and machine gun fire.

Sensing the Japanese retreat, General Buckner sent word to both army and marines to apply unrelenting pressure to prevent Ushijima from reestablishing his army in a new position.

The Sixth Marine Division moved into Naha and encountered little resistance as they pressed toward the Kokuba Estuary. On the east coast, the army, likewise, met only nominal resistance.

In support of the Japanese retreat, the eighth kamikaze attack hit the American fleet on May 27. A dozen ships were damaged or sunk. Losses were 52 KIA, 288 WIA, and 290 MIA. The Japanese lost more than 100 planes.

The attack did not alter the scheduled change in operations command. At midnight, Task Force Thirty-one replaced Task Force Fifty-one. General Buckner now reported directly to Admiral Nimitz. The men fighting on land didn't notice the change. Their problems were mud, more mud, and iron-willed Japanese protecting Ushijima's retreat.

On the evening of May 24 the USS *Mississippi*, with her fourteen-inch rifles, led an attack on the 300-acre Shuri Castle grounds. She was joined by the battleship *Colorado*, with sixteen-inch guns. Under almost continuous shelling, the twenty-foot-thick walls began to crumble on May 27.

Little noted at the time, the *Mississippi* was the second battleship named "Mississippi" to train its sights on Shuri Castle. In 1853 Commodore Matthew Perry had visited Okinawa on his fleet's ship, the *Mississippi*. At the time, one said how poor the Okinawans were and commented that they appeared to be a mouse in the eagle's (Japan's) talons. Now the talons were those of the American eagle.

The Sixth Recon had moved into Naha on May 28 when our commander, Major Anthony Walker, received a message of his new appointment from Lieutenant Colonel Victor Krulak: "You are hereby named acting Mayor of Naha. The appointment . . . carries all pay and emoluments accruing to the office . . . to be collected from Imperial Treasury."

On May 29 the army Seventy-seventh, designated to take Shuri Castle, was days away, facing the backbone of enemy resistance. At the same time, the First Marine Division broke out of its position and quickly topped Shuri Ridge. Shuri Castle lay straight ahead and commanded the area.

At this point, Lieutenant Colonel C. W. Shelburne requested permission from General del Valle to storm the castle. Because of the danger of a counterattack from the fortress, permission was granted. By mid-morning, the marines occupied Shuri Castle, although they barely avoided disaster. The army Seventy-seventh had scheduled a heavy artillery barrage and air attack on Shuri Castle. Preparations were complete, and the time had been set. Just minutes before the attack was to begin, word was received that marines were on the castle grounds. Frantic messages were sent out, barely in time to stop the assault.

One of the marines who attacked Shuri Castle was Captain Julius Dusenbury, leading Company A. His outfit fought mud and a party of Japanese defenders before they reached the castle. Dusenbury, from South Carolina as was General Buckner, had a private mission that he raced to complete.

He ran into the once beautiful and elegant courtyard. From that point, he could see a flagpole on the parapet. He ran up the parapet, removed his helmet as he raced along, and took out an American flag, which he quickly ran up the pole. It was the Stars and Bars of the Confederacy!

Chapter 23

RECON GOES TO
SUGAR LOAF HILL

"Hit the deck!" yelled Sergeant McDougal, as if he needed to say anything. Shells were exploding about 150 feet away.

"Chronis, get on your radio and tell that cockeyed artillery captain to lift his sights." It was the commander giving orders, and he was cussing mad. But the artillery spotter on the hill had seen the error and already made changes.

It was too late for George Taylor. A chunk of smoking shrapnel had burned through his shoe and buried itself in his foot. Doc Redinger helped the injured man away.

"What about the rest of us, Doc?" someone called out. "Taylor can make it on his own."

"I can only take care of one of you at a time, and this is George's turn," he replied.

Guard duty on the seawall was terrible. It was so dark that the sky didn't reflect light off the water, and the men just waited—listening and responding with their emotions. It began to rain, and the lapping of the waves began to sound like enemy voices. Were the Japanese trying another landing?

Sweetpee punched Jim Smith. "Red, wake up! I've got to talk to somebody or I'll go bananas."

"I'm not asleep. Good thing, too, or you'd be joining Taylor in the hospital, getting my rifle barrel extracted from your asshole."

The harmless threat didn't bother Sweetpee. In the silence that followed, the rain poured.

"I hate rain, mud, Japs, and this whole damned island," lamented the frustrated guard.

"You should have joined the navy," said Red.

"Crap! Sailors float on 'wet'."

"Guess you heard the navy made a fake small boat landing on Oroku Peninsula.

"Yeah, Red, now the navy; next it'll be the marines for the real thing. That's us!"

Sweetpee stiffened and fumbled with his poncho, trying to get his rifle from where he'd been keeping it dry. The hair on the nape of his neck stood from what he heard. That scream! Sounded like a woman right in front of him, on the lip of his foxhole. An explosion shook the earth.

Red, who had scrunched down, came up pawing for his weapon.

"What in God's name was that?" he yelled.

A flare burst and he peered out into the gloom. There was another scream, like a woman yelling in his ear. An explosion splattered mud in the foxhole. The makeshift poncho cover was swept away.

"Hellfire, Sweetpee, that's some kind of Jap shell."

"The bastards are shelling us with something new," observed Sweetpee.

"Sounded like a screaming mimi."

"What's a screaming mimi?"

"Hell, I don't know, but that's what it sounded like."

It was about noon the next day when Mac returned from headquarters.

"I've got some bad news, and some worse news. The bad news is those screaming shells you heard last night are eight-inch rockets, a new weapon the Japs are throwing at us. They're not very accurate—all the more reason to take cover when you hear one.

"The worse news is that John Sheffield, one of our replacements, was hit."

"Is he going to be okay?" asked an apprehensive Red. He had told me the day before that he had a feeling that someone was going to get it today, said if anything happened to him for me to contact his folks.

"He was decapitated by shrapnel during the shelling."

The rain, the heat, and the rotting dead Japanese brought hordes of flies. Big green blowflies were on everything. To eat, a soldier had to hold food with one hand and brush off flies with the other, as best he could.

The day dawned gray and misty. Mac appeared at my hole.

"Ozark, take a work detail and bury those dead Nips." In the work group were Walker, Sweetpee, and Winn.

"You hear any firing last night?"

"Not much, a little after the shelling."

Mac moved on.

"Wonder what that was about?" asked Sweetpee.

"Dunno."

In a few minutes, Mac was back. He reported that Buddy, our foxhole digger, had threatened to shoot him during the night when he woke him for his watch. Said he did shoot into the air. He was concerned.

"Is he still digging?" I asked Mac.

"Yeah. I was just over there. Well, get ready to move out. We got orders to reinforce the Fourth Regiment up near a place called Sugar Loaf Hill."

"Good God, Sarge, it's pouring rain and the mud is A-hole deep," griped Sweetpee.

"Not my orders; I just pass them along."

The Recon Marines slogged along. Some wore ponchos, but the rain ran off our helmets and down our necks. All of us were wet and covered with mud below the knees.

"Wait up!" came a desperate call from someone back in the pack. "I just lost a shoe in the friggin' mud."

We carried our rifles slung muzzle-down to keep out the rain. If anything was said among the sullen men, it was a gripe.

I peeked out from under the brim of my helmet to see a stick in the mud. I looked again and recognized it as an M-1. As we plodded closer, I saw that it marked a casualty. Beside the rifle was a marine's shoe half-buried in the gunk. Above the shoe was a man's leg—just a leg, standing there, as if it were ready to walk off. We passed as if in solemn review, looked, and moved on. Not a word was said. Just the sound of shoes sucking mud and rain pelting on ponchos and helmets.

A lightning flash exposed four men standing in the road. We tensed at the sight, but no one made a menacing move. Who were they? What were they doing there? Lightning flashed again; they were dressed as marines.

"We're up here to support a company of the Fourth. Is that you?"

"Yes, I guess it is." came the reply. There was nothing in the voice to cause alarm. Just a subdued voice in the rain.

"Where's your commander?" asked Mac.

"He's dead."

"Who are you?"

"Baker Company. Most of them are dead."

"Where's your commanding officer?"

"He's dead."

"Who's in charge?"

"Guess I am," said the little man. Mac noted that he was soaked and covered with mud. He began to feel sorry for him.

"Where's the rest of your outfit?"

"We're all that's left."

"Well, you can return to your headquarters. We'll take over."

"We don't know where it is." Mac felt a vein of pity empty into his heart.

"Stay with us. We'll help you tomorrow, if there is a tomorrow."

At their destination, the men dug foxholes in the mud and watched the water trickle into them. Some sat on their helmets and removed their shoes, pouring out muddy water. Off came bloody socks, revealing shriveled feet.

"Look at that!" said Sweetpee. "My foot's as wrinkled as grandma's washboard."

"That's nothing," said Pappy. "Look at this bloody sock. My feet are a swollen mass of blisters."

Some of the men tried to find something with which to make shelters. Others sat resignedly in their muddy holes, soaking in the rain.

The marines wished fervently that the Japanese would be content to stay in their dry caves up on the hill. Everyone was sleepless, miserable, and mad—angry at the world, angry at the Japanese, angry at the mud, and spoiling for a fight.

Bang!

I lifted my dripping poncho and stared into the dark. Nothing was moving. I heard nothing but the sound of pelting rain.

"Corpsman! Corpsman!" yelled a voice in the dark. I reached for my rifle as I listened. I slowly pulled it to my side and slipped a finger inside the trigger guard.

The word was being passed. It was Buddy. He had accidentally shot his foot.

"Accident, hell!" said Sweetpee.

The night passed with bitching, cussing, but no Japanese. At daylight, Mac summoned me.

"You knew Buddy pretty well. Go up there and get his things. We're pulling out."

My stomach was churning so hard that I was getting sick. There in the muddy hole was bloody water. I gathered Buddy's pack and rifle and turned to go, when I noticed something in the bloody soup. I picked it up and began puking uncontrollably. It was Buddy's big toe.

The old camp looked like heaven as the bedraggled men returned and flopped down to rest and sleep.

"Ozark! Sweetpee! Take Daniels and Zimmerman with you on the water detail."

"Damn!" I said. I had just made myself comfortable. "Well, let's get to it, Sweetpee. Gather the canteens."

The canteens had to be carried about a quarter-mile to an artesian well, where the water wasn't contaminated. We went off with the canteens jangling, filled them, and returned. The clouds were scurrying, breaking up. The steady rain had turned to showers.

As the water detail approached camp, we could see Major Walker talking to a group of men.

"Wonder what's up," said Sweetpee.

"You men have all volunteered to make a night reconnaissance across the Asato Gawa into Naha. God Almighty, I'd like to go with you. But General Shepherd won't hear of it." Major Walker's voice was gruff, raspy. "Find out what you can about the enemy's strength. You'll be saving lives.

"Now, men, this mission I consider to be beyond the call of duty. I'm going to submit the name of every man for a medal." He paused and surveyed each man. "Good Luck. Dismissed."

Before we could distribute the canteens, an artillery observation plane flew over. While I was watching, a puff of black smoke appeared near the plane, and its right wing came off. The plane went into a spin. The wing drifted away in the stiff breeze over Naha Bay. When the plane was a couple hundred feet above the water, the pilot either jumped or fell out. No parachute opened, and he plunged into the water with a huge splash. The plane followed with another splash. Then the wing splashed down. Soon the rhythmic waves covered everything.

A Navy LCI came in to investigate and drew enemy fire. It left. The navy blasted the coast with tremendous shelling. Then an LCVP approached. It drew machine gun fire but kept coming.

I was called away, but I talked to Charley Payne about it later. He said that the ship rescued a man, presumably the pilot, from the mast of a sunken ship in the harbor.

Chapter 24

RECON OCCUPIES NAHA

As soon as the commander left, teams were given instructions by Sergeant Manion.

"There are four teams of four. Each team has a leader. Just before dark, each of you is to paint your face. Divide into couples and help each other with the camouflage. You'll be swimming fully clothed with cartridge belt, canteen, and bayonet. Each quad will enter the water at two-minute intervals. Be quiet and assemble on the opposite bank.

"Do we wear helmets?" asked a knucklehead.

"Unless your head is bulletproof," said Manion.

He started to walk away.

"Sarge!" Manion stopped.

"Yes."

"Don't we have a password?"

"I'm glad you asked. Listen to this, each of you—*snap!* If you hear someone or something, snap your fingers once. A friendly will answer by snapping two times. So, if you hear a snap, Wampler, what do you do?"

"Snap my fingers twice."

"Right. Now, don't forget. Your life may depend on it."

"Night patrol, gather round," Manion shouted. Rain began pouring.

"We're to secure. Nips have been sighted in the area, and our mission has been canceled for tonight."

It was raining, and men sat in their holes like drowned rats, watching amtracks move along the seawall to prevent an attack from the sea.

Thunder, lightning, shelling! Recon noncoms didn't bother to assign watches. No one could sleep. Morning slipped in, misty and gray. Slowly, the grumpy men began to stir. By noon, the clouds were breaking up, and it was announced that the night patrol was on again.

Clouds scurried over the sliver of a moon as a command post was established on the bank of the Asato Gawa. The tide was out, and the men waded silently into the waist-deep, mud-bottomed stream.

Major Walker and others watched as men moved into the water. The night was dark. Word had been passed to all units that flares were prohibited until further notice. There was enough skylight reflected off the water for the Recon observers to see silhouettes of the men. The only sound was the tide washing gently against the shoreline.

"Just a couple more minutes," Commander Walker said, "and they'll be safely across."

Suddenly, rifle fire broke out across the river.

"Goddamn Japs!" said one of the officers, with deep emotion in his voice.

Japanese shelling started. Big missiles screeched, rumbled, and exploded in the distance. One of the rear echelons was catching hell. Then some rounds hit Recon.

"Take cover, men. Back to your foxholes," ordered an officer.

Across the Asato Gawa, Team Leader Ray Keel instructed his men to take off their boondockers and pour out the water.

"Wring out your socks; we don't want sloshing," he instructed. "Check each other's gear. We don't want anything rattling." William Gadbois recalled the two other members of this team were B.A.Fisher and Al Wizbicki. After they had gone about the length of a football field, they ran into a Japanese patrol. Keel kneeled, and so did the others.

A flare went off, and they could see shadows of Japanese nearby. They said something to the marines that was not understood. Keel fired his carbine, and so did Gadbois. Some Japanese grunted but did not fire.

The marines ran back to the rendezvous point. When another team returned, they fired at them. No one was hit.

A third team, led by Sergeant Manion, had a grenade thrown at them. It exploded in a cabbage patch. Mud splattered on Elbert "Pappy" Woodhams. He thought that he was wounded and would bleed to death, but he wasn't hurt.

The fourth team walked up a draw away from the river. As they left the draw, they came to a stone wall, which they followed until there was a gap opening onto a road.

"Listen!" whispered the leader. Men bumped into each other in the dark as they halted. A shuffling noise was moving down the road toward them. "Take cover. Pass the word."

The four marines flattened themselves along the roadside. It was a Japanese guard detail going to their posts. When they could no longer be heard, one of the marines jumped up and said excitedly, "That Jap kicked gravel in my face. He was so close I could have tripped him."

"Be glad you didn't," said a more mature team member.

The patrol moved along the road for a mile or so, until they topped a small hill. In the distance was a building. Lights could be seen in the windows. Antennas could be seen on the roof. Voices and laughter came from an upstairs room.

"Lets go up there and throw a grenade through the window," said a man who was beginning to feel brave. "We can wipe them out."

"Could be," replied the leader,"but this is a fact-finding mission. Don't fire unless fired upon."

On the way back down the road, they heard a scrunch, and barely had time to get down before a lone bike rider approached. Probably a civilian.

"Down!" urged the leader, at the gap in the wall. As the men fell, they heard the unmistakable pop of a stick grenade being charged. The explosion deafened the marines. Debris flew on them and smoke hung in the air. By the time it was quiet, the attacker was gone. Not a shot was fired.The leader called the roll of his men. All were okay except Wampler, who said, "I've been hit."

"Can you walk?"

"I think so, but I'm bleeding. My leg's all wet."

"Okay, come up here next to me."

The group moved down the draw to the Asato Gawa. They removed their shoes and tied the laces together, and slung their shoes around their necks. They had to swim because the tide was coming in and the water was deeper.

"I made a mistake," said the leader. "Now you know why you should never come back the way you went out on patrol."

Wampler's leg kept him from swimming well, and as he sank lower into the water his helmet filled and pulled him to the bottom. When he bounced up, he was disoriented and saw a Japanese soldier swimming a short distance away. He fired and heard the bullet strike.

As he climbed the muddy bank, he said, "I shot a Jap back there. He was following us."

"I heard the shot, but I didn't see any Jap."

"I know I got him."

"Where's your limp? Where were you hit?"

"Right here . . . somewhere." He was feeling his hip.

"You faker," laughed Manion, the leader. "A piece of that grenade hit your magazine clip and bent it, see! Then it punched a hole in your canteen. That wet you felt was water."

"Son of a gun."

Keel came in holding his helmet. A bullet had drilled a hole though it. "There's your Jap," Manion said, looking at Lucky.

Sheffield was a new man to Recon, transferred in only two days earlier. After the enemy shelling, he was missing. When Manion returned from the mission, he ordered men to search for Sheffield. "He probably ran off and hid somewhere," said one of the searchers.

"Here's his helmet. Oh my God!"

"What is it?" asked Manion.

"There's blood in it." Nearby, they found Sheffield's body. The flesh had been stripped from his legs by shrapnel.

"Jesus! We never got to know him—he's just a face that passed our way," lamented Preacher.

A cold rain fell as Recon massed to move out. Wampler shivered every time his cold dungarees touched his skin. His nerves were knotted. He was shaking.

"Cold, Wampler?"

"Some, Doc." He tried to smile.

"We'll be moving soon, then you'll get warmed up."

Artillery shells thundered overhead, with fire blinking red in their tails.

"Thank God they're ours," said Doc.

"Okay, Recon, let's go." It was Lieutenant Autry, waving his arm forward.

Recon crossed over the engineer's bridge spanning the Asato Gawa, up the southern bank and into the rubble of Naha. Two men ran across an opening in a garden wall as bullets splattered the dirt behind them.

Enemy dead littered the street, their brown bodies turning black with decay. Those wearing jackets were so bloated that their buttons were about to pop off.

We had taken refuge behind a wall, recalled Corpsman George Willis, when he was called to treat Roger Pushee of Rutland, Vermont. He had been shot in the head. To reach him, Willis had to run across an opening.

He heard Sergeants Manion and Woodward yelling for him to get down. He saw bullets kicking up dirt at his heels. He dove into a shell crater, but it was filled with water. He came up blubbering water and mud. The sergeants laughed. The corpsman crawled to the wounded man, treated him, and dragged him to safety, but Pushee later died of his wound.

"Dang blast this mud," said Pappy to Sweetpee as they stood guard outside an abandoned house where their squad was sleeping. "It's about to pull off my shoe. It's more like glue than mud."

"I noticed it's a different color, too," added Sweetpee, "more like chocolate."

"Maybe it is."

"Is what?"

"Chocolate," said Pappy. "I've heard of Mississippi mud pies. They're chocolate."

"Why don't you taste it?"

"You kiddin'?"

"No. I'll taste it." Sweetpee dipped his finger into the gooey substance and touched it gingerly to his tongue. "Hmmm, tastes sweet."

"Yeah!"

"Like molasses."

"What you guys mumbling about? You're supposed to be quiet on guard duty." It was Mac checking the perimeter.

"The mud, Sarge. It tastes sweet."

"Well, it should. That building up the street was a sugar factory before it was blown up. Syrup spilled all over."

Morning brought more rain, buckets of it. I slipped on the rubber pants I had kept ever since the landing. The squad managed a smoky fire with salvaged wet wood and made hot coffee.

"I don't feel so good," said Sheridan "Pappy" Yost, our bugler.

"You sick?" asked Doc.

"No. I had a dream last night. I was on a ship waving goodbye to my wife and boy, but the ship was up in the clouds. And I was playing taps on my bugle. I just feel that my time is . . ."

"We all have weird dreams out here," explained Doc.

Enemy shells began falling, and everyone jumped for shelter.

"Corpsman!"

It was Hutchison, one of the men in another platoon. He had been hit in the arm with shrapnel. Nothing fatal. But he had been wounded before, so he'd be going stateside—a Hollywood wound.

Our artillery opened up, and the enemy shelling stopped.

Crack, crack, crack! It sounded like a string of firecrackers going off. Snipers had pinned the marine squad down in the mud.

"Ozark," yelled Mac, "see that wall ahead? See if you can get up there."

I crawled in the water-filled ditch. The rubber navy pants had felt good until now. The cool water flowed in around my hips. I raised my body out of the water and a bullet ripped through my backpack. I slipped out of the straps and crawled ahead. Mud flew in my face, followed by the sound of the nearby rifle.

"Ozark, move back!" It was Ace Brown calling.

Just as I sprang to my feet, a rifle fired. I fell forward with a splash, not hurt—just a reflex. As I lay there, I wondered what to do. Maybe the sniper would think I was dead. I figured it was about fifty yards to safety. If I could make it in two twenty-five-yard bounds, maybe the enemy wouldn't have time to sight me in.

During the first leg, I heard no shots. I lay in the water-logged ditch while catching my breath. Then I jumped up and ran, zigzagging, toward Ace. Bullets were flying thick and fast, but I made it. I was scared, shaking like a leaf in a windstorm.

Ace was smoking. I took out a cigarette and asked for a light. Ace held out his cigarette, but his hand was shaking so much I couldn't light my weed. I held Ace's hand to steady it, but we were both shaking. "Here, use my lighter."

A nambu opened up, followed by the dreaded call for a corpsman. A new man in our outfit was hit. A bullet went through his helmet and lodged in his neck. He complained of blurred vision and was evacuated.

Marines saw some snipers pulling out and fired at them. The major called for a smoke screen, and Recon retreated to the "sugar house."

"Rain, rain, go away," said Sweetpee the next morning. He was fanning the smoke from the open fire where he was trying to dry clothes.

"We're moving out at 1230, pass the word," someone yelled.

As Recon approached the area where they had been fired on the previous day, nothing happened. Apparently, the enemy had pulled out. Then we moved over a red-dirt knoll, and all hell broke loose— nambu and rifle fire. Two men were hit. One was Sheridan Yost. He was killed instantly.

"Corpsman!" yelled a nearby rifleman, desperation in his voice. He began sobbing so hard he couldn't call again. Doc went to him.

Pappy Yost was a father to us. He was older, and a little pudgy. He had a wife and son. All of us agreed to sell our souvenirs to the sailors and flyboys and send the money to Yost's widow for the education of their son.

My fondest memory of Yost was seeing him on the beach at Guadalcanal. I could close my eyes and see him there, framed by the coconut palms and the ocean in the background. The trumpet was tilted toward the sky, and he was practicing the melancholy melody of taps. Pleasant dreams, Yost. You served your time in purgatory.

Recon moved on.

"Don't bunch up," yelled Mac. The Recon men were attracted to the sight of the fresh meat and blood of Japanese who had been killed during the retreat. Body parts were splattered on a wall. It was sickening. Sweetpee felt knots forming in his stomach. He moved on.

A private gathered souvenirs. He was loaded with a Japanese rifle, rising sun flag, and a broken-handled sword. He looked at a shattered watch and Japanese field glasses, but didn't take them.

When a Japanese machine gun opened up, he dropped everything and ran for cover. Curtis watched him and shook his head. Then he walked up to the wall behind which the machine gun was chattering. He lifted himself up by his fingertips until he could see over. He dropped down as bullets chipped away the wall where his head was. He methodically removed the pin from a grenade, held it a couple of seconds, then tossed it over the wall. The machine gun was silenced. He walked away.

Recon moved back to the bivouac area. We guarded a bulldozer clearing a road of debris, carefully watching for mines in the old roadway.

Night brought another downpour of rain. Lieutenant Autry moved his platoon into an abandoned warehouse, where the Twenty-ninth Weapons Section had set up a 37mm gun.

Naha! We were billeted in a warehouse on the Kokuba Riber (#1 at top center of photo). Two men were killed by Nambu machine gun fire on Oroku Peninsula (top of photo). We blew bank nearby (2) but found no money—just records. Bridge (3) was top target for Japanese. Shot two enemy off one day as they tried to blow it up; another we fired at blew himself up. (4) Where we stayed on Onayama. VanHeuvelen to the hospital. Center of island (Ona Yama) is Naha mayor's house. At left tip of island is cave we stayed in, also a warehouse. O'Brien hit near mayor's home. Bridge (9) later made into pontoon bridge. (10) Two Japanese shot here trying to escape in a boat. (11) Oroku Peninsula in the distance. (12) Water points. Several marines were killed attempting to get water. Our squad (13) was the outpost for the water points. (14) Tank blown up near the bend in the river; a few miles in the distance, big battles raged on the Oroku—many died. (17) Sweeney was strafed and killed while riding in a Jeep with his radio on a road near the river. Objects in the river are sunken Japanese boats. (19) Torii, Okinawan temple gate. (21) Our C.P. (24) Office building. Our command post was on the island.

Torii stands alone over leveled city of Naha, Okinawa.

Two Okinawan villages, both partially destroyed.

Naha, where every foot of hallowed soil has a memory.

Another view of Naha, the Okinawan capital.

Okinawan airfield at Naha with wrecked hangars.

Wrecked fishing boat in dry dock at Naha Harbor, Okinawa.

One of few surviving buildings in Naha. Note shell holes in walls.

Still standing is the wreckage of the post office in Naha, Okinawa.

Wrecked train in Naha railroad yards. Coaches looked like U.S. streetcars.

Crossroads, Naha, Okinawa.

One of the least damaged streets in Naha, Okinawa.

From the south, looking back on what was Naha, Okinawa's capital city.

Beached Japanese ships in Naha, Okinawa, harbor. In the distance is Oroku Peninsula, site of heavy fighting.

Green recruits, going to the line. "Good luck! I got mine—a million dollar wound."

Chapter 25

THE BANK ROBBERS

Recon took refuge in a concrete warehouse on the Kokuba Estuary the night of May 28. It was good to get out of the rain and mud, we agreed. The two-story building had a flat roof and no windows or doors—they'd been blown out.

"Look at that!" said Charley Payne, our BARman. He pointed to puffs of cement coming from a stack of cement bags. There was no sound, but the puffs seemed to be small explosions.

"Get down! Everybody take cover!" It was the battle-wise Manion giving orders, looking out for his boys. A bullet whizzed by and ping-ponged around the concrete walls.

Payne didn't appear to understand. He jumped up and ran across the open building.

"What's going on?" he yelled.

"Japs . . ." I started to answer, but I never finished.

I saw Payne's eyes turn wild, and he stopped transfixed. He slowly sank to a sitting position, grabbed his crotch and screamed, "Right in the fuckin' balls!" A bullet had gone through his wrist—then the scrotum. He seemed unaware of his wrist.

"Corpsman!" I yelled. Doc appeared and helped Payne to a jeep for a trip to the field hospital.

I took the concrete stairs two at a time to the second floor. The Recon men there were unaware of what had happened. I spread the news, and Sweetpee grabbed Payne's BAR, and by doing so became the center of the squad's fire team.

More Japanese fire rained down on the warehouse from across the Kokuba Estuary.

"Chronis! Bring that radio over here," instructed one of the officers. He made a call, and before long the weapons company was setting up the 37mm gun. It was brought into the building and placed to shoot through the open window. It was protected by bags of cement. I introduced myself to the gunner, who said his name was Ski. As I turned away, Ski stepped over to the window and sat down on the sill. I glanced back to warn him, only to see him topple over to the floor. His body made a few traumatic quivers.

"Corpsman!" I shouted. But it was too late. The bullet had hit him in the neck, severing his spinal chord. The man was carried away, and the restless men settled down.

Sweetpee came up to me. "Sergeant Manion had just come in with his dauber down. That new man—what's his name . . ."

"Sweeney."

"Well, he was out on a communications detail. They were laying wire when one of our planes flew over, low and slow. He waved at the pilot and took a bullet through the top of his head. Guess the pilot thought he was a Jap. Our men are mad as hell. They shot at the plane with their rifles. The pilot's probably back on a carrier now, bragging about the Jap he shot!"

"Sweeney. Wasn't he the one that used his helmet for everything—wash, cook, shave, food?" asked Red Smith, who had walked up sporting his handlebar mustache.

"Yeah. And he believed in pre-destiny. He probably wasn't wearing that helmet when he got hit," I said. "He had said when his time was up, it was up."

"Listen up!" It was Lieutenant Donald Grubb, the new officer of the Third Platoon. He was an energetic New Englander. "We've got a mission tomorrow that you'll be telling your grandchildren about. We're going to rob the Bank of Naha, and it's all legal. Intelligence wants to know if there's any information hidden in the vault."

"Up here!" came a call from the second floor. Several men grabbed their weapons and ran up the stairs. Sweetpee arrived in time to fire the

BAR at about a dozen enemy soldiers who were running into a house. One fell at the doorway and was dragged into the building.

Later, I was standing watch with Ace Brown. We had relieved the machine gun crew at dark. It was raining. Ace had the second shift and was half asleep when I heard a light noise. I heard it again. I woke Ace.

"Did you hear that?" I asked. Ace's mouth was so dry that he couldn't speak. He uncovered the machine gun.

"There it is again," whispered Ace. *Meow!* A spotted house cat nonchalantly walked into the open.

Later we heard a similar noise again. It was a rat, probably the one the cat was searching for.

I woke to the *rat-a-tat-tat* reveille of enemy machine gun bullets on the concrete wall. It was barely daylight on an overcast day. I broke out a C-ration fig bar and went out to the machine gun placement. I was searching the distant hill with field glasses when I caught a glimpse of something moving. It was so close it blurred the corner of the lens.

"I couldn't have been more startled if someone had slapped me in the face with a wet towel," I later told Ace. Right there on the bridge was a Jap, crouched down. He was wearing a brown uniform and a helmet.

I thought of turning the machine gun on him. Then I noticed some of our guys in the line of fire. I picked up my M-1 and walked into the warehouse, then up the steps where I could shoot down at him.

"Any of you guys want to shoot a Nip?" I asked. A bunch of guys came running to the big window opening. There he was, plain as day.

"How did you spot him?" asked Mac.

"The stupid SOB was wearing green camouflage on his helmet." He looked like a bush. There was no green on the bridge except him.

While we were firing, another Japanese appeared on the bridge. After a few shots were fired at him, he flew about ten feet in the air. He had blown himself up.

Recon had lost so many men. We were probably at about fifty percent of capacity. As much as replacements were needed, the old-timers were skeptical of the new men—some came with only boot camp training, most without combat experience.

However, the new men were not without their own concerns. We heard about a replacement in another platoon.

· "I'm to report to Lieutenant Curtis," he said. Curtis stood. He
was wearing combat boots, a kimono, and a derby hat. He was
smoking a cigar. The recruit looked bewildered.

"Sir!" he said, and saluted as his eyes roamed over the officer's
appearance.

"Jesus!" yelled Curtis. "Don't call me that. You'll get me killed."

The replacement gave up and walked away, wondering what he
had done to get his leader killed that wearing a kimono wouldn't.

Some of the marines found a wind-up phonograph in the rubble,
along with Japanese and a few American records: "You're Just Too
Marvelous" by Jo Stafford; "There's a Small Hotel" by Frances
Langford; and "Come Out, Come Out Wherever You Are" by
Frank Sinatra. Every time they played the Sinatra record, the
Japanese responded by firing their machine gun from across the
estuary, chipping concrete and splintering wooden window frames.

McDougal took his squad on a mission to blow up caves where
Japanese were believed to be hiding near the seawall. We were working as a demolition team. We threw a dynamite charge into the
mouth of a cave but saw it land in water. We ran for safety, but the
charge didn't explode. After I was sure the fuse was out, I returned
to see what had happened. As I approached the cave, I could see
that the fuse was still smoking.

I ran like hell, but it wasn't fast enough. The blast picked me up
by the seat of the pants and pushed me down the hill while rocks,
mud, smoke, and other stuff whizzed by my head. I didn't go back
to see if the cave was closed.

Some men couldn't resist searching the caves for souvenirs. The
way I heard it, Paul Rallis of Old Orchard, Maine, was souvenir
hunting in a cave, when he was shot at. He fell to the floor and lay
there a long time, but when he moved he drew fire. Obviously,
someone could hear him. He became aware of how bright the lumi-
nous dial was on his watch and how loud it was ticking. He took it
off his wrist and buried it.

When he started to crawl, he was aware of the noise his dungarees made as they scraped the ground. He took them off and
crawled out of the cave only in his skivvies.

The cave patrol moved to a beautiful old shrine overlooking the
blue waters of the East China Sea. The stone steps were worn
smooth from thousands of footsteps over the years. Shell holes and

debris are all around, but the shrine was not damaged, not a scratch. It was a divine wonder—a miracle!

The patrol returned, ready for their next mission. Recon was to blow the vault at the Naha Bank. This was a rare privilege without the normal dire consequences, an experience of a lifetime.

Ace Brown and I approached the massive, battle-scarred building with trepidation. The front door was ajar. We were suspicious that Japanese were inside. Even if they weren't, here was the ideal place for booby traps. I pushed the door open wider with my rifle barrel.

"See anything?" asked Ace.

"Just papers and junk all over the floor."

"See the vault?" asked Mac, who had come up behind us, carrying a pack containing explosives.

"Not yet," I answered. Then I spied it. "Yeah, there it is."

The men moved in quickly to secure the lobby—and to look for souvenirs. Mac removed a thick, dough-like gray substance from the pack. He shaped it like a cone and stuck it on the hinge of the vault door. He poked primacord in it and yelled, "Fire in the hole!"

We scrambled for the door. *Whooom!* The blast filled the building with smoke and dust. I was the first one in the vault.

"Hell, I can't see anything." Others rushed past me for the vault. "Hey, guys, look for important papers or maps," I added.

"Boy, am I going to have a time when we get to Japan!" said Kvaase, stuffing his pockets with yen.

As the men moved along, searching the vault boxes, it became evident that the valuables had been cleaned out.

Sweetpee joined a group outside the bank, who were joking about what they would tell their folks back home.

"Who will believe me when I say I robbed a bank—and got away with it?"

That night I was standing guard at the machine gun emplacement. I could hear the Japanese below me on the Kokuba River. I was very quiet, waiting for an opportunity to attack, when I felt something coiling around my leg. It was too dark to see, and I didn't dare shoot or call out with the enemy so close. My heart sank in fear. Marines had been warned of the three types of poisonous snakes on Okinawa. One was the Habu. It had deadly fangs and grew to eight feet long, we had been warned.

A flare popped open, and I saw the animal's tail.

"One of these nights I'm going to kill that darned spotted cat," I muttered.

Another flare popped and danced toward the bridge over the Kokuba Estuary to Ona Yama, a small island.

I saw something in the water near the bridge, just a silhouette that seemed to move. But it was difficult to be sure. I nudged Sweetpee and whispered, "I think someone's out there near the bridge. You look during the next flare." The flares were about ten minutes apart.

Pop! The flare lighted the area eerily. There they were. Two Japanese were standing in hip-deep water by a bridge pier. The flare went out before we could shoot.

Pop! Another flare lit, but the Japanese were gone.

Whaamm! Scintillating sparks flew out in all directions. The concussion from the blast nearly knocked us down.

Pop! The flare lit up the damage. To me, it looked like only the pier's steel reinforcing rods were left.

Pop! "Hey, Sweetpee, look at that. Those Nips are back to finish the bridge." I sent a hail of machine gun tracers toward them.

Pop! The Japanese were gone. But I couldn't sleep, even after I had been relieved. I wondered if the Japanese would try to finish the job—or worse, try to finish off the machine gun crew that had fired on them.

At first light, I searched the bridge with field glasses. The damaged pier looked useless. Then I discovered wires dangling from charges placed on other piers. We had saved the bridge for the marines to cross.

Sweetpee and I were celebrating when we heard that two men in the second platoon had been wounded. They came across a cave while on patrol and attempted to blast it with a grenade. Japanese in the cave had blasted them. I wondered if they were replacements.

I slapped my arm. "Damn, something bit me," I said.

"Me, too!" said Sweetpee, slapping at his face. "Mosquitoes!" he yelled, "millions of them!"

The warm, wet weather had brought out flying hordes. Marines spent the day searching for a place to get away from the bloodsuckers. Toward evening, they built a smoky fire and stood in it.

"Don't know which is worse, burning eyeballs or giving blood to the mosquitoes," said Sweetpee.

The thump of a boat on the estuary below us was cause to forget our personal misery.

"There's a rowboat tied down there," said Sweetpee.

"I see it, and there are five Japs trying to get into it," I added. "The tide has gone out since they tied up; now they have to expose themselves to get to the boat."

"Let's have some fun." Sweetpee squeezed off two or three rounds, and the Japanese retreated to the safety of the bank.

"What's going on?" asked Ace.

"We're shooting at Japs down there trying to get into their boat," Sweetpee said. The Japanese were back, and he pumped out the remaining rounds in his clip. The Japanese ran for cover.

"Let me get into that," said Ace. They were soon back, and Ace fired a few rounds at them. By this time, I was firing and laughing at the show the Japanese were performing. Each time they would try to get to their boat, we would fire and laugh. They ran out. We fired. They ran back. They ran out. We fired. They ran back. We laughed and laughed. Others joined us, and we practiced on live targets. This went on until it was too dark to see.

By the morning light, the boat was gone, and so were the Japanese.

"What happened to them, Ozark?"

"We never knew. Maybe we sank the boat. Maybe they floated it on high tide and rowed to Ona Yama."

"We may find out," said Mac as he walked up. "Recon is scheduled to make a daylight amphibious landing on Ona Yama island."

Chapter 26

RECON CONQUERS
ONA YAMA

Recon was roused at 0330. It was dark and chilly. We ate cold C-rations for breakfast. No fires were allowed. They could alert the enemy to our invasion plan.

"God, I'm tired," said Sweetpee, lying with his head on his pack. He had prepared to leave before he went on guard duty. "I got only two hours' sleep."

A while later, the fuzzy roar of an incoming shell got Sweetpee's attention. Then it exploded on Ona Yama. He jumped up.

"How'n hell can a guy get any rest?"

"Haven't you heard, Sweetpee? There's a war going on," said an amused Mac.

The night silence was shattered by more naval shells exploding on Ona Yama. The big-gun fire lasted for fifteen minutes while Recon stood by on the Kokuba riverbank. "What the hell they trying to do, sink it," cried Sweetpee.

I didn't say anything, but I felt small, insignificant compared to the barrage.

As soon as the shelling stopped, Recon was ordered to board armored amphibians for the dash across the estuary to the island.

The tractor the first squad was on had steering difficulty, and the coxswain asked us troops to help guide it by moving from side to side—for example, more men on the starboard side meant that the tractor would go right. We clung to the gun turret as we moved from side to side.

"This damned tub will probably sink of its own weight or stall before we land," complained Ace Brown.

"Or decide on its own to take us out to sea," I added.

At the beach, we scrambled off the amphibs and ran for cover. Smoke shrouded the area to protect the landing, but Japanese on the hills beyond the estuary were beginning to lob in shells.

At the cackling sound of a nambu, the first squad took cover behind some buildings. We watched and waited as the breeze cleared out the smoke, foot by foot. Each object that was cleared was studied carefully for movement.

There was a flurry of small-arms fire, followed by the cry, "Corpsman!" We hesitated.

"Move out!" yelled Mac.

A machine gun chuckled, and we invaders hit the dirt.

"Shit!" It was one of the new men; he had dived into a stinking cesspool. No one wanted to be near him.

Sweetpee and I crawled up to a concrete wall. As we moved along it, bullets were chipping away at the top. Chunks were flying into the air. More men crowded against the wall, and it began to fall over. It was merely sitting on the ground. Men grabbed to hold it up, exposing their fingers.

"See that round cistern over there?" I said, motioning with my head.

"Yeah," replied Sweetpee, feeling the wall beginning to fall.

"Let's make a dash for it."

The two of us rose in a crouch and zigzagged as we ran. Bullets spatted around us. We dove in, and Sweetpee landed on top of me. We sputtered as we found ourselves waist-deep in water. We remained hunkered down, listening to the gunfire. Then we heard grenades exploding. The gunfire ceased.

"Corpsman! Corpsman!" The calls were coming from different places.

Sweetpee and I ventured glances over the concrete rim. Men were walking around. The Japanese guns had been silenced. Two crumpled men in brown uniforms lay in a puddle of their own blood. Flies were already beginning to lay their maggot eggs in the torn flesh.

Jim Smith came hobbling up to Doc Redinger. He was in pain

and jumping around. Each time he hopped, his red handlebar mustache flopped up and down like a hound dog's ears.

"Acts like he's got the hotfoot," said Ace, smiling. Red grimaced, and Ace's smile vanished. Doc ripped open Smith's trouser leg, exposing a raw, bleeding wound.

"You've been shot through the hip, but there's no exit wound," said Doc, as he continued to examine Red.

"Ah, here's the bullet! You've got three balls, but one won't do you any good—it's spent."

After the initial skirmish, Recon put up a defense around the island. Then we began a thorough search of the island for remaining enemy.

Lieutenant Curtis had two men with him who were searching the abandoned buildings and houses. Several large buildings had stacks and stacks of bolts of cloth in various colors. Obviously, the island was the center for clothing manufacturing.

In the corner of one building, he saw loose netting, like that used for window treatments.

"Hmmm," he thought, "that would make good mosquito and fly control for my bed."

Just as he reached for the netting, he noticed that he wasn't the first with that idea. A Japanese soldier was lying under the net sound asleep. From the corner of his eye, he saw movement under another piece of netting. He fired at the one moving and took him down. The startled sleeper woke in time to see what he was up against, but it did him no good. Needless to say, Curtis got his netting.

"The way he's charged up," said one of his companions, "any insect getting close to his bed will get zapped with static electricity."

Everyone was nervous this first night on Ona Yama. It was new territory, and no one knew what to expect. Two men guarding a dark road with a machine gun were brought to attention by a noise.

"Sounds like a bunch of them," the gunner said. He triggered the machine gun and it began chattering away. Suddenly, the trigger-happy newcomer was yanked from the gun. Sergeant Tabb had him in an armlock. "What you firing at?"

"Japanese."

"Since when do Japanese bleat like sheep?"

The newcomer had a burial detail the next day—sixteen sheep.

Meanwhile, Lieutenant Curtis had found a cave for their protection, but the sides were shale, and slabs kept falling off due to the heavy rains. The roof was dripping, but Curtis was so exhausted that he was asleep on his feet. He sat down and pulled his poncho over his head.

"What if there are Japanese back there in this cave and they find we are camped on their front porch?" asked Sammy Zaidain.

"Sammy, if they haven't complained I don't think we should ask their permission now.

"Christ almighty," I screamed, holding my head. "What is that?" It sounded like a screaming kamikaze was coming directly into our location. A groggy Sweetpee came to life and tried to stand but fell dizzily. He was not fully awake.

"What was that, a screaming mimi?"

"I never heard it called that," Mac laughed. "It's a big rocket. And it'll scare the hell out of you. They store them in caves and roll them out on rails, I hear. Dampness in the caves keeps some of them from exploding, but if they do, they make a helluva hole. Last night one killed a marine in the second platoon and injured two more. But our CP in the pagoda was lucky. One hit the tile roof and glanced off. If it hadn't, I'd be acting lieutenant today." As he was leaving, Mac called back, "Try to get some sleep. I expect all hell to break loose tonight. You'll be standing watch on the beach, and chances are good the Japs will try to blow the bridge across the estuary."

A cove, protected by a small point of land jutting into the estuary, served as cover for the machine gun, a light 30-caliber. Ray Spears from Texas and another marine were manning it. They had been instructed to keep a sharp lookout for anything unusual.

They had set up their machine gun at the water's edge, when a mortar shell knocked out the gun. Shrapnel and flying coral rock cut limbs off the tree above them. Spears said his back hurt and his ears were ringing. He thought he was going to die, but no one was seriously hurt.

It was dark, and the tide was coming in, when Spears and the others saw objects moving on the water.

"Wake up! Boats! And they're headed toward the bridge." Spears began firing. Flares popped. In the dancing blue light, others opened fire. Sporadic fire continued as the objects moved relentlessly toward the bridge. But the bridge didn't blow.

The mystery was solved at daylight. Empty oil drums accompanied by a half-sunken wood boat were part of the flotsam that had drifted in on the tide.

"Well, they could have been full of explosives," said Ace.

A big, red-faced sun rose through the mist as Recon counted casualties. Three more men had been lost. A direct hit by a mortar shell had ripped through a radio man's tent. Bits and pieces of the radio were mixed with bits and pieces of the marine. His dog tags went to grave registration.

Two marines had strayed from their outfit and were stranded on the island after dark. When challenged, they didn't know the password and were cut down as they ran.

I was sickened by the news that so many of my buddies had been killed or wounded. I felt the pressure of the loss and the constant weight of thoughts that I might be next. It was a too-tight headband that I couldn't remove. At times, I began to welcome death.

Finally, Major Walker called in a 37mm gun from the Sixth Artillery Section. At first, the cave location wasn't known, but a wisp of blue smoke finally gave away the gun's position. It was firing from nearly a mile away through a port not much larger than a seabag.

After the Japanese gun was located, a Lieutenant Goddespotti mounted his 37mm gun on the roof of the concrete warehouse where we were staying. "It's a textbook situation for bore sighting!" said the happy gunner, as he did a little jig. He looked through the open barrel, made a few adjustments for distance and wind, loaded the gun carefully, and pulled the lanyard. The gun fired, and for a few seconds it appeared he had missed.

Lieutenant Christie was watching through field glasses.

"Bunghole!" he shouted.

"What did you say?" asked the gunner.

"Bunghole. It's something I learned as a kid. It went like this:" Bunghole! Bunghole! Papa shot a bear. Shot him in the A-hole and never touched a hair."

Evening brought a meal of 10-in-1 rations, a huge improvement over C or K rations. But we dreaded the night. Japanese come out of their hiding places like vampires. The shelling continued, but it was farther away. Still, the terrifying screaming mimis roar in.

It had been days since the regiments crossed the bridge; now came transports with supplies and souvenir hunters in jeeps. These guys were stupid. Two sailors were driving into a known Japanese mine field when Sergeant Manion intercepted them. They said that they thought marines were firing just to scare them. Manion chewed them out, but good!

The constant traffic had stirred a dust cloud over the Recon area. Noise and dust made it hard to sleep. I wished it would rain again, and settle the dust.

Recon men now had time to thoroughly search the island. We rummaged through junkyards of discarded airplane parts and machine tools. We searched a doctor's office and found a roomful of sewing machines and piles and piles of cloth. We took anything we could use to make our miserable lives more comfortable. Most of the Japanese were gone, but hords of flies and mosquitoes and droves of fleas are back. Rats, cats, and even dogs prowl the night.

Some of our souvenir-hunting men were surprised when they searched a house. Lawrence Poteet stepped on a loose floor board. He lifted it to see a Japanese pointing a pistol at him. He jumped back and the shot missed. The marines surrounded the house and set it on fire with phosphorus grenades. Two Japanese ran out of the flames and were shot. Poteet got the pistol that had been fired at him.

Days were full of rumors. Some said Recon's mission on Okinawa had ended. They'd heard we'd be going to Hawaii or Guam; maybe the States. Wouldn't that be grand?

Slopchute scuttlebutt, that's what it was called.

Shelled again last night, I wrote. I wondered if my letter would pass censorship.

I didn't mention that a missile had penetrated a solid wall near where some of the gang were harmonizing. The projectile went out through another wall, through a blanket airing on a line and disappeared into the estuary.

Sweetpee killed an old rooster that's been crowing reveille every morning, I wrote in the letter to Mother. *He's boiling it in his helmet. I'll bet it never gets tender enough to eat. Hope he remembered to add salt.*

We're eating a lot better, I added. I didn't note that men were coming down with dysentery. That would be censored. I didn't say anything about the nightly shelling for the same reason. Casualties were mounting in Recon.

I finished my letter and opened my barber shop. I was cutting Sweetpee's shaggy hair when some unknown marines came by. That wasn't unusual now; soldiers, sailors, and flyboys were snooping for souvenirs—marines, too.

The three marines called themselves the "Burpee Boys." Two looked beefy enough to be football linemen. The other was a skinny little fart, just big enough to be the equipment manager. They called themselves Big Burp, Little Burp, and Hiccup. They have a never-ending routine.

Sweetpee was laughing so hard at their German submarine routine that I couldn't cut his hair.

The three would shove each other's arms up like a conning tower, all the while yelling, "Octoon! Spittoon! Typhoon!" Then the little guy would have his nose by the big one's shoulder, and the third one would yell, "Inspection, armpits!" And so it went. By the time they left, my side hurt from laughing and my feet hurt from standing.

That night Spears and Lawrence Poteet had the estuary watch, when they heard someone approaching.

"What's the password?" whispered Spears.

"Hot dog," said Poteet.

"Not you. There's someone coming."

"What's the password?" yelled Spears, a little too loud.

"Hot dog. Keep it down."

"Bun," said Poteet, giving the countersign. It was Sergeant Manion with a message. "Listen, the company CP was hit, and we don't know whether it was wiped out or not. So be alert to anything."

Nothing happened at the outpost, but by daylight there were two sleepy marines. Manion came by.

"What happened at the CP?" asked Spears.

"A shell exploded in a tree above them. Shrapnel killed two, and three or four more were wounded. The major is up there now."

"Do you know who got it?"

"Not yet. It's a mess. You know, body parts, ammunition, and gun parts—everything is all messed up."

"You want us to stay here until we're relieved?"

"Yes. Just so you're forewarned, we will be along later looking for volunteers."

"Volunteers?"

"We need a patrol to make a night reconnaissance on the Oroku Peninsula."

Ancestral burial tombs near Naha. Japanese soldiers fortified themselves here among their ancestors. Some stayed permanently.

In these tombs, enemy soldiers lay in wait, then "Bang!"

Nile of company headquarters looks at the result of a night attack. He used a .45 pistol with plenty of knock-down power. C.P. was set up on the road in the background. (Below) Lieutenant Autry looks at what remains. Hot, muggy weather caused film to lose its silver emulsion, creating spots.

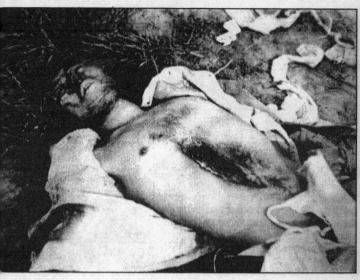

Another enemy dead.

Where the living mingled with the dead.

Dust shall return to dust.

Enemy dead.

Chapter 27

OROKU NIGHT PATROL

The men of Recon knew something was up. All the officers and noncoms had been called to the company CP for a meeting. Now it was two hours later, and they were still there. It was rumored that General Shepherd was with them.

"Must be something big," I said.

We didn't have to wait long for the news, because we could see Lieutenant Autry and Sergeant Tabb coming down the hill toward their seawall position.

"We need volunteers for a night foray over there on the Oroku," Autry said, pointing to the land across the Kokuba Estuary. "You will go in four rubber boats. Sergeant Tabb and Sergeant McDougal will fill in the details." Autry left.

"General Shepherd . . ." Tabb began.

"Manion stood, five feet six inches of solid man, and began to talk. There wasn't a man in the outfit who wouldn't follow him into the fires of hell.

"General Shepherd . . ."

There was a murmur among the men. "I knew it. Told you so. Now will you believe me?"

"Knock it off! As I was saying, General Shepherd wants to know what's behind the Nishikoku Beaches over there on the Oroku Peninsula. You'll go in four rubber boats, four men to the boat. This will be a full-scale, black-face reconnaissance. There'll be no flares for four hours before midnight.

"What are we looking for?" asked one of the new faces.

"Anything and everything out of the ordinary. Be alert to anything that would impede an amphibious landing. Any of you men who want to volunteer can find me at my foxhole.

"Just one more thing. Major Walker says he feels this mission is by far the most important thing Recon has been called on to do. He said this is beyond the call of duty. Any man who volunteers for this mission will be recommended for the Silver Star. Dismissed."

"Golly, this must be important with a capital I," said Ernest "Black Cat" Rasar.

"Sure sounds scary, like the whole landing depends on us," said Sweetpee.

"Well, I'm not going to volunteer. I learned in boot camp never to volunteer for nuthin'," said a private.

Dan Kvaase recalled how he volunteered to join one of the four-man teams: "I had thought and thought about volunteering. It was during the night, and the moon was bright. I went over to Lieutenant Curtis and asked him what he thought were the chances of coming back. 'I don't know, maybe fifty-fifty.' "

"And those coming back will be put in for the Silver Star? That's a very important medal, isn't it?"

"One of the highest our country offers. But it's not only those coming back; Major Walker said all volunteers will be recommended."

We wore soft caps, dungarees, and cartridge belts, and were armed with .45 pistols.

We were told a navy gunboat was standing by in case of emergency. That sounded good: A warm bed, hot food, shower, and other comforts. But it never happened.

We rowed our rubber boats around the estuary and pulled it onto the beach, climbed the beach, and came out on a road. We took the road, and in about a mile we came up behind some Japanese. We could hear them rattling mess gear.

Leader Fuller Curtis whispered for the team to return to the beach. On the way back, we ran into a Japanese patrol. One of the

Japanese threw a grenade. It went off with an orange flash in a ditch about two feet deep. No one was hurt.

Dan ran. He heard footsteps behind him and ran faster. He heard the metallic sound of a rifle bolt. He ran all the way to the beach, where others were waiting.

We jumped into our boat to go and someone asked, "Where's Rivers?" Rivers was a big man who had clubbed a Japanese to death with his pistol earlier.

"We have to go back," said Curtis. "Marines don't leave their buddies."

At the beach, Rivers came running to us from his hiding place. No flares were to be fired, but one went off and the Japanese began firing at us.

We were paddling like fury, and bullets were zipping around, when suddenly we bumped into something and stopped. We had hit a big mine, but were too small to set it off.

When we arrived back at the CP, it was nearly 0300, and Major Walker was preparing a rescue mission. We were supposed to have returned at midnight.

Some of the other teams also had difficulty. One led by Gardner O'Brien couldn't find their boat. They thought of trying to swim back although the tide would carry them out to sea, but the thought of a trigger-happy sailor seeing them in the water caused hesitation. At last they found their boat and paddled back. They found an anxious Major Walker, but he was glad to see them return. He gave each a swig of whiskey from his bottle.

Another team was walking along, when the leader pointed upward. They were under a huge net. Then they heard Japanese voices. The team leader motioned his men to move to the side of the road and take cover while he crawled ahead. As he approached, he could see a small fire and men moving around. He made a mental note of its location and returned.

"It's a gun battery."

The Recon party retreated and moved on. They came to a low hill and crawled to the top. In the distance was the bombed-out structure of Machinato Airfield. They walked under a stark doorway in a wall to see several natives rummaging through debris. As the men stood still in the doorway, a woman approached. She said nothing. The men followed her until she left the road.

The leader noticed the time. They had already been out too long.

"Back to the beach," he whispered

The patrol was more relaxed now, not as cautious. They were surprised by a navy star shell. Each froze in his tracks, no movement to give them away, but someone was coming down the road, closer and closer. They could see his rifle now. It was a soldier. And that damned flare just wouldn't burn out. The Japanese did not appear to be alarmed as he approached. He spoke. The Leader said nothing, but slipped his hand around his .45 and slid it from the holster. Burning in his mind were his instructions: *This is a reconnaissance mission. Do not fire unless fired upon.*

The soldier, realizing he faced an enemy patrol, quickly lifted his rifle, but he was too late. "That damned flare could have got us killed!" said Sweetpee.

"There's always someone who doesn't get the word," added another.

"Be quiet back there."

The patrol moved out at double-time. They were late, so they stayed on the road, a different one than before, but it went in the direction of the beach. There was a bend in the road, and just beyond was a house with lights burning. Men and women could be heard talking and laughing. As they came closer, they could smell food cooking.

Keel pulled a hand grenade from his belt.

"Hey, Sergeant, let me take 'em. This grenade will do the job. I'll just toss it through the open window."

"No! No firing. That's the Major's orders."

Keel had a sudden inspiration. "We ought to at least let those happy bastards know we were here. What you say?"

"No firing. That's an order."

"Okay. No firing."

Keel crept to the open window, stood in full view, and took a deep breath. Then he initiated his own banzai attack. He let out a blood-curdling scream that was something between a rebel yell and an Indian war whoop. It sounded like *YaaaHOOO!* He saw a few startled faces, but mostly heels, as the building was immediately vacated. A few new doorways were made, and the cooking fire was knocked over. Keel didn't stay any longer, and when he caught up to the patrol they were already moving—fast! He looked back to see the building in flames.

At the beach, they saw that a Japapese patrol had found their boat. A firefight broke out. The marines were not accustomed to firing .45s, and the Japanese were anxious to leave in the dark. A lot of bullets were whizzing through empty space.

We found our boat and got out of there. Back at the squad area, some of the men were having difficulty.

Meanwhile, back on the beach, Don Rice was in the third squad, second platoon with Krystofik, Williams, and James. Rice recalled the squad's experience:

> We were in a trench along the Oroku riverbank when a nambu opened up. I crawled about twenty feet on the bottom of the Jap trench, then attempted to peer over the trench wall. The nambu opened up again, hitting the dirt directly in front of me. I ducked, but a bullet ricocheted and hit me in the temple, knocking me out.
>
> That night, mortar shells began dropping on us. One had our number. It hit the trench bank and came to rest about a foot from James' head, but didn't explode. We crawled into a dry water tank and spent the night there. The tank was for water to supply a nearby hut where we spent off-duty time. It was below the crest of the hill and out of view of the enemy.

After four hours in enemy territory, Recon patrols had returned to tell of some hair-raising encounters, but we reported that the Oroku Peninsula was lightly defended.

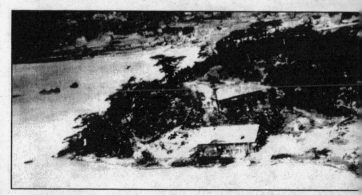

Section of Onayama showing Oroku Peninsula in background. Japanese supplies in foreground: lumber, engines; and in the building: nails, airplane wings, diving suits. House above warehouse was blown to bits before we arrived. At point of island is a submarine pen.

Onayama Island, foreground, with house marked "here" where our squad stayed after capturing the island. Beach shell holes and wrecked barges are visible. The blown bridge was replaced by pontoons. Across the water are the foothills of Oroku Peninsula. See Torii gate in left foreground—up that road is where marine Bereman was killed.

Gun hidden in cave on Oroku Peninsula in southern part of Okinawa. Guns were fired, then pulled back to safety.

Chapter 28

MARINES TAKE OROKU

Capture of Shuri Castle by no means ended the fighting at strong points south of Shuri along the Kokuba Gawa, where machine guns were ensconced in tombs and caves.

An attempt was made over loudspeakers to get the holdouts to surrender. Their answer was a swarm of bullets. A sniper killed Lieutenant Colonel Woodhouse, a favorite officer of Marine General Shepherd.

As the Japanese withdrawal was completed, resistance eased, and Ushijima's guards pulled back. Both army and marine divisions made rapid progress as the weather improved and the sun finally broke through. The Fifth Marines crossed the Kokuba Gawa near Tsukasan, several miles east of Naha on a railroad bridge.

On May 31 General Shepherd was instructed to study the feasibility of bypassing the Kokuba Gawa Estuary at Naha and making a landing directly on the Oroku Peninsula's Nishikoko Beaches from the sea. Accordingly, Major Anthony Walker's Recon Company had made a night reconnaissance of the area. All units were notified to restrict flares and star shells until after 0300.

Meanwhile, the army units along the east coast of Okinawa

swept toward the entrance to the Chinen Peninsula, placing themselves in a position to cut it off from the main island.

On the west coast, the amphibious marine landing was curtailed because only seventy-two landing craft were available. It was decided to attempt the landing with only one regiment, Colonel Shapley's Fourth. The Twenty-ninth was alerted to be ready to follow as soon as the beachhead was secured and landing craft were available.

At the same time, Major Walker's Recon Company was to board boats and take Ona Yama, a small island in the estuary near Naha. From this vantage point, they were to protect the Sixth Engineers while they replaced the bridge across the Kokuba Gawa.

In a sweeping move farther inland, marines seized the ridge west of Gisushi. While they were trying to seal caves in the area, a white phosphorus grenade set off an underground ammo dump that literally blew up the escarpment hill, killing three and wounding seventeen marines.

The amphibious assault units were ready to invade Oroku Peninsula by June 3. After severe artillery and naval gunfire shelling that rocked the beach on the morning of June 4, the marines moved in and landed with little resistance. They advanced to the airfield by dark.

Minefields, mud, and breakdowns delayed progress. Communications men had better luck. They unreeled trunk wires across the Kokuba Estuary and anchored them to the mast of a sunken ship.

During the Oroku invasion, the Japanese began using eight-inch screaming rockets that were terrorizing, but not accurate.

Mud and hilltop strongpoints made progress by the invaders jagged but steady. One hill, called Little Sugar Loaf, was particularly nettlesome.

On June 6 fire from Senaga Shima, a small island some five hundred yards off the Oroku coast, caused considerable concern. The Japanese were firing heavy artillery and 20mm cannons from concealed positions. The marines returned fire and called for an air strike. As planes dropped bomb after high-explosive bomb on the little island, marines alternately clapped their hands and cheered as they saw the explosion and flying debris, then clapped their hands over their ears as the sound waves approached.

By June 7 the warm sun was out and the soil was becoming dry enough for wheeled traffic. After the airfield was secured, the marines faced a tangle of hills, with a maze of caves and gun emplacements. Their attack seesawed over and around these obstacles. Sometimes troops would be moving at right angles to the main line of advance.

Stubborn resistance was faced by Major E.F. Carney on a hill near Tamikamiya. He knew if he went over the hill his troops would face a rain of fire as they moved down the back slope. So he sent a fire team into a cave that led through the hill instead. Once the cave was open, other men followed. This tactic was so successful that it would be used time after time.

By June 10 Admiral Minoru Ota could see his defense cracking as the marines were again successfully using the combined "tanks-accompanied-by-infantry" offense. He dispatched a message to Ushijima's new headquarters on the Kiyamu Peninsula that enemy tanks were attacking his cave headquarters and his navy forces were dying gloriously at that very moment. He ended the message by wishing Ushijima success.

Although Japanese commanders seldom issue direct orders, it was Ushijima's desire for Admiral Ota to withdraw to the Kiyamu Peninsula where naval and army forces would stand and perish together. In fact, General Ushijima sent Admiral Ota a message saying so.

But the message arrived too late. Admiral Ota, who had misunderstood an earlier message when Shuri fell and began withdrawing from the Oroku Peninsula, had firmly decided to make his last stand where he was.

June 13 turned out to be a rout of the Japanese. The demoralized troops went wild—some surrendered, others fought with grenades or committed suicide. At one point, the Japanese asked the marines to pause in their assault so that those committing suicide could have a moment of peace before their final act.

After the battle, marines searched for Ota's headquarters cave, where they found three hundred dead, all badly wounded bodies of troops in the medical center. They had been injected with cyanide to end their suffering. It was reported that they were given a choice of death or surrender. Some were so injured that they had to crawl to the cave entrance to surrender. Others simply held out their arms to the doctors as they passed by with syringes of potassium cyanide. Only sobbing could be heard.

Marines found hundreds of bodies on the stinking cave floor.

Blood, pus, rot, and mud caused an unbearable stench. The search continued until Admiral Ota's body was found on June 15. He and five officers, dressed in full, pressed uniforms, had lain down on beds with their hands clasped behind their necks. Their bloody throats had been cut.

The battle for Oroku Peninsula was at an end. General Shepherd notified General Geiger that organized resistance on the Oroku Peninsula was over. During the ten days of fighting, nearly 5,000 Japanese were killed and 200 surrendered. The Americans had lost 1,608 marines either killed or wounded.

Chapter 29

RECON IINVADES SENAGA SHIMA

Rising out of the East China Sea like a huge battleship was the heavily fortified island Senaga Shima. Following the amphibian landing June 6 on the Oroku Peninsula, the Fourth Marines pushed rapidly inland to protect their right flank. But this brought them under fire from a 20mm cannon and a large naval gun in a cave located on Senaga to their rear.

Marines shoved inland and supplies came ashore. Senaga, only a few acres in size, was like a pesky boil on their backsides.

A previous Recon night patrol on June 10 had determined that Senaga was not heavily defended, so General Shepherd ordered Recon to invade the island, which lay about five hundred yards off the Okinawan coast and at low tide was accessible on foot.

Early on the morning of June 14, Recon, reinforced by Company C of the Twenty-ninth Regiment, launched their attack on Senaga Shima.

I was roused at 0315 to prepare for the invasion. It was dark, and the all-night pounding of the little island by artillery had kept me awake.

Men of Recon grumbled as they amassed at the Okinawa seawall, which was protected by amphibian tractors. A heavy barrage of artillery broke out for a final softening up.

"If they keep this up, they'll sink the damned island," I said, as I watched sparks fly from the explosions.

"Damn, those are powerful shells. My eardrums are popping," said Sweetpee. Fragments from the shells showered into the water near them. Covering smoke shells followed.

"Move out! Pass the word. Move out!" The order permeated the waiting marines. They rose and began crossing the coral corridor. After only a few yards on the tidal flat, a machine gun opened up. Tracer bullets were coming from the seawall.

"Holy shit!" yelled Wizbicki. "It's one of ours!" Recon broke ranks and ran for the shore of Senaga Shima. Never was an island assaulted more quickly. Fortunately, there was no enemy resistance, or Recon would have been caught in the crossfire.

Dawn broke to expose an island of precipices, caves, boulders, and faults, but little overgrowth—just a few screw pines.

"This is nothin' but a goddamned mountain desert," I said. "Well, I can climb the rocks as long as there are no Japanese behind them".

Struggling, slipping, and climbing, I reached the top of the escarpment.

"Would you look at that view?" Sweetpee stood to look as rifle fire chattered away down the side of the cliff. Both men dropped to their knees.

"Hey, Major, there's a Nip down here in this cave!" a marine called out. There was no answer. Since marines were taught not to draw attention to their officers in combat, this was a blatant violation.

"There's a Jap down here!" the marine replacement yelled desperately.

"What do you want me to do?" replied the Major. "Come down there and grapple with him?" The major sounded disgusted. The conversation was punctuated by a rifle shot.

"Whoa!" I yelled. "Land mines!" I knelt, probing the dusty coral with my K-bar knife. From behind the safety of a large rock, my rifle fire exploded the mine. The marines left the path on top of the island and began working their way down the mountainside.

Sweetpee, Winn, and I made our way into the mouth of a large cave. We approached cautiously, leapfrogging. A wrecked naval gun, ammunition, and stored seabags were found, along with quantities of fish, rice, and fruit. We loaded our pockets for a feast.

As Winn and Watson approached another cave, a Japanese shot at them, and another threw a grenade at Winn. Neither was hurt. The Japanese ran back into the cave. Winn called for an interpreter, who told the Japanese to come out because the cave was to be sealed.

Two Japanese came out unarmed. They said that others were in the cave. No amount of coaxing persuaded the others to surrender. The cave was sealed with explosives.

Three marines appeared with a beautiful silk flag. This set off a frenzy of souvenir hunting. Recon guys combed the caves and found more food, clothes, guns, and ammo—even fountain pens and wristwatches.

As evening approached, Senaga Shima was declared secure. Recon Company bivouacked on the westward side of the island, where we witnessed a beautiful sunset. A cool breeze picked up, followed by a star-studded night sky. I had the first duty, and as I watched, a shooting star headed east. Could it be, I thought, that Mother would be watching, could see the same star?

Now that the Okinawa campaign was drawing down, I found myself thinking more about Mother. How long would it be?

"Hear that?" whispered Sweetpee. "Right out there, someone slipped on the rocks." A rock broke loose and bounced down the bank. "To-ma-reh!" shouted Sweetpee. No answer. "What's the password?" Sound of someone running. Ozark fired at the sound.

"I don't think you hit him," said Sweetpee. The remainder of the night was uneventful.

After washing in a clear-water shell hole and eating a C-ration breakfast, Sweetpee and I climbed to the top of the escarpment. It was a beautiful day, and we had a spectacular view of the battle for Oroku Peninsula. The enemy was pounded from sea, air, and land. Smoke and sound outlined the area of attack. It was a real live movie. What a show!

War was a magician. There was a ship near the tip of Senaga, firing inland. *Wham!* The whole island shook. The ship was gone. The same thing happened to buildings or bridges. One moment they were there—the next, they were gone. While I was taking a bath in the clear-water shell hole, I happened to look out to sea where something moving had caught my eye. It was "Black Cat" Rasar.

I recalled Cat swimming in the ocean at Guadalcanal. Not much bothered him, but one night, on a mock amphibious landing in shark-infested water, Black Cat found himself swimming in strange company. On a previous night, in rubber boats, they had felt a thump and had seen the ominous dorsal fin, and Cat had laid his hand on the creature and yelled at the top of his voice, "Shark!" Moments later, the animal was determined to be a huge turtle.

There was news when I returned to the bivouac area. Recon had a new commander. Major Walker had been transferred to one of the regiments, and Lieutenant Christie, our executive officer, was taking over. And Recon was moving out, back to the mainland.

Back on Ona Yama, Recon was relegated to patrol and cave-closing duty. Watson and I made up one team. We climbed a ridge and found a number of dead Japanese. Some were barefoot, and others wore sandals with the big toe split from the sole.

"That shoe is called a *tabi*," I said.

"Where'd you hear that?"

"One of the Intelligence guys back at HQ."

Most of the dead were wearing leggings. We searched the bodies of those that weren't too rotted or bloated. Watson kicked one of the turgid bodies and it exploded, blowing disintegrating flesh parts on both of us.

"Keep your friggin' feet to yourself!" I shouted, wiping and smearing rotted guts and squirming maggots from my jacket.

We sat on the apron of a tomb to eat lunch, but our appetites wouldn't come. The smell of putrid flesh was on our hands and in the air, and the pesky flies gagged us, big green flies with repulsive, iridescent bodies and devil-like red eyes. I tried to eat a cracker, but a swarm of flies covered it.

When Watson and I returned, we learned that Red Smith and another injured man had gotten together on Guam, where they were recovering from wounds. There was scuttlebutt that Recon might soon go to Guam.

Watson and I were assigned to a work detail sandbagging the seawall.

"Ya' know, this reminds me of the keep-busy duty we had on the 'Canal," said Ray Spears.

"We're in a kind of twilight zone," I said. "Men are still getting killed, but I understand there's a post exchange at the airbase. I heard we'll soon be paid, have an issue of warm beer, and an outdoor movie."

"I'd settle for a shower. This humid weather is as bad as summers back home."

"Huh-oh, look who's coming," I said. It was Sergeant Tabb.

"Come on, you guys, we have more caves to blow. Lieutenant Curtis will be going with us."

Our party moved along a road near the caves, lugging fifty-pound boxes of TNT. Explosives were taken from the boxes as needed and carried to the caves. After one cave was blown, Walker and I sat down to rest.

"Did you hear anything?" asked Kermit Davis.

"No," I said, listening.

"How's everything going?" asked Fuller Curtis, who walked up.

"Okay, but Walker thought he heard something after we blew that last cave."

Then they all heard it—the sound of a child crying somewhere in the rubble of the cave. Curtis sprang into action. He found the mouth of the cave closed, but dust and smoke were billowing from a side entrance. He disappeared into the hole while Walker and I watched in disbelief. Soon Curtis appeared with a child, unharmed but frightened.

Several of the cave-sealing parties gathered in the shade under a clump of trees to eat lunch. We were admiring a dagger that Hays had found. It was a ceremonial dagger, probably belonged to a samurai for *sepulca* (hari-kiri). In addition to Japanese characters, the handle and a scabbard had a curious design.

"Looks like a hex," said Walker.

"A what?" asked Davis.

"Hex. A design Amish put on barns and houses in Pennsylvania to ward off evil spirits. It's a little like African voodoo."

"It's a beautiful souvenir," I said.

"Oh, I'm not going to keep it. I'm going to trade it to one of those flyboys for the best sour-mash bourbon whiskey there is, then I'm going on a pukin' toot."

"You won't have to wait long," I said. I saw a jeep approaching. Two pilots hopped out. Their clothes were clean and pressed.

"You fellas have any souvenirs?" asked an airman with a mustache and a Vandyke beard.

"Hays has," I said, as I pointed to him. Hays showed them the dagger and they began to haggle. Finally, they went to the jeep and items changed hands.

The grove of trees was located on a slope. Before the resting

Marines was a grassy swale, and on the opposite side was a driveway to a fenced cemetery. The jeep was moving into the driveway to turn around and Hays was returning with four bottles of an amber-colored liquid when it sounded like lightning had struck.

"Thunderations!" yelled Hays. As he hit the deck, bottles broke and amber fluid spilled out and soaked through the gravel. He looked as if he wanted to cry.

I looked up to see the jeep as high as the treetops and disintegrating. Wheels and pieces of metal showered the grassy vale.

"What happened?" asked a Marine.

"Land mine," said Fisher.

Although marines searched the area, only pieces of the airmen were recovered. Only the dagger handle with the design was found.

"I think I'll keep it as a souvenir," said Hays.

I found half of a lip with a mustache still on it.

Back at camp, Recon men found the area saturated with non-combatants. Marines began to feel superior to these late arrivals.

That night was not peaceful. Five Japanese infiltrators slipped into the Recon area. Four were shot outright in a firefight. One ran off and was chased by Doc Redinger. The Japanese turned to fight, but when he saw Doc's size, he decided to run. It was too late, though. Doc decked him with his fist, and a rifleman came up and finished him off.

The following day was hot and hazy. The men lounged, wrote letters, read, and visited. At dusk, the green bottle flies were relieved by hordes of mosquitoes. We placed extra flares on the perimeter after the previous night's Japanese invasion. Sweetpee and I set them out with tripwires attached.

The gray dawn had barely lifted when a loud call broke the silence: "Corpsman!"

Some goofball had wandered into a flare. It went off and shot right up his rear end.

"What a bloody mess," I said. Blood, crap, and flesh was all around, and the sound of the guy screaming bloody murder was still ringing in my ears.

"Assemble!" came the order. "Rifle inspection."

"I haven't had my rifle inspected since we left the 'Canal," complained Sweetpee.

"What'n hell's this crap?" bitched Hays. "Yesterday we were in slaughter land, blowing caves. We were looking at and smelling dead Japanese with their bellies ripped open and their guts hanging out, their heads blown off, meat rotting off their bones. Hell, there's a war going on, and some peacetime officer wants to show his authority by having us stand at attention while he inspects rifles."

The new commanding officer, Christy, came by about dark. The guys bitched to him about the state of affairs until they found out he was a regular guy and had been fighting with the Recon Company, Sixth Marine Division, ever since they landed.

Some time later, it was suggested that a swig of liquor would taste good, whereupon Doc produced a quantity of sick-bay alcohol. Nerves loosened, talk loosened, and time slipped by.

"Say, fellows," said Christy, "I think it's past my bedtime." He raised his butt about three inches off the ground before his arms gave way. He fell back on the ground. Someone threw a blanket on him, and he lay there all night.

We woke to a beautiful summer morning. The sun rays shooting through multi-colored clouds reminded me of the rising sun on the Japanese flag. I was in a melancholy mood, thinking of my mother and home. Sweetpee saw me looking downcast and suggested we go sightseeing up near the prisoner compound.

The mood wasn't improved when we saw two old withered Okinawan men trying to bury an already half-buried Japanese.

Then we heard that a tank crew we had known at the seawall was killed when the tank hit a mine.

Back at camp, we learned of an issue of hammocks. I stretched my hammock between two trees but noticed that one tree had been weakened by shrapnel. At dark, several men went to see an outdoor movie, *Bull Fighter*, starring Laurel and Hardy.

During the movie, there was a horrendous explosion that shook the ground and lighted the entire area.

"God Almighty! What was that?" I exclaimed.

"A ship blew up over there in the harbor," my companion said. We scrambled up the hillside for a better view. We watched as the ship burned down to the water.

"Wonder what happened?" I asked.

"Probably a mine."

"Could have been a kamikaze."

Fire was still on Sweetpee's mind the next morning when he and others of the first squad were called for a new kind of fireteam. A village was burning, and firefighters were needed. It wasn't until the fire was out that we learned the village was an ammunition dump.

Things were looking up back in camp.

"Look at that!" said Lucky. A gallon of sliced peaches, and a date pudding for dessert.

"Listen up, you guys," said Mac. "There's going to be a ceremony at the Sixth Marine Division Cemetery since this is Independence Day. We'll be boarding trucks for the trip in thirty minutes."

"You know," said Mac, "back home we'd be having a picnic in the park with fried chicken, baked beans, potato salad, and a tank full of ice-cold watermelons."

The six-bys jostled along the dusty road and began to climb above sea level. The East China Sea was calm and reflected the sunlight.

"Lord Almighty," said Mac. It was breathtakingly beautiful.

Across the road were row after row of white crosses. I thought of our wounded and dead: William Sheffield, Norman Slattery, Sheridan Yost, Spellman, Pushee, Smith, Payne, Hutchison, and Newton, and the numerous others who were wounded and transferred.

The speeches were soon over, and the honor guard fired the salute. The bark of the guns shattered the silence, then the peaceful, restful notes of taps echoed over the landscape.

"Sleep with the angels," I whispered.

Back at the compound, I rushed out eagerly when I heard "Mail call." But there was no letter for me.

Later, Preacher was called to the CP, and I drifted that way to see what was going on. I wished I hadn't. I watched as Preacher wrote on each unclaimed letter: KIA, WIA, or MIA.

Sixth Marine Division on Okinawa.

Taps: Forever American soil.

Senega Shima, the rock full of enemy-infested caves that Recon Company captured. Senega Shima is about 300 yards off the coast of Okinawa. Our platoon invaded the island.

Senega Shima as seen from Okinawa. Our company secured the small island, but our time was not synchronized with a tank guarding the seawall. They opened fire, and we took the island in a hurry.

Cemetery ceremony honored those who gave their tomorrows so that we can have today. This was on Independence Day. Arrow marks my approximate position.

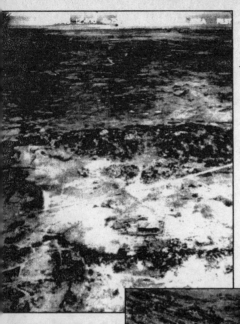

Aerial view of front line on June 2 at 2:45 P.M. Note shell holes in rice paddies, top center. Data at top of photo shows area, altitude, date, time, and that this is a restricted photo.

Aerial reconnaissance view of southern Okinawa, not far from where the last remnants of the Japanese forces were pushed into the sea. Terraced fields in foreground.

Chapter 30

BATTLE ENDS, USHIJIMA DIES

With the capture of Oroku Peninsula by the marines and the Chinen Peninsula by the army, the tip of Okinawa narrowed precipitously. Recon was squeezed out, and, after the capture of Senaga Shima, we were relegated to cave blowing and guard duty.

Mud and heavy rains in early June slowed the Tenth Army's advance southward, but they managed to keep pressure on the retreating Japanese by slogging forward, often without supplies.

River crossings, rough terrain, lack of supplies, lack of artillery coverage, and evacuation of dead and wounded—all were far more difficult enemies than the Japanese.

The weather broke somewhat by June 10 and marines captured Yuza Hill, placing them forward of the Army's Ninty-sixth Division which had been stopped cold by Japanese defenses on the fortified Yuza Dake Escarpment. The American Tenth Army suffered heavy casualties, including the marines, before they advanced to Kunishi Ridge, the western anchor of the Japanese line of defense.

The approach to this fortress was a broad valley with grassy plains and rice paddies. The ridge was honeycombed with caves and tunnels, bristling with artillery, anti-tank guns, and troops. Only two roads were available for marine tanks to use, and both were covered in depth by Ushijima's army. Marines approaching the ridge were forced to retreat. As a result, a night attack was planned.

General Buckner had been sending messages to General Ushijima, urging him to surrender. When more than a dozen Japanese wearing white hats appeared, the marines assumed that they were surrendering and suspended action, but when hailed, all but six Japanese ran. Shortly thereafter a heavy Japanese mortar barrage ended the short truce.

The night attack proceeded at 0300. The Japanese were surprised at daybreak, and several groups were wiped out before they could eat breakfast. Marines had a foothold on the ridge, but when reinforcements tried to move up, they were cut down. Tanks came to their support but were forced to withdraw under heavy enemy artillery. Marines tried again under cover of smoke, but were forced back. Tank artillery battered the tombs suspected of harboring the enemy, then a third attempt was made under smoke. It, too, was forced back.

Now the troops who had established a foothold on the ridge were suffering. They needed both supplies and replacements. By midafternoon, tanks were able to deliver supplies. Then they tried to deliver troops by concealing them in each tank's compartment and delivering them through the bottom escape hatches. Nine tanks were able to deliver fifty-four troops this way before dark. They brought back twenty-two wounded.

After midnight, a company of marines moved to the ridge without resistance. But, oddly, Japanese were still in the ridge, with access to both forward and reverse slopes.

The battle for Kunishi raged on, with bombardments from air, land, and sea, including naval rockets. Tanks finally opened the road toward the center of the ridge and did yeomen service by delivering both men and supplies to marines on the ridge. Wounded were evacuated inside and outside tanks' some were lashed to the tanks and sandbagged there for their protection.

The Japanese were noticed laying smoke to screen an operation in Kunishi Village, so marines gave them a mortar barrage. Later, when the village was taken, wrecked mortars, machine guns, and other ordinance was found.

On June 14 at 0330 marines used flares to light their way to the crest of Kunishi without opposition, but support troops were denied from joining those in assault. Tanks tried to lend support but were turned back by anti-tank fire.

Air drops of supplies missed their mark and fell into enemy hands. Pressure on the assault troops lasted all day and all night. One marine company supported by gun and flamethrowing tanks made some progress.

For the next several days, the battle seesawed. Casualties mounted while naval and artillery explosives rained down on enemy positions.

Advancing through Kunishi Village on June 16, marines found a number of Japanese soldiers wandering in a daze. During the afternoon, the Pinnacle, a strong point, was taken.

The Army Ninety-sixth Division attempted to clear out a stretch of Kunishi Ridge and was blasted by Japanese defenders, although an armored bulldozer had made a road sufficient for tanks. The tanks were unable to give sustaining support, because they were needed to evacuate the wounded.

By June 17 Kunishi Ridge was bypassed and became a mopping-up operation. Marines to the east were battling for Mezado Ridge and Kuwango Ridge. Enemy fire was intense from caves and brushy hillsides, yet marines made progress. After dark, the Japanese counterattacked, but their success was limited before it failed. The enemy's left flank was exposed, and the way opened to enclose the remaining Japanese troops on Kiyamu Peninsula.

Meanwhile, the army was moving down the Pacific side of the island, encountering strong enemy positions on the Yaeju Dake-Yuza Dake Escarpment. Naval gunfire and artillery smothered the enemy as the Tenth Army proceeded toward the tip of Okinawa, hill by hill, and moved up to Hill 89, Ushijima's headquarters near Mabuni.

General del Valle selected Lieutenant Colonel P. E. Wallace to make a fatal thrust through the Japanese defense to the ocean. General Buckner was at Wallace's observation post on Mezado Ridge watching the marines' progress on June 18 at noon, when he decided to leave. Apparently, a Japanese artillery crew saw the cluster of men. Five shells were fired, spraying coral shards, one of which struck General Buckner in the chest and killed him.

Another tragedy occurred on June 18, in what became known as the Cave of the Virgins. A number of Okinawan high school girls had joined the Japanese in defense of their island home. These girls were mostly nurses and nurses' aids.

Known as the Himeyuri girls, from the name of their school, 155 of these girls worked under terrible, stifling conditions. They were required to do such hideous tasks as cleaning amputees who couldn't manage to defecate alone, or hold a penis while a man without arms urinated. Bad air in the caves contributed to the spread of tuberculosis.

American troops approached the girls' cave and asked for those inside to surrender. The Americans had no idea who was in the cave. When no one came out, they tossed in white phosphorus grenades, and some reports indicate flamethrowers were also used against the helpless girls. Of the 155, 123 girls were killed outright.

By June 19 General Ushijima knew that the end was near, but he had no thought of surrender. He and Cho had sneered at Buckner's note urging surrender. The American didn't understand the way of the Samurai.

Ushijima sent farewell messages to Japan and Formosa, then congratulated all the local units he could contact, exhorting them to fight to the last man for the emperor. Most of the staff officers had dressed as civilians to escape north. Some had orders to form guerrilla units and fight on.

Colonel Yahara's mission was to escape and report to Imperial Headquarters in Japan, an almost impossible mission, as he was quite tall and stood out among the usual soldiers or Okinawans.

Fighting like cornered animals, the Japanese near Makabe on Hills 79, 81, and others, fought to their deaths. Tadashi Kojo's Twenty-second Regiment made a final stand at Maesato Village. Kojo sent his last message to Ushijima.

Desperate Japanese had to be burned from their holes screaming and kicking. Marines followed flamethrowers, scampering over rocks so hot that they blistered their feet through their shoes. Finally, they cut a swath to the coastal cliffs at the island's end.

As General Ushijima was toasting his officers during their farewell dinner, a Tenth Army tank delivered a shell directly into the cave mouth on Hill 89. It was an ominous sign.

On June 21 General Shepherd notified General Geiger that organized resistance in his area had ended.

At 0300 June 22, Lieutenant General Cho bowed to General Ushijima, both in full uniform, and said that since the cave was dark he would lead the way. The small party stepped into the open moonlight and out onto a ledge above the shimmering waters of the Pacific Ocean. A white death quilt was placed on the rocks.

As they knelt and bowed to the east in honor of their emperor, approaching marines heard voices and began throwing grenades.

Ushijima, then Cho, bared their bellies to the moonlight and thrust in the hari-kiri knives to commit seppuka. As blood spurted, the adjutant, as commanded, brought his sword down on their bared necks with all his strength. Two shouts, two strokes, and it was over.

Partly in honor of Ushijima, the last Okinawan kamikaze attack followed, with thirty different raids.

General Cho wrote his epitaph: "I depart without regret, fear, shame, or obligations." He added, "on the 20th year of the Showa Era." He signed his name and stated his age as fifty-one years.

On June 21 the Army's Seventh Division captured Hill 89. Okinawa was declared secured. The eighty-three days of battle were over. More than one thousand Japanese soldiers and conscripts surrendered, along with four thousand civilians.

Soldiers mopping up in the area of Hill 85 on June 25 found the bodies of Generals Ushijima and Cho buried near the base of a cliff.

What price war? In the battle for Okinawa, 100,000 Japanese were killed. American casualties were 49,151. The marines lost 2,938 killed, 13,705 wounded. The army had 4,675 KIA, 18,099 WIA. The navy lost 4,907 KIA and 4,824 WIA. Japan lost more than 3,000 planes, including 1,900 kamikazes. The U.S. lost 36 ships, with more than 368 damaged.

My squad with Japanese flag. Front row, l to r: Walker, Bordoni, Wynn, and Payne. Back row: VanHeuvelen, McDougal, Brown, and Boan. Some men risked their lives for a souvenir like that flag.

Chapter 31

GUAM AND
THE ATOMIC BOMB

Sweetpee and I had just returned from a cave-blowing expedition. We were sweaty and dirty. We decided to explore a Japanese junkyard before returning to our company area. We were looking for anything that would make living conditions more comfortable, but we were careful not to venture into the far end of the yard, as it came within view of a large cave that hadn't been sealed. Anyone venturing into that area came under sniper fire from the cave.

"Wonder what we could do with this?" asked Sweetpee. He was holding what appeared to be a small electric motor.

I looked up from the pile of metal I was searching. Out of the corner of my eye, I saw someone approaching. This wasn't unusual anymore. Hundreds were coming and going across the Ona Yama bridge to the Oroku Peninsula.

"I wonder how far it is to the front line now," I said. "Someone asked me yesterday if I was in the Quartermaster Corps."

"I hear General Shepherd has declared the marines have secured and we'll be leaving Okinawa soon."

"Attention!" yelled the visitor.

At first Sweetpee and I hardly knew what to do. We hadn't heard that command in months. We straightened up to see a naval officer facing us. His pants were neatly pressed, and the creases in his short shirtsleeves had a knife edge. He wore a navy cap with a small amount of braid and scrambled-eggs decoration. The gold bar of an ensign was on his shirt collar.

"What do you guys think you are doing? Don't you realize this is war reparations? Drop that object, soldier!" Sweetpee dropped the object like it was a hot potato, but he felt like throwing it at the officer. He resented being called a soldier, and he resented being ordered around by a shavetail junior officer who had never seen a front line. In fact, Sweetpee felt superior to the officer.

"God, you guys look awful. What's that smell?"

"Cordite," I said.

"What did you say?"

"Cordite, sir. We use it . . ."

"Never mind. Who's your superior officer? I ought to run you in."

"Colonel Anthony Walker," said Ozark.

"At ease," ordered the officer. "You men have any souvenirs, or know where I can get some?"

"We don't have any, sir," said Ozark. Then he remembered the cave. "But there's a cave up that path. Some may be in it."

The officer took off walking at a brisk pace.

"You think he'll find anything, Ozark?"

"Yeah, a hot reception." As we watched in anticipation, rifle fire broke out. The officer came back running at full speed. He tripped and fell. Sweetpee thought he had been shot, until he saw him jump up and run. His hat flew off. We applauded as he ran by. He hesitated momentarily with a horrified expression, then ran on.

"He didn't even say goodbye," commented Sweetpee.

"What was that all about?" Mac asked as he arrived.

"Oh, that sailor found the Jap sniper," said Ozark.

"Well, you men better get your seabags packed—we're pulling out." Mac left.

"You think we ought to return the officer's hat, Ozark?"

"Naw, let the Jap have it for a souvenir."

Later we learned that someone from the navy had registered a complaint with Lieutenant Autry, but no one seemed to know who had offended the ensign.

"What kind of crap is this?" bellyached Fred Westphal of Wichita, Kansas. "Here we are loading seabags on a six-by to leave and we're supposed to stand watch."

"The old Marine Corps doesn't change, does it, Westphal?" said John Wynn.

"Recon is heading for Guam, but where after that?" Scuttlebutt was thick as Okinawa mud.

"I heard a couple guys talking," said Westphal. "They said we're going to hit Japan's main island this fall—and we're to be the first ashore. Casualties are estimated to be one hundred percent."

After a bloody battle like Okinawa, foot marines become numb to the dangers of combat.

"If my number's up, there's nothing I can do about it," said Newton Wood.

"Don't think that way," said Sweetpee. "Marines are trained to have battle smarts. They know things to do to improve their odds."

Recon Marines assembled at 0430, climbed aboard trucks, and headed for debarkation at Naha. I stowed my gear and came on deck as the ship left the harbor. As I stood at the rail, I looked back at Okinawa. A flare shot above the trees and drifted away. Wind was blowing in the pines and the boughs appeared to be waving good-bye. We were silent as Okinawa slipped away into a blue line on the horizon.

"Look!" said Lucky. Ahead was a convoy of LSTs; there must have been about twenty of them, rolling with the ocean swells. As we watched, the PA system announced, *Chow down*. At the bulkhead door was a posted list of those with guard duty. I had the midnight shift with Fisher, a replacement from New York.

It wasn't long after Fisher took over for me that the gentle swells lulled me to sleep.

"Wake up, Ozark!" whispered an excited Fisher.

"What is it?"

"I don't know, but I hear strange sounds."

I listened and began to laugh at the city slicker.

"You ever been on a farm, Fisher?"

"Never."

"Well, you have now. Listen and you'll hear cats meowing, dogs barking, pigs grunting, and chickens cackling. At daylight, you'll hear roosters crowing. Those sounds are the mascots these guys are bringing with them."

At breakfast, I ate eggs, bacon, and fried potatoes. I was surprised at how good navy chow tasted. However, some disagreed.

The ship was heading into a storm and was wallowing in the waves. Doc Redinger was busy with the seasick.

Dinner was literally a mess. Sick men had puked all over the stainless steel tables and the deck. I slid in and waded out, eating only an apple.

I couldn't sleep. I wasn't seasick, but a trash barrel loosely lashed to the bulkhead kept sliding back and forth, scraping on the deck. The sound was relentless.

Recon Marines gradually established a routine: eating, sleeping, inspection, and guard duty. We often talked of navy food.

"I can't remember when I last had boiled eggs for breakfast," said Redinger.

"Can you believe how these swabbies eat?" said Sweetpee. "I thought all they had were navy beans, but last night we had steak and ice cream. Maybe being a peacetime seagoing bellhop wouldn't be so bad."

"Land!" someone shouted. In the distance, I saw a rounded island with a fringe of palms, and above that, grassy hills.

"Look at the sailboat masts," yelled Sweetpee as we neared Apra Harbor. "They're as thick as a box of toothpicks."

"I hear music," said George Mays. Sure enough the Third Division Marine Band was giving Recon a welcome. That wasn't all—a convoy of six-bys were waiting to take us to our new quarters. The trucks went through Agana, the capital, and on to a well-kept tent area.

"Look at that!" yelled Sweetpee, "we're going to live in style." "Sonofabitch," he added, as the trucks sped through the area. The trucks stopped along a dirt road.

"Everybody out!" yelled Mac.

"Damn it to hell, Sarge," there's nothing here but jungle," said Fisher.

"We're going to change that. By tomorrow night, this will look like Thoid Avenue, New York City," he joked.

Recon men hacked away the undergrowth and erected wooden platform tents. At nightfall we were issued beer. Some went to the outdoor movie, but my outfit stayed in its large tent.

Most of us had headaches the next morning, but after breakfast we felt better. Then we went to the supply tent for bedding, tables, boxes, and several fifty-gallon metal drums for trash.

"Wow! Look at the beer issue—fifteen cans," said Sweetpee, who was bunking next to Fisher. By the third can of beer, Daniels was coaxing Zimmerman to say something in Yankee. When Zimmerman responded, Daniels would laugh hysterically. Fisher would then prompt Daniels to say something in Rebel.

"Remember that flag they ran up the pole at Shuri Castle? That was the Stars and Bars of the Confederacy," said Daniels as he rose on unsteady legs, sloshing beer from the can.

"That was not!" countered Zimmerman. "It was the Stars and Stripes, the flag of the Union, and we won the war."

Some men were playing cards, joking and laughing. One group was trying to harmonize their singing. No one was paying attention to the argument that was developing between Zimmerman and Daniels. Surely, they didn't intend to do each other bodily harm. Everyone in the tent was armed.

There was a loud *bang*, a kind of reverberating sound. It came from outside the tent in the dark. Silence fell like an ax in the tent. There it was again—*bang!*

"It's a fight!" yelled an observer, and everyone rushed to the tent doorway. "They're knocking each other into the trash barrels."

"Wouldn't you know it," I commented, "they didn't get enough combat on Okinawa, so now they're fighting a war that happened a hundred years ago."

It was hot and humid on Guam, and most of the men on work details stripped to the waist. I developed a fungus on my chest and the base hospital gave me some medicine.

"What's that purple stuff on your chest?" asked Sweetpee

"Potassium permanganate. It's for my fungus."

"Boy, I hope you don't get it like Chronis did on the 'Canal. That green hairy stuff was growing right out of his ears."

One day three officers came to the tent area.

"We're looking for Boan," one of them said.

"We don't have any Boan here," said Alex. "You must mean Ozark."

"No, his name is Jim Boan from the University of Missouri," said a dark-eyed officer. He had the build of a football player.

"Ozark, come out here and see if you know these guys," yelled Sweetpee.

I knew them, all right. They were fraternity brothers. They

pinned bars on my shirt collar and took me to the Officers' Club. They talked of old times and enjoyed themselves, but my combat experience was far different from theirs. We had drifted apart.

Somehow, I felt sorry for them and their sheltered lives. What could they tell people they did during the war? Served on Guam . . . in communications, in quartermasters, training recruits, in logistics, making inspections, map reading.

Later, I was outside the tent looking at the lights of Agana. It was a sultry night. Suddenly, there was a distant rumble. It was August 6, and I wondered if it could be an earthquake. As I listened, the rumble became louder, closer. Now I could make out a wave of voices.

Bomb—I definitely heard the word, and I wondered if Agana was the target. The enormous excitement was beyond what was expected from a bomb. Then I heard more.

Atomic Bomb! End of the war!"

Where? Japan? Tokyo? No, some place called Hiroshima. Thousands killed. As more information came in it arrived on wave after wave of shouts of joy coming up the mountainside from Agana.

The paths between tent rows were gravelled and the beer-drinking men were dancing there, making the gravel fly. They were yelling and singing. Some were praising President Truman for saving their lives. Everyone thought they'd soon be going home.

"Kiss Operation Coronet goodbye!" screamed Sweetpee. "Coronet" was the rumored code name for the invasion of the Tokyo plains in the spring. Marines were told to expect heavy casualties. Even women and children would have to be killed because they would make sneak attacks with grenades, knives, and guns.

Three days later, a more subdued celebration swept over the island when it was announced that a neutron bomb had obliterated Nagasaki.

Recon men were criticizing Russia for entering the war. They felt that Stalin was doing it to get his hands on the northern Japanese islands.

It was official. Hirohito had unconditionally surrendered Imperial Japan.

I was disheartened. At mail call I didn't get a letter from Mother. This is the second mail call that I hadn't heard from her.

"There's more bad news, Ozark, we're not going home," said Sweetpee, who had just returned from the CP.

"Damn," I said. "I was counting on seeing my mother. I've been going over in my mind what I'd say to her.

"Sorry to say it, Ozark, but looks like it'll be occupational duty either in Japan or China."

"China?"

"Yeah, repatriation of those monkeys who tried to wipe out the entire Chinese population."

"Well, at least no one will be shooting at us." I said.

"Oh, one other item of interest at the CP. Pompous General MacArthur is credited with winning the Pacific War and will accept Japan's surrender on the deck of the Battleship *Missouri*."

"I have cross-referenced language booklets in both Japanese and Chinese," I said. "I'd sell one cheap, but I don't know which one."

Lieutenant Autry called for assembly. "Secure this place, and place your seabags in front of the tents. Recon is moving out," he announced. After chow at the mess tent, we were surprised when they returned.

"What did they do?" I asked as I looked over the area. Everything was gone: seabags, their tents. Only a gravel path in the jungle remained.

Trucks were waiting. We boarded and rolled down Marine Dive toward Agana and the docks beyond. Dusk descended and the harbor light blinked in the distance. It began to rain, and the lights splashed golden spears across the dark waters.

"My pack is soaked and the straps are buried in my shoulders," complained Sweetpee.

"My rifle's getting soaked, and it'll rust before I get aboard ship," mumbled another marine. "Wonder why we'll need rifles in China?"

China! I thought. I'd always heard that no marine was complete until he had served in China. Now I was about to become a China marine.

Company tent rows on Guam. Marines slept on folding cots.

Old U. S. Post Office, Agana, Guam.

Pango Bay, Guam. Sixth Marine Division area is on cliffs behind the camera.

Native jungle home in the cliffs back of Agana. Coconut, banana, and papaya tress shown in picture bore edible fruit.

Part of Agana, the capital of Guam, nestled against the hills that make Orote Peninsula.

Civilian bus depot, Guam.

Street in Agana parallel to Marine Drive. Concrete buildings billeted marines before the war.

"Guam Grill"—a restaurant restricted for military personnel. Tables were usually on the balcony, where Guanamians ate and drank.

Governor's home at Agana, Guam.

Marine mess halls on Guam.

Agana Heights village, Telefofo, was typical of U.S.-constructed buildings for natives.

"Be careful with that Nip saber, Buck; it was hard come by."

The author standing in front of the Recon Company area on Guam.

The author in front of Base Hospital 113, Guam.

Author and a buddy explore Guam.

Marine Drive, a modern highway on Guam.

Postcard.

Chapter 32

TSINGTAO, CHINA

The USS *Dade*, known as APA 99, nosed out of the Apra, Guam, harbor and headed west with the Recon Marines in her compartments below deck.

"Damn, this soaked pack is heavy," said Dutch Grossman as he stripped the straps from his shoulders and dumped the pack on a bunk, "and my rifle could be used as a squirt gun."

"Yeah, first thing we gotta do is clean and dry our pieces; they'll have a rifle inspection for sure tomorrow, and there better be no rust," said Westphal.

"What do they think we are, monkeys?" I questioned, looking at the bunks—six rows, six high. "I'm glad I got here in time for a lower."

Sweetpee and I stowed our gear and went topside. On the fantail we saw a radio-operated five-inch gun. Forward were lifeboats, winches, hatches, capstans, and other seagoing equipment. We noticed that the forward deck was wide and steeply inclined to the bow.

Rain had stopped, and the lights sparkled on the water: big white lights, green lights, blue lights, red lights, some flashing, some winking signals rhythmically.

"Look, Sweetpee, it's a symphony of lights," I observed.

Recon men returned to our compartment and stripped to our skivvies to sleep.

"God almighty it's hot down here," said Bardoni.

"Did you see that, Ozark?" said Sweetpee.

"What?" Only the safety light was on, and it was difficult to see anything clearly.

"That shadow at the compartment door."

"I didn't see anything."

"It was Ace. He just left with a blanket. He's going to sleep topside, where it's cooler. Tomorrow night he's going to have company—me."

The USS *Dade* sliced its way through the waves, gently rolling with the swells. The sun was almost unbearable. The deck was hot enough to fry an egg, and we marines were crowded into the shade of deck boats and large objects. The heat sapped our well of tolerance. Some played cards. Most tried to sleep.

I went to the bow anchor winch, where I could look at the foamy spray and watch the flying fish leap from the water.

"It's cooler today," I wrote Mother. The boys here talk a lot of home, speaking of multi-colored leaves dancing in the breeze, grass turning brown, fall flowers blooming, hummingbirds humming, girls dressed in gay colors, and football games.

Tooweet! It was the boatswain's whistle. "Now hear this . . ." A description of our location followed. The convoy was in the China Sea, cutting low through the Ryukyus near Formosa, northwest of Okinawa.

The wind picked up. The sea became whitecrested and choppy. Wind blew up a gale and ripped the tops off the crested waves, blowing stinging spindrift into our faces. The convoy continued its relentless course northwest. Ships were rolling, and the chilly wind brought tears to the eyes of the marines on deck. Some sniffed while others turned seasick.

"I'd sure like to be home for Christmas," said Ace, who unknowingly was speaking for all. There was a spray of wind-blown foam.

"That blowing foam reminds me of snowflakes—the way they scurry across a road," said a nearby marine.

"Wouldn't it be fun to walk into the living room near the Christmas tree with an armful of presents and surprise everyone?" said Sweetpee.

"Gee!" said Lucky, with a distant look in his eyes.

Whoomp! Whoomp! A destroyer passed the *Dade* with black smoke pouring from its stack and water roiling in its wake.

Ace, Lucky, Sweetpee, and I watched it pass in awe.

"Wonder what that's about?" I said.

"Probably saw or heard something, maybe a submarine," said Ace. As we watched, a battleship and two more destroyers appeared in the convoy. They wallowed smoothly like whales in their element.

"Look! There's land!" yelled Ace.

Ahead was a jagged brown coastline far different from the small green caps of the jungle islands.

China shone in the brilliant fall sunlight. And as I watched, the gray, red, and green colors of Tsingtao appeared against a mountain backdrop. Other marines appeared on deck. Behind them sixteen ships were moving into the harbor. Ahead were red tile roofs of buildings, church steeples, and radio towers.

As the ship dropped anchor, we watched the Chinese. Two boys appear, paddling a boat. A basket was hanging over the bow and seashells were on the bottom in a net. Marines threw them cigarettes, candy, and T-shirts. Other boats quickly assembled.

"These people are wearing pajamas," said Joseph Calvetti from Patterson, New Jersey.

"No," said Mac, "they're wearing kimonos or padded coats and loose-fitting pants."

I noticed old trucks that appeared to be burning wood or coal parked nearby.

"Look at those trucks," said Fisher. "The steering wheel is on the wrong side, but the names are Ford, Chrysler, Oldsmobile. How can they do that?"

"This is China," said Sweetpee. "Don't you know they do everything backwards?"

Marines boarded the trucks which appeared to run on gas fumes and headed to downtown Tsingtao. People cheered as the marines passed, but they weren't all Chinese. Some faces were pink, white, or ruddy. Some held their thumbs up. We were told this meant, 'friend'.

There was a mass of humanity, walking, riding bicycles, pulling rickshaws, handling carts, carrying baskets balanced on poles, or sitting beside the wares they were selling. There were armed soldiers in the street.

Walls surrounded many homes. Glass shards were embedded in the concrete on top the walls. Heads appeared in the upper floor windows to watch the American marines go by.

As the trucks rolled on concrete strips in the road, presumably to prevent ruts, a marine threw a handful of coins to the cheering crowd. There was a mad scramble for the coins. A man pulling a rickshaw abandoned his passenger to search for coins.

Trucks passed vendors with trays of fried fish, bowls of spaghetti, pears, racks of mirrors, jewelry chains, wreaths with flags, even Chiang Kai-shek's picture.

Carts were loaded with celery, sweet potatoes, chairs, tables, and dry goods as the trucks passed through a market. Most carts were pulled by people, but some were powered by shaggy ponies.

The trucks stopped at a large brick building. It could be in the States. Someone said it was once a university. We dismounted and took our gear to the top floor, which was a long open hall equipped with bunks. Above was a string of electric lights.

Recon had arrived in China.

Turned out the building was the Grand Hotel.

Sweetpee, Hays, and I were anxious to see the city. We hailed rickshaws and headed downtown on Shantung Road. Venders were everywhere, selling coal, food, and many other items in baskets of all sizes and shapes.

We marveled at the physiques of the men pulling the rickshaws. They must have run miles every day to produce those lean, hard muscles.

On the way downtown, we passed Saint Michael's Cathedral Church, a prominent landmark. When we stop, many beggars surrounded us, calling: "*Cuma-shaw! Cuma-shaw!*" meaning, "Give me something."

We were hounded by children who held out their hands and begged. We noticed fingers missing and were greatly concerned. The children are victims of leprosy. We ran to our rickshaws and moved on.

At the beach, we saw many people swimming.

"Say," said Otis Spears, from Texas, "that looks like a lot of fun."

"Yeah," said Sweetpee, "If the sharks are fasting."

I was growing a mustache, but I needed a shave and a haircut. We stopped at a barbershop. There were four barbers, not unlike in the

States, but all had little plastic cups under their noses held by elastic bands around their heads.

"What are those things?" I asked.

"I guess they don't want to smell you," said Sweetpee with a smile.

I pointed to the item and gestured to his barber. He shook his head. Finally, someone who understood a little English said that they were breath deflectors. The barbers all ate garlic.

The first squad, along with most others, had acquired a houseboy to keep their quarters tidy. When I walked in with a fresh haircut and trimmed mustache, the boy pointed to me and giggled into his hand. I wondered what was amusing the youngster.

"*Loquasit!*" he said, or something like that. Later I learned that it meant "very fine."

I smiled and offered the boy some Chinese scrip. It was about 1,800 dollars to one American. I was hoping to buy the Chinese boy a meal of steak and eggs. But the boy demurred. That was not his taste. He took only a few of the scrip bills and headed off for his favorite meal.

Soon after the houseboy left, Recon had a visitor, a German civilian probably eighteen to twenty years old. He related how Germans and White Russians had occupied that part of China years ago. He was their descendant.

Johnny Winn raced into the room, his short legs churning.

"There's an officer and an enlisted man coming for inspection. They're checking rifles, bunks, equipment, everything."

The men turned to and began to police the place. After the inspection, the officer announced who would stand guard duty, who would go on mess duty, and the time and place of parade drills.

"Here we go again," said Sweetpee, "back to spit-and-polish marines."

Then the officer announced weekend liberty, and that took the sting out of his orders. To start the holiday, several of my outfit decided to go to the horseraces. We were shocked when we saw the horses.

"Those are plow ponies, not race horses," complained Doc Redinger, who had been to the races at Ak-Sar-Ben in Omaha.

"This is no Kentucky Derby, I'll agree," I said.

After the races, we walked out to see several venders selling fruit and vegetables.

"Don't eat any of that stuff," I said to Fisher.

"Why not?"

"It's fertilized with human shit."

"What?"

"Night soil, human waste, and it's diseased," added Sweetpee. "Weren't you present when they told us about it?"

About that time, a two-wheeled cart with what looked like a huge barrel mounted on it came into view.

"There's one of those honey wagons now," said Doc.

"Hold your nose," yelled Sweetpee.

Fisher didn't. Fisher gagged.

I was remembering the honey wagon while I was on guard duty, and I smiled to myself when I thought about Fisher. Then I looked up and saw a shooting star, and it was followed by several more. Mother Nature was putting on a show. Again I wondered if the stars were visible back home. I tried to remember what day and what time of day it would be back home in Missouri. Mother was often on my mind during these lonely nights on guard duty.

Girls seem to be on the minds of most of the Tsingtao marines. My new friend was in charge of building maintenance had a crew of about a dozen Chinese led by a head man. He told the leader he needed a woman, and in a few days a beautiful Chinese girl appeared in his room and had been there ever since.

The marines were all young and virile, with an overabundance of libido. Every weekend, we'd have liberty, and marines made their desires known to the rickshaw men, and they knew where to take them.

One of the young virgins who had his first experience with a woman became excited and ripped loose the ligament on his penis. Doc had to take him to the hospital. Guess he spent his free time in quarters, but he may have been the lucky one. Doc told him about a marine in another outfit who had contracted a venereal disease. When he went to urinate, he had to play his penis like a piccolo. Another had to grab hold of the urinal because it hurt so much.

Sweetpee told me about a date he had been on one Saturday night.

I don't know how it came about, but three of us had dates with Chinese girls down near the harbor statue on Shantung Road. I was having a devil of a time trying to talk with her in the dark. I was trying to convince her I needed to make love, and she was trying to convince me to take her to America. Neither of us was doing a convincing job, and it ended in a wrestling tussle.

Damned if I didn't fall into a foxhole some enterprising Jap had dug. By the time I got out, my desires for the Chinese girl were gone.

I kept writing letters home:

We're going to have a big football game here between the 22nd and the 29th Regiments. It will be held in Tsingtao Stadium. It's football weather here now, and we think about the big games back home. This should be a good game. We have a number of ex–college players in the Marines.

Thanksgiving and Christmas are just around the corner, so we're all looking to a big feast of turkey with all the trimmings, but it won't be like home. We have a pagoda-illustrated Christmas card planned. I'll send you one. Don't tell, but I bought a beautiful Chinese tea set to send Mother. The place where I bought it assured me that it will be packed well for shipment.

Some of the men are rotating home. It's a sad parting as one group after another leaves. My time to come home will be soon, and words can't express how anxious I am to be with you.

Tsingtao, China, Christmas card.

Pagoda near Tsingtao.

Christmas card from Tsingtao, China.

Convoy en route to Tsingtao, China, from Guam.

Panorama of Tsingtao. Cleared area in center of photo is a tent camp. Bay is at left, and St. Michael's Cathedral is in distant right.

Grand Hotel, where we were billeted in Tsingtao, China.

Edgewater Beach Hotel, Tsingtao, as officers' quarters. In harbor (right) beyond buildings is U.S. transport ship.

"Loquasit," our houseboy said when he saw this picture. It means "very fine." Picture was taken in Tsingtao.

Shantung University, Twenty-second Marine area, Tsingtao, principal city of Shantung Province, Shantung Peninsula.

Street scene in Tsingtao, China.

"Hey, Joe! Peanuts, Joe!" shouted the street vendors in pidgin English to passing marines.

Street vendors on Chefoo Road. Coal paddies (briquettes) in foreground.

Christmas decorations over a street in Tsingtao. Chinese policeman in center of photo; Chinese soldier at right.

Money exchange center, Tsingtao. One U.S. dollar equaled approximately 1,800 Chinese puppet currency units.

"Cumma-shaw!" asked the Tsingtao beggar. ("Give me something.")

Street in Tsingtao. Chinese sailors at right; beyond them on the crossroad is a rickshaw. Spike in mall is a statue. Harbor is at end of street. Building at right was a hotel, then housing Recon Company. Building at left was for Japanese soldiers.

Wedding procession on Shantung Road. Group was led by musicians.

"U.S. Bar" in downtown Tsingtao. This was a rickshaw center, like a taxi stand. Protection for the shops were shuttered windows and barred doors.

Twenty-second Marine Regiment marching down Shantung Road, Tsingtao, China.

One of the gardens in "Temple of all Religions"—Red Swastika. Concrete slide in the center is sacred—to be used only by gods—and one sacrilegious marine.

Unloading hogs from Chinese junk. Hogs had to swim ashore.

Drinking water came from street pumps (fire hydrants). Water was carried in buckets, one on each end of a bamboo pole over the shoulder.

Chinese on dock overlooking small boat harbor, Tsingtao.

Stadium and racetrack are in the left background. This was the site of the Japanese surrender. In the distant background is the China (or Yellow) Sea.

Beach where swimming was fun—if the sharks were fasting! Tsingtao, China.

Enlisted men's club, Tsingtao, was sponsored by Red Cross. There was a naval signal light on top of the building.

Pagoda Pier. This was the liberty dock for sailors. In distance at left of pagoda is a lighthouse.

Skyline of Tsingtao from Pagoda Pier. Chinese junks in foreground. St. Michael's is outside picture to the left.

Strand Park, Strand Beach, and Strand Hotel in background. Tsingtao.

Race track, Tsingtao. Chinese would bet on any old "plow pony."

Towering above the Tsingtao skyline is St. Michael's Cathedral.

Street scene in front of St. Michael's.

View of Tsingtao from the top of St. Michael's. In foreground, see how buildings follow the streets, leaving the inside open for a courtyard.

U.S. Post Office, Tsingtao, China.

Sixth Marine Division Headquarters, Tsingtao. Note guard in guardhouse at gate. General Shepherd's office was in this building.

Japense victory monument at Shantung and Dei Hsien roads, Tsingtao.

Football? Yes, the Twenty-ninth versus the Twenty-second regiments of the Sixth Marine Dvision in Tsingtao stadium.

View near the park on the outskirts of Tsingtao.

Restaurant at intersectin of Shantung and Hupii.

Entrance to shrine in the Japanese section of Tsingtao.

Sixth Marine Headquarters, Tsingtao.

Scuttled Japanese ships in small boat harbor of Tsingtao. Note rising sun insignia.

Enlisted at _____ COLUMBIA, MISSOURI _____ on the _____ 30TH _____ day of
_____ MARCH _____ 1942, to serve EARL ENDS _____ years

Born _____ 1 SEPTEMBER, 1921 _____ at _____ DREASMYVILLE, MISSOURI _____

When enlisted was _____ 66 1/2 _____ inches high, with _____ BLUE _____ eyes, _____ BROWN _____ hair,
complexion: _____ FAIR _____ citizenship: _____ U. S. _____

Previous service: _____ NONE _____

Rank and type of warrant at time of discharge: CORP (LINE TEMP) RANK FR 12JAN46

Weapons qualification: _____ EXPERT - RIFLE - 21DEC43 _____

Special m' g qualifications: INTELLIGENCE MAN; MACHINE GUN CREWMAN _____

Service (sea and foreign): _____ PACIFIC AREA FROM 10NOV44 - 31DEC45 _____

Wounds received in service: _____ NONE _____

Battles, engagements, skirmishes, expeditions IN ACTION AT OKINAWA, RYUKYU ISLANDS FROM
1APR45 - 9JUL45; OCCUPATION OF CHINA FROM 12OCT45 - 12DEC45

Remarks: GOOD-CONDUCT MEDAL PERIOD COMMENCES 13JUL43; NO OFFENSES SINCE THAT DATE;
ADDED ACT B 1JUL45; AUTH: ART 3-17 MCM CHG #6, CMC SERIAL NO-586450, DATED 29
NOV45

Character of service excellent.

Serial number _____ 389873 _____   SECOND LIEUTENANT   U. S. M. C.

Is physically qualified for discharge. Requires neither treatment nor hospitalization.
I certify that this is the actual print of the right index finger of the man herein mentioned.

COMDR.   U. S. N. R

Monthly rate of pay when discharged _____ $56.70 _____

I hereby certify that the within named man has been furnished travel allowance at the rate of
five _____ cents per mile from _____ SAN DIEGO, CALIF. _____ to _____ GREAT LAKES, ILL. _____
and paid $ _____ 152.83 _____ in full to date of discharge.

(Signature of man)   SECOND LIEUTENANT   U. S. M. C.
                                                     BY DIRECTION

DUE TO WAR CONDITIONS THE INFORMATION ON THIS CERTIFICATE IS INCOMPLETE

The author's discharge papers.

Chapter 33

COMING HOME

Lieutenant Autry came to the barracks door and shouted, "Jim Boan and Ray VanHeuvelen, report to headquarters immediately."

We donned headgear and met at the barracks door.

"What's this all about, Ozark?"

"Don't know, but I hope it's good news."

We announced ourselves to a lieutenant at headquarters.

"You two men get your gear together. You're going back to the States," he said. "Be prepared to leave by 0100."

Sweetpee and I both felt like shouting and throwing our caps in the air, but we settled on giving each other broad smiles. We were dismissed. As we reached the door, the lieutenant called out.

"Boan!"

"Yes, Sir."

"Here's a letter for you."

I took the letter, and once outside the door, we did a little celebrating. Then I looked at the letter. It was from Mother.

"Dear Son, I don't know how to tell you this. But a terrible thing has happened to me. I don't want to alarm you, but I thought you should be prepared." It was signed "Mother." Big block letters at the bottom of the page read, "LOVE YOU."

I couldn't believe that was all of the message. I turned the page over, but the back was blank. I handed the letter to Sweetpee.

"What do you make of this?"

Sweetpee read the letter, then read it again. He handed it to me and I read it again.

"I don't like to say this," began Sweetpee, "but it sounds to me like she's suffered the same fate as your birth mother and grandmother.

"Oh, God, Sweetpee, I hope you're wrong. I don't think I could stand to see her hurting."

We walked on in silence and parted at the barracks door. I read the letter over and over and talked to myself about what could have happened. I lay on my bunk with my eyes closed.

"Why couldn't they tell me what happened?"

"You say something, Ozark?" asked Sweetpee.

"No, I was just wondering."

"You better gather your wandering mind and pack, if you're leaving today."

I packed my seabag and prepared to leave. I felt better after telling everyone goodbye, and they had best wishes for me.

As the ship pulled out of the harbor, I watched the steeples of Saint Michael's church disappear. Only a gray blob remained of the town, and then it disappeared and just the brown hills remained, then disappeared.

"Yippee! I'm going home!" called out Sweetpee, standing by the deck rail and shouting at the ocean.

I smiled as I felt the ship's propellers strain against the waves. At times it shuddered. It seemed to be in a hurry, and it couldn't move fast enough for me. Day after day and night after night, the ship surged forward, but there never seemed to be a destination. I had forgotten how big the Pacific Ocean was.

Then one morning the Golden Gate Bridge loomed out of the fog. The men on deck cheered. Soon the entire shoreline shone with beautiful white buildings. We were home, back in the good old USA.

The ship docked at Treasure Island in San Francisco's bay, and we were told we could have liberty that night in San Francisco. I made plans to call home, and I began rehearsing what I would say. I was still thinking when we were called to line up for chow.

Being regimented into a controlled line was foreign to us veterans. We hadn't been in a formal line for months, some of us for years, and we didn't take kindly to some white-capped swabbie telling us what to do. We lined up in a column of crowds.

After being told repeatedly to fall in behind the yellow line, the petty officer left and reappeared in a jeep. He began driving down the yellow line and forcing us behind it. About a third of the way through the crowd, a half-dozen marines grabbed the jeep and began to rock it back and forth. The driver bailed out and ran. The officer stayed in the jeep until he lost his seat, then he jumped out. SPs appeared and forced the marines to behave.

We lost our liberty.

At mess, I consoled myself by drinking a pitcher of whole milk. "I have never tasted anything so good since I left the farm," I told Sweetpee.

The next day was January 12, 1946.

"See this certificate?" I said to Sweetpee. "I'm going to hold it all the way to Missouri." I was holding my discharge.

It was a sober, tearful goodbye when he and I hugged at the train station. "I love you like a brother," choked Sweetpee.

"Me, too," I managed. Then, when I was more composed, I said, simply, *"Semper Fi."* We parted, and I boarded the train without looking back; I didn't want my old buddy to see me cry.

When the train arrived at St. Louis, there was snow on the ground, the first I had seen in two years. The statues in the park at the station looked stark, naked, permanent. I walked up to one and said, "Good to see you again. This ol' hillbilly is back, and he came through with hardly a scratch."

On the train to my destination, Jefferson City, I tried to imagine who would meet me and how they would have changed since I left.

As the train pulled in, I saw my father, and my brother still in army uniform.

As expected, it was a tearful reunion. Mother was noticeably absent.

"We'll go see her," said my brother, John.

We went directly to the hospital, and I followed them to her room.

The first thing I saw was Mother. Her face was flushed with fever. I gasped and knelt beside her. It was the bane of all the Thacker women, tuberculosis. Doctors had given her all the antibiotics they dared.

I burst into tears and left the room sobbing. I never saw her alive again. After the funeral, I bought an old Plymouth with a sail ship as a hood ornament. Cars were scarce, but this one would do, even if I had to carry a five-gallon can of oil in the trunk.

"Where do you think you'll go?" asked my brother.

"I don't know. Maybe out west. I gotta get away."

"I'll come if you want company."

"No. I have to make this trip alone."

When I returned, I was the same old Ozark again.

"I've made up my mind," I told my family, "I'm going back to school and get my degree. The GI Bill of Rights will pay for most of it."

That fall, when I arrived at the University of Missouri, I found everything had changed. Quonset huts housed married veteran students. Student attitudes were more focused, serious—the social demeanor was gone.

"Ozark," my fraternity president said, "do you suppose you could find another place to stay? We need the room in the fraternity house for the neophytes."

"Even my own fraternity doesn't want me," I told my new roommate. "This isn't a sleepy college town anymore."

On December 7 I walked through the fallen leaves to the exact spot where I had stood five years earlier when I had first heard that the Japanese had bombed Pearl Harbor. I reminisced how the world had changed, how much smaller it seemed.

Even as I stood there, a cloud appeared on the distant horizon. There was a new fear arising about Communist Russia and China. Someone once said, I recalled:

> It is the soldier, sailor, airman, and marine, not the reporter, who has given us freedom of the press.
>
> It is the soldier, sailor, airman, and marine, not the poet, who has given us freedom of speech.
>
> It is the soldier, sailor, airman, and marine, not the campus organizer, who has given us freedom to demonstrate.
>
> It is the soldier, sailor, airman, and marine who salutes the flag, who serves beneath the flag, and whose coffin is draped by the flag, who allows the protester to burn the flag.

Sixth Division Cemetery, Okinawa.

BIBLIOGRAPHY

All the World's Fighting Ships. London: Conway Maritime Press, 1980.

Astor, Gerald, *Operation Iceberg*. New York: Donald I. Fine, Inc., 1995.

Berry, Henry. *Semper Fi, Mac*. New York: Berkeley, 1983.

Brown, Joseph Rust. *We Stole To Live*. Cape Girardeau, Missouri: privately published 1982.

Feifer, George. *Tennozan*. New York: Ticknor & Fields, 1992.

Garzke, William H. Jr. and Robert O. Dulin *Battleships*. Annapolis, Maryland: Naval Institute Press, 1985.

Hallas, James H. *Killing Ground on Okinawa*. Westport, Connecticut: Praeger, 1996.

Leckie, Robert. *Delivered from Evil—The Saga of World War II*. New York: Harper & Row, 1987.

————. *Okinawa: The Last Battle of World War II*. New York: Viking Penguin, 1995.

Manchester, William. *Goodbye Darkness: A Memoir of the Pacific War*. Boston: Little, Brown Co., 1980.

Marine Corps Gazette. September 1946.

McCormick, John. *The Right Kind of War*. New York: Penguin Books, 1992.

Meyer, S.L., ed. *The Rise And Fall of Imperial Japan*, New York: The Military Press, 1984.

Newcomb, Richard F. *Iwo Jima*. New York: Bantam, 1995.

Nichols, Charles S. Jr., Major USMC, and Henry I. Shaw Jr. *Okinawa: Victory in the Pacific*. Paducah, Kentucky: The Battery Press, 1989.

Reader's Digest Illustrated Story of World War II. Pleasantville, New York,:Reader's Digest Assoc., 1969.

Sledge, E. B. *With The Old Breed at Peleliu and Okinawa*. Novato, California: Presidio Press, 1990.

Steinberg, Rafael, ed. *Island Fighting,* Chicago: Time-Life Books, 1978.

Sulzberger, C.L. *The American Heritage Picture History of World War II*. New York: American Heritage Publishing Co., 1966.

Tregaskis, Richard. *Guadalcanal Diary.* New York: Random House, 1943.

Walker, Anthony, Lt. Col. *Memorial to the Men of Reconnaissance Company*. Middletown, Rhode Island: privately published 50th anniversary tribute, 1995.

Wheeler, Richard. *IWO.* Annapolis, Maryland: Naval Institute Press, 1980.

World War II Magazine. August 24, 1984.

Yahara, Hiromichi, Col. *The Battle For Okinawa.* New York: John Wiley & Sons, 1995.

Young, Peter, Brigadier, ed. *Atlas of the Second World War*. New York: Berkley, 1974.

———. *World War 1939–45, A Short History.* New York: Thomas Y. Crowell Co., 1966.

ROSTER OF THE SIXTH MARINE DIVISION
RECONNAISSANCE COMPANY, 1 APRIL 1945

OFFICERS

Autry, Robert L., 1st. Lt.
Christie, William J., 1st Lt.
Curtis, Paul F., 2nd Lt.
Newton, Reason G., 1st Lt.
Walker, Anthony, Maj.

NONCOM. OFFICERS

Bolan, John J., Jr., Cpl.
Buchanan, James T., Sgt.
Carmichael, Hughie, Cpl.
Clunn, William F., Cpl.
Cossen, William C., Sgt. Maj.
Curry, William C., Cpl.
Curtis, Fuller, Cpl.
Curtis, Walter I., Cpl.
Daniel, James T., Jr., Cpl.

Dawson, William H., Cpl.
Evans, Iola, Cpl.
Hardacre, Joseph J., Cpl.
Hays, Harold R., Cpl.
Krysztofik, John J., Cpl.
McDougal, Robert J., Sgt.
Manion, Harry C., Sgt.
Meck, Chester R., Cpl.
Moore, Buford M., Jr., Platoon Sgt.
Nelson, Raymond D., Staff Sgt.
O'Brien, Gardner C., Cpl.
Richards, Raymond J., Cpl.
Tabb, James C., Gunnery Sgt.
Wizbicki, Alexander J., Cpl.
Woodward, James G., Gunnery Sgt.
Zaidayn, Sam P., Cpl.
Zimmerman, Alfred D., Cpl.

Chief Cook

Kollar, Frank P.

Assistant Cooks

Bailey, Clarence J.
Brakey, Bud A.

Privates and Privates First Class

Aikins, George, Jr., PFC
Baxter, James L., Pvt.
Blankenship, Thomas E., Pvt.
Boan, James O., PFC
Bordoni, Anthony F., PFC
Boydell, Earl M., Jr., PFC
Brandes, Zack, Sr., PFC
Brown, August C., PFC
Burak, Zigmund J., PFC
Burien, Willie M., Pvt.
Burkart, James K., Pvt.
Calvetti, Joseph A., Pvt.
Cochran, Marshall E., PFC
Cone, John F., PFC
Cooper, Marvin W., Pvt.
Davis, Kermit R., PFC
Drake, Robert A., Pvt.
Ellis, William E., Pvt.
Ferris, William T., Pvt.
Fisher, Berry A., Jr., Pvt.
Gadbois, William F., Pvt.
Goulden, Francis S., Pvt.
Grace, John N., Jr., PFC

Grossman, Edward T. III, Pvt.
Guenther, Norman F., PFC
Hansen, Earl H., Pvt.
Hart, John J., Jr., Pvt.
Hays, John J., Jr., Pvt.
Hobe, Theodore J., Pvt.
Hutchinson, John H., PFC
Hencinski, Anthony F., PFC
James, Earl F., Pvt.
Joyce, John O., Pvt.
Keel, Raymond L., Pvt.
Kvasse, John D., Pvt.
Lindsay, James M., Jr., PFC
Loes, Joseph H., Pvt.
Martin, Joseph F., PFC
Masely, Metro, Jr., PFC
Mays, George G., Pvt.
McCollough, Francis E., PFC
McConnell, James E., PFC
Miller, Darwin L., PFC
Miller, Ray H., Pvt.
O'Brien, Edward F., PFC
Osborn, Edwin G., Pvt.
Payne, Charles H., PFC
Payne, James R., Pvt.
Phillips, Lyle W., Pvt.
Phillips, Robert L., Pvt.
Posey, William G., PFC
Poteet, Lawrence T., Pvt.
Pushee, Roger C., Pvt.
Rallis, Paul A., PFC
Rasar, Ernest E., PFC
Rice, Donald N., Pvt.

Rodgers, Ernest W., Pvt.

Shimp, William A., Pvt.

Spears, Otis R., Pvt.

Spellman, William M., Pvt.

Slattery, Norman D., PFC

Smith, John E., PFC

Smith, Jim C., Pvt.

Sweeney, William J., PFC

Taylor, George H., PFC

VanHeuvelen, Raymond H., Pvt.

Walker, Herbert G., PFC

Wampler, Don M., Pvt.

Warren, Harold N., Pvt.

West, Donald B., Pvt.

Westphal, Fred E. T., Pvt.

Wheeler, Julian J., PFC

Will, William K., PFC

Willett, William R., Pvt.

Williams, Robert A., Pvt.

Wills, Ernest J., PFC

Wilson, Fred E., Pvt.

Wilson, R. M., Pvt.

Winn, Johnny D., Pvt.

Wood, Newton C., Pvt.

Woodhams, Elbert C., Pvt.

Yost, Sheridan C., PFC

Zemetra, John A., Pvt.

Zgainer, Edward G., PFC

PHARMACISTS MATES

Bridger, 2nd Class

Redinger, Harold F., Chief

Wilkerson, John H., 2nd Class

Willis, George E., 2nd Class

JIM BOAN entered the Marine Corps after graduating from the University of Missouri. Following his discharge he worked in an advertising agency for many years. He founded a newspaper which he published for ten years before retiring. In his retirement, Boan continues to write articles and stories for various magazines.